D0628531

Tennessee

ROBERT BRANDT

Revised by Monique Peterson
Photography by Joe Allen

COMPASS AMERICAN GUIDES
An Imprint of Fodor's Travel Publications

Compass American Guides: Tennessee

Editor: Jennifer Paull
Designer: Siobhan O'Hare
Compass Editorial Director: Paul Eisenberg
Compass Creative Director: Fabrizio La Rocca
Editorial Production: Linda K. Schmidt
Photo Editor and Archival Researcher: Melanie Marin
Map Design: Mark Stroud, Moon Street Cartography
Cover Photo: Joseph Allen

Second Edition

ISBN 1–4000–1618–5
ISBN-13 978–1–4000–1618–1

The details in this book are based on information supplied to us at press time, but changes occur all the time, and the publisher cannot accept responsibility for facts that become outdated or for inadvertent errors or omissions.

Compass American Guides, 1745 Broadway, New York, NY 10019
PRINTED IN CHINA

10 9 8 7 6 5 4 3 2 1

To Anne, who always has fun when she travels.

TENNESSEE

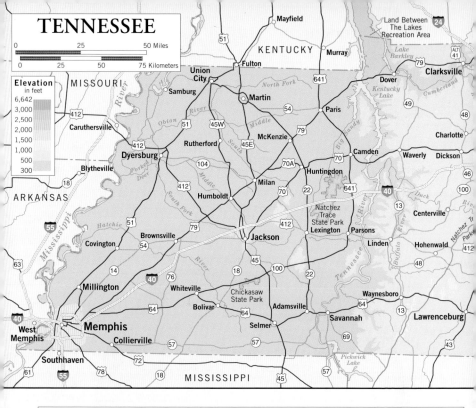

Elevation
in feet
6,642
3,000
2,500
2,000
1,500
1,000
500
300

MISSOURI

ARKANSAS

KENTUCKY

MISSISSIPPI

Land Between The Lakes Recreation Area

0   25   50 Miles
0   25   50   75 Kilometers

CLIMATE CHART

Weather Station	TEMPERATURES				RECORDS		PRECIPITATION				TOTAL ANNUAL	
	Jan	Apr	Jul	Oct	High	Low	Jan	Apr	Jul	Oct	Rain	Snow
Bristol	45/26	68/44	85/64	70/45	102°	-25°	3.4"	3.4"	4.5"	2.4"	41"	18'
Chattanooga	50/30	71/47	90/69	71/49	106°	-10°	5.3"	4.3"	4.8"	3.2"	53"	4"
Crossville	48/28	70/47	86/62	71/47	103°	-14°	5.4"	4.6"	5.4"	3.4"	54"	12"
Clarksville	44/29	70/47	92/68	70/47	112°	-14°	5.6"	4.5"	3.8"	3.1"	49"	12"
Gatlinburg	48/25	72/42	86/61	71/42	105°	-13°	4.8"	4.9"	6.1"	3.1"	57"	13"
Jackson	51/31	72/50	92/68	74/50	110°	-21°	5.0"	4.5"	3.7"	3.2"	49"	8"
Knoxville	49/29	70/47	89/68	71/49	104°	-24°	4.5"	3.6"	4.5"	2.8"	47"	13"
Memphis	50/31	73/52	91/73	76/51	108°	-13°	4.6"	5.8"	4.0"	2.4"	52"	5"
Nashville	48/29	70/49	90/69	71/49	107°	-17°	4.4"	4.1"	3.8"	2.6"	47"	11"

MILEAGE CHART

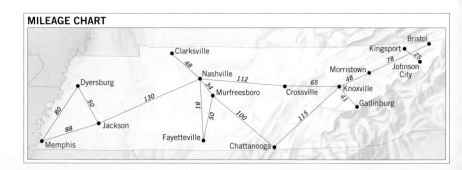

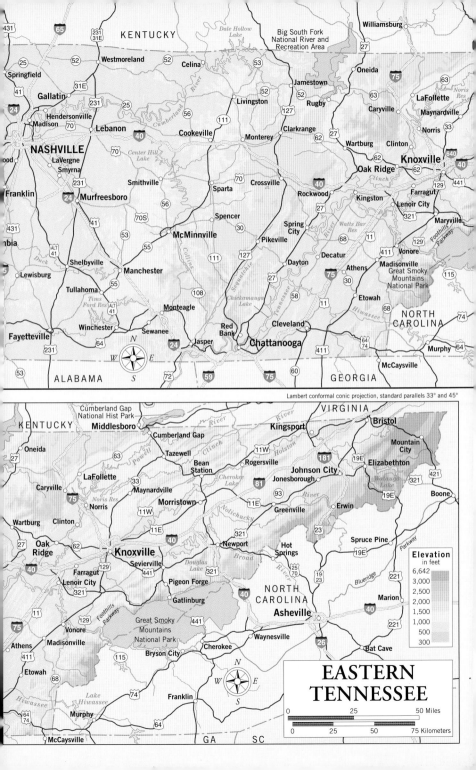

EASTERN TENNESSEE

Lambert conformal conic projection, standard parallels 33° and 45°

Elevation
in feet

6,642
3,000
2,500
2,000
1,500
1,000
500
300

0   25   50 Miles

0   25   50   75 Kilometers

C O N T E N T S

Literary Excerpts

Topical Essays

Maps

CHAPTER DIVISIONS

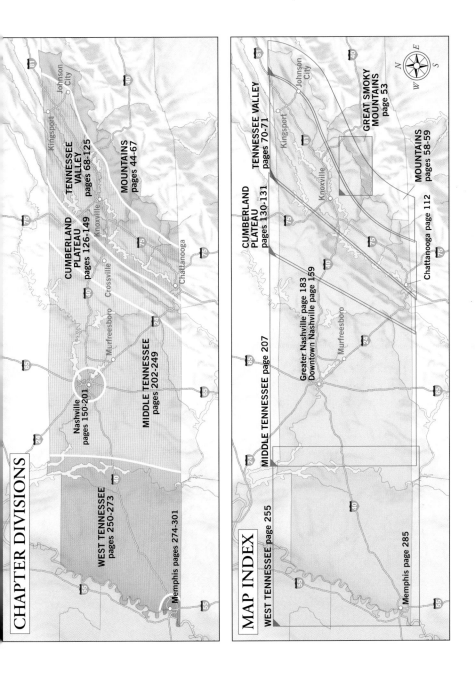

TENNESSEE VALLEY
pages 68-125

MOUNTAINS
pages 44-67

CUMBERLAND PLATEAU
pages 126-149

MIDDLE TENNESSEE
pages 202-249

Nashville
pages 150-201

WEST TENNESSEE
pages 250-273

Memphis pages 274-301

Johnson City

Kingsport

Knoxville

Crossville

Chattanooga

Murfreesboro

MAP INDEX

TENNESSEE VALLEY
pages 70-71

GREAT SMOKY MOUNTAINS
page 53

CUMBERLAND PLATEAU
pages 130-131

MOUNTAINS
pages 58-59

Chattanooga page 112

Greater Nashville page 183
Downtown Nashville page 159

MIDDLE TENNESSEE page 207

WEST TENNESSEE page 255

Memphis page 285

Johnson City

Kingsport

Knoxville

Murfreesboro

N
W E
S

O V E R V I E W

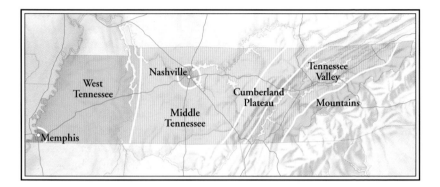

West
Tennessee

Nashville

Middle
Tennessee

Cumberland
Plateau

Tennessee
Valley

Mountains

Memphis

MOUNTAINS

pages 44–67

The tall mountains along Tennessee's eastern border are protected by the Great Smoky Mountains National Park and the two sections of the Cherokee National Forest straddling it. Dense forests, clear, rushing streams, mountaintop "balds," dazzling displays of wildflowers, and more than a thousand miles of trails make this one of the nation's most popular vacation spots. Sprawling tourist towns near the Smokies provide every type of entertainment and shopping imaginable, ranging from the tasteful to the tacky.

Rhododendrons carpet Roan Mountain.

"Cuzin" Raye plays guitar at the Museum of Appalachia.

TENNESSEE VALLEY

pages 68–125

Part of the Great Appalachian Valley that reaches from Canada to Alabama, the valley in Tennessee is actually a series of parallel ridges and valleys. It's where East Tennesseans live and work, though there is no shortage of recreation options on the chain of TVA lakes. The valley's historic sites and museums are most often visited on a trip to the mountains that flank it. Chattanooga, with the fabulous Tennessee Aquarium, pivotal Civil War battlegrounds, and railroad history, is a popular destination in its own right.

CUMBERLAND PLATEAU

pages 126–149

The plateau in Tennessee is part of the larger Appalachian Plateau stretching from New York into the Deep South. This rolling forested upland, sliced by deep rugged gorges harboring swift streams, is a vast outdoor playground. Highlights include Cumberland Gap, the Big South Fork, Fall Creek Falls, South Cum-

Northrup Falls at Caditz Cove.

berland Recreation Area, the late-1800s British colony of Rugby, and the Oxford-inspired Gothic campus of the University of the South at Sewanee.

Shop window along Lower Broadway.

NASHVILLE

pages 150–201

Nashville is best known as Music City, headquarters of the world's country music business, but the talented composers, writers, arrangers, and musicians in this, America's second largest recording center, make all kinds of music besides country. There is much to see beyond music-related sites. Andrew Jackson's Hermitage is one of several splendid antebellum plantation houses open to the public. A replica of the original Parthenon in Athens sets the tone in this city, noted for classical architecture. Nashville is a center of higher education, Tennessee's state capital, and the setting for a network of parks and greenways that protects a pleasing and varied natural environment.

Centennial Park's Parthenon.

MIDDLE TENNESSEE

pages 202–249

The Midstate, which takes in the sprawling Nashville metropolitan area, has two major landforms, the Central Basin and the Highland Rim surrounding it. The Basin, a rich agricultural area, is a rolling mosaic of field and forest dotted with stately houses from both the frontier and antebellum periods. Outdoor recreation is the main attraction on the more forested Highland Rim. Middle Tennessee highlights include Jack Daniel's Distillery and key Civil War sites at Murfreesboro, Franklin, Spring Hill, and Fort Donelson.

Rolling farmland in Middle Tennessee.

Lowland swamp along the Wolf River.

WEST TENNESSEE

pages 250–273

The West state's dominant features are two rivers that border it, the Tennessee on the east, impounded now into Kentucky Lake, and the mighty Mississippi on the west. Chains of wildlife refuges and other preserves line each of the big rivers. Shiloh, scene of a great Civil War battle, is on the Tennessee; and near the Mississippi River, Reelfoot Lake, created during an earthquake in the early 1800s, is one of the Southeast's noted natural areas. The growing and ginning of cotton created great wealth in the Delta region, which accounts for the grand town houses in several of the Deep South towns.

MEMPHIS

pages 274–301

The Bluff City's boast that it's the "home of the blues" and the "birthplace of rock 'n' roll" reflects the city's rich musical tradition, kept alive by museums, the studio where Elvis cut his first record, Graceland, his home, and at clubs offering music day and night on historic Beale Street. Aside from music sites, Memphis has Mud Island, the park and museum showcasing the Mississippi River, the National Civil Rights Museum at the Lorraine Motel, where Martin Luther King, Jr., was assassinated, and one of the nation's finest smaller art museums, the Brooks, in scenic Overton Park. Memphis is host to a year-round lineup of festivals and events dedicated to music—and the other big thing for which the city is famous, barbecue.

The Carl Drew Blues Band performs at a club on Beale Street.

HISTORY AND CULTURE
The "Three States" of Tennessee

MOTORISTS ENTERING THE STATE in the 1960s were puzzled by the signs along the interstates reading: "WELCOME TO THE THREE STATES OF TENNESSEE." The next governor ordered them removed. He said they were divisive. Maybe so. But it's true that Tennesseans have always conceived of their state in thirds: East, Middle, and West. Tennessee's constitution distinguishes between the three "Grand Divisions." The state's flag has three stars. The three divisions are different in just about every way —physically, historically, and culturally. So how did this come about? How did a single state evolve into three states? Because of the land, the lay of the land.

■ LANDSCAPE

Tennessee acquired its borders when someone applied a quill pen to a map and extended the north and south boundaries of North Carolina from the Appalachian crest all the way to the Mississippi River. The resulting 450-by-100-mile parallelogram slices through nine distinct topographic regions, giving Tennessee the most varied landscape and most diverse ecology of any non-coastal state. Environments range from high mountains covered in boreal forests in the East to cypress-filled

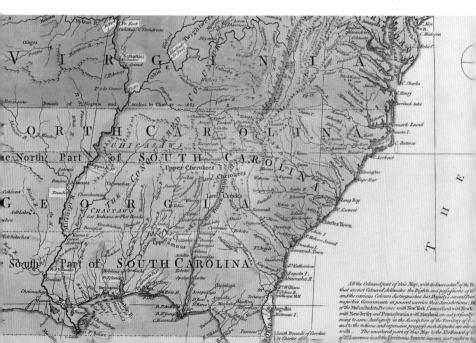

In his painting Tennessee, *A. H. Wyant depicted the gorge where the Tennessee River cuts through the Cumberland Mountains. (Metropolitan Museum of Art, New York City)*

swamps in the West. In between lie narrow valleys between rows of parallel ridges, forested mountain tableland cut by deep gorges, undulating wooded uplands, and rolling farm country. This varied landscape has produced distinct cultures and economies that evolved largely in isolation from each other.

■ THE FRONTIER

William and Lydia Bean get credit for building the first permanent house in Tennessee, a log cabin along the Watauga River at the site of a hunting camp used by William's friend Daniel Boone. The Beans were among the settlers who filtered into the valleys of present-day Upper East Tennessee from colonial Virginia and the Carolinas in the late 1760s. King George III had tried to restrain them with his 1763 proclamation prohibiting westward expansion beyond the Appalachian crest. The king was kindly disposed to his Cherokee allies, who claimed the land.

(opposite) In 1755, Briton John Huske drew "A New and Accurate Map of North America," on which he claimed to have corrected "the Errors of all preceding British, French and Dutch Maps." This detail illustrates England's assertion that its colonies' borders extended west indefinitely. Here the territory that would become Tennessee is part of North Carolina. (Library of Congress)

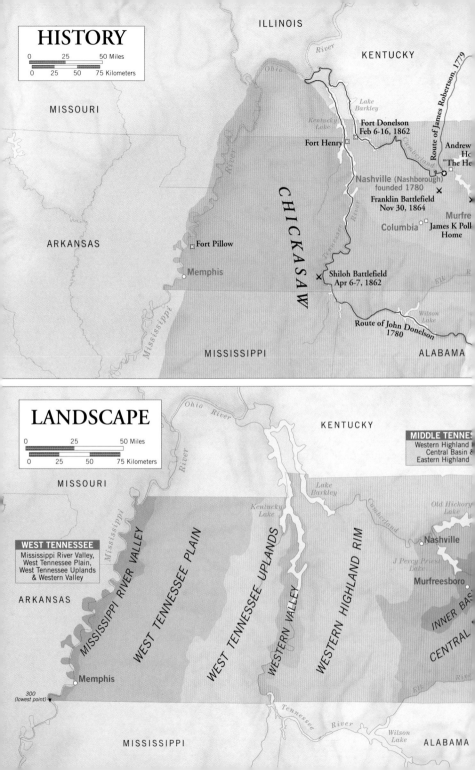

HISTORY

0   25   50 Miles
0   25   50   75 Kilometers

ILLINOIS

KENTUCKY

MISSOURI

Ohio   River

Lake
Barkley

Kentucky
Lake

Fort Donelson
Feb 6-16, 1862

Fort Henry

Route of James Robertson, 1779

Andrew Ho
"The He

Nashville (Nashborough)
founded 1780

×

Franklin Battlefield
Nov 30, 1864

Murfre

Columbia

James K Poll
Home

ARKANSAS

Fort Pillow

Memphis

CHICKASAW

Tennessee   River

×   Shiloh Battlefield
Apr 6-7, 1862

Elk   R

Wilson
Lake

Route of John Donelson
1780

Mississippi

MISSISSIPPI

ALABAMA

LANDSCAPE

0   25   50 Miles
0   25   50   75 Kilometers

Ohio   River

KENTUCKY

MIDDLE TENNES
Western Highland
Central Basin &
Eastern Highland

MISSOURI

River

Lake
Barkley

Kentucky
Lake

Old Hickory
Lake

Cumberland

Nashville

WEST TENNESSEE
Mississippi River Valley,
West Tennessee Plain,
West Tennessee Uplands
& Western Valley

MISSISSIPPI RIVER VALLEY

WEST TENNESSEE PLAIN

WEST TENNESSEE UPLANDS

WESTERN VALLEY

WESTERN HIGHLAND RIM

J Percy Priest
Lake

Murfreesboro

ARKANSAS

Mississippi

INNER BAS

CENTRAL

300
(lowest point)

Memphis

Tennessee   River

Elk

Wilson
Lake

MISSISSIPPI

ALABAMA

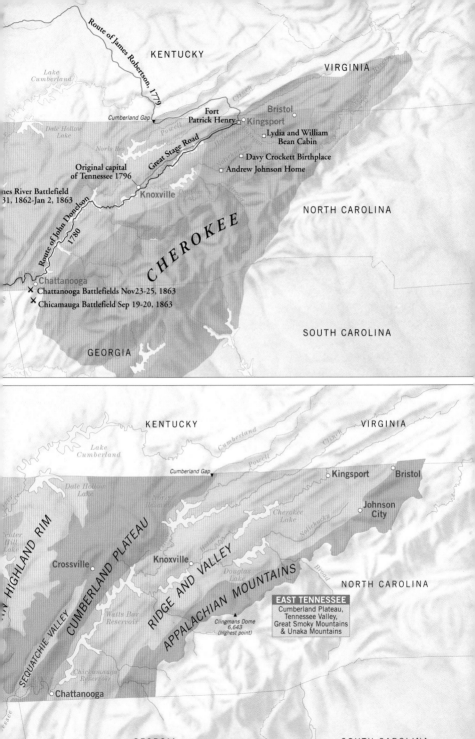

Route of James Robertson, 1779

KENTUCKY

VIRGINIA

Lake Cumberland

Dale Hollow Lake

Cumberland Gap

Fort Patrick Henry

Kingsport

Bristol

Lydia and William Bean Cabin

Davy Crockett Birthplace

Andrew Johnson Home

Norris Res.

Great Stage Road

Original capital of Tennessee 1796

Knoxville

NORTH CAROLINA

nes River Battlefield
31, 1862-Jan 2, 1863

Route of John Donelson 1780

CHEROKEE

Chattanooga

✕ Chattanooga Battlefields Nov 23-25, 1863
✕ Chicamauga Battlefield Sep 19-20, 1863

GEORGIA

SOUTH CAROLINA

KENTUCKY

VIRGINIA

Lake Cumberland

Dale Hollow Lake

Cumberland

Powell

Cumberland Gap

Kingsport

Bristol

Johnson City

Cherokee Lake

Center Hill Lake

N HIGHLAND RIM

CUMBERLAND PLATEAU

Crossville

Norris Reservoir

Knoxville

RIDGE AND VALLEY

Douglas Lake

APPALACHIAN MOUNTAINS

NORTH CAROLINA

Broad

SEQUATCHIE VALLEY

Watts Bar Reservoir

Clingmans Dome 6,643 (highest point)

EAST TENNESSEE
Cumberland Plateau, Tennessee Valley, Great Smoky Mountains & Unaka Mountains

Chickamauga Reservoir

Chattanooga

GEORGIA

SOUTH CAROLINA

For decades the Cherokees were allies of the British. This engraving of Cherokee diplomatic chieftain Attakullakulla (far right) and six other Cherokee chiefs was made during their 1730 visit to King George II. This engraving is the only known likeness of Chief Attakullakulla, who 45 years later would negotiate the vast Transylvania Purchase. (Smithsonian Institution)

The relative peace between the natives and the settlers ended with the outbreak of the American Revolution. The ink was hardly dry on the Declaration of Independence when, in July 1776, the Cherokees launched well-coordinated attacks on the settlements. They captured Lydia Bean and took her to their towns, where only the intervention of Cherokee "Beloved Woman" Nancy Ward saved her from being burned at the stake. The 1776 attack started a cycle of violence and land cessions that by 1819 confined the Cherokees to a small wedge of land in the southeast corner of the state around where Chattanooga would later develop. Most Cherokees by then lived in Georgia. After Tennessee's and Georgia's remaining Cherokees were rounded up in 1838 and herded west on the deadly "Trail of Tears," white settlement of East Tennessee was complete.

The settlement of Middle Tennessee has its origin in the grandiose Transylvania Purchase of 1775 by which North Carolina land speculator Richard Henderson negotiated the purchase from the Cherokees of much of what would become Kentucky and Tennessee. Henderson wanted to make his dubious land title stick, so he recruited John Donelson and James Robertson to lead the "Great Leap Westward," the 1779–80 migration to the lush Cumberland River country. After the threat of Indian attacks faded around 1794, settlement spread out from the Nashville region, and by 1810, it had filled most of the middle part of the state.

The pioneers were never happy being part of North Carolina. North Carolina was never happy with them. So it ceded what would become Tennessee to the United States. In 1790, President George Washington appointed a land-hungry North Carolinian, William Blount, as governor of the new Southwest Territory. Blount's first capital was at Rocky Mount (1790–1792), his second at White's Fort near the confluence of the Holston and French Broad Rivers. The town that grew up here was named in honor of Secretary of War Henry Knox. Tennessee was admitted to the Union in 1796 as the 16th state. As Tennessee grew, the capital moved with the political winds—from Knoxville to Nashville and back, then to Murfreesboro and finally to Nashville in 1826.

Tennesseans started to cast a covetous eye farther west as the frontier period was winding down in East and Middle Tennessee. A scattering of Chickasaw farming villages existed in the fertile land west of the Tennessee River, and all the area was important as hunting grounds for deer, bear, and turkey. Pressure to open West Tennessee to settlement grew stronger and stronger, until finally, in 1818, the U.S. government appointed Andrew Jackson to negotiate

In this portrait of James Robertson (attributed to Henry Benbridge), the wagon train in the background refers to the subject's significance: with John Donelson, he led a migration of settlers into Cumberland Valley country, purchased in 1775 by speculator Richard Henderson. (Tennessee State Museum)

a deal in which the Chickasaws gave up their claim. By 1825, counties were established, Memphis and other towns were laid out, land was cleared, and the growing and harvesting of cotton was underway.

■ ANTEBELLUM YEARS

Tennessee was most clearly divided into "three states" during the four decades before the Civil War. The economy was based on agriculture, and the lay of the land dictated how it was practiced. The hills and valleys of East Tennessee remained as they were during frontier times, a region of small farms where families raised corn, wheat, and livestock for their own consumption and for barter with their neighbors. West Tennessee, on the other hand, is relatively flat and generally fertile. The slave-based, cash-crop plantation economy of the Old South took hold in a big way in the cotton country of West Tennessee. Middle Tennessee was in the middle, both literally and figuratively. There were rich plantations in the Midstate's heartland, notably Wessyngton, the largest plantation in Tennessee, which grew tobacco on its 20,000 acres—but most middle Tennessee farms were smaller than

Thomas W. Wood painted Southern Cornfield, Nashville *in 1861.*
(Courtesy of the T. W. Wood Gallery and Arts Center, Montpelier, Vermont)

*Among Emil Bott's river-and-steamboat paintings is this one of the Cumberland River near
Nashville. The fact that steamboats could navigate the Cumberland and Mississippi Rivers—
and not the Tennessee—served to separate East and West Tennessee from each other, if not from
other states. (Tennessee State Museum, Nashville)*

those in the West, and they usually weren't devoted to a single crop. The region
was a leading exporter of mules, horses, hogs, and sheep.

Transportation, or lack of it, played a major role in the evolution of sectional
differences. Steamboats began chugging up and down the Cumberland and Mississippi Rivers in the 1820s, affording access to outside markets for agricultural
products and bringing in manufactured goods to Middle and West Tennessee.
Nashville and Memphis grew into important river ports. The western Tennessee
River was navigated from the Ohio River to Florence, Alabama, but the upper
reaches to Chattanooga and Knoxville were seldom navigable. This made it next
to impossible to ship anything in or out, further separating the East from the rest
of the state. When railroads were built in the 1850s, they ran north-south, not
east-west through Tennessee. A rail line connected Knoxville to Virginia and
Georgia, but not to the rest of Tennessee. A passenger could get from Nashville to
Louisville, Kentucky, by direct rail, but not to Memphis.

The antebellum decades have been called the "golden age" of Tennessee politics. Andrew Jackson, who emerged as a national hero after leading the defeat of the British at New Orleans in 1815, was elected president in 1828. He dominated politics in Tennessee and the nation for years and gave voice to the aspirations of the common man. Being the controlling and hot-tempered man that he was, Jackson was bound to make enemies, and by the mid-1830s, an anti-Jackson movement was firmly in place in national politics. Tennessee's second president, James K. Polk, a Jackson disciple, was elected in 1844. Anti-Jackson sentiment was strong enough in Tennessee to prevent Polk from carrying his home state.

The great majority of Tennesseans in those days were yeoman farmers. Most didn't own slaves, and the majority of those who did owned one or two and worked the fields alongside them. Slaves made up 25 percent of the state's population by 1860, but their distribution was uneven. East Tennessee was nine percent slave, Middle Tennessee 29 percent, and West Tennessee 34 percent. Social and sectional divisions became more pronounced, as the planters in the Middle and West grew in wealth and influence. Most of the small farmers of East Tennessee had no use for slaves, and opposition to slavery gained an early foothold there.

ANDREW JACKSON ON SELFISH PURPOSES

*I*t is to be regretted that the rich and powerful too often bend the acts of government to their selfish purposes. Distinctions in society will always exist under every just government. Equality of talents, of education, or of wealth cannot be produced by human institutions. In the full enjoyment of the gifts of Heaven and the fruits of superior industry, economy, and virtue, every man is equally entitled to protection by law; but when the laws undertake to add to these natural advantages artificial distinctions, to grant titles, gratuities, and more exclusive privileges, to make the rich richer and the potent more powerful, the humble members of society—the farmers, mechanics, and laborers—who have neither the time nor the means of securing like favors to themselves, have a right to complain of the injustice of their Government. There are no necessary evils in government. Its evils exist only in its abuses. If it would confine itself to equal protection, and, as Heaven does its rains, shower its favors alike on high and the low, the rich and the poor, it would be an unqualified blessing.

—President Andrew Jackson, 1832

This anonymously painted scene depicts James K. Polk speaking to a Knoxville audience on July 4, 1840. At the time he was campaigning for his own second gubernatorial term and for the election of Martin Van Buren to the presidency. (Tennessee State Museum, Nashville)

Though fewer than a quarter of the white families statewide owned slaves, slavery emerged as the number-one political issue of the 1850s. Slave owners exerted power and influence far beyond their numbers as they reacted to fears of slave rebellions and abolitionist rumblings in East Tennessee and in the North. The nation moved closer and closer to disaster as the election of 1860 approached.

■ CIVIL WAR

Tennesseans, or, to be exact, the white males who could vote in those days, initially rebuffed the Deep South states, which seceded after the 1860 election of President Abraham Lincoln. In a Tennessee referendum in February 1861, the East voted "no" to secession, the West voted "yes," and the Middle tipped the scales against it. Attitudes changed after Confederates fired on Fort Sumter, and Lincoln called for troops in April 1861. In a vote in June, the Middle Tennessee vote switched from a majority against to 88 percent for secession.

The Civil War ravaged Tennessee like no other state except Virginia. The state was a major battleground. Geography and politics dictated that it would be. Tennessee's border, stretching from the mountains to the Mississippi, was the Confederacy's western border. And because of the sharply divided loyalties—more pronounced in East Tennessee, but present everywhere—Tennessee was one place where, literally, brother fought brother and neighbor fought neighbor. In an engagement near Memphis, for example, the Second Tennessee Cavalry–Confederate fought the Second Tennessee Cavalry–Union.

The conduct of the war produced a curious result. Secession sentiment was strongest where the plantation economy was the strongest, in West Tennessee and in the Middle Tennessee heartland. Yet those regions were the first to fall to Union occupation. Pro-Union East Tennessee stayed under Confederate control much

Born and raised in the northeastern United States, artist Gilbert Gaul nonethelesss sympathized with the romance of the Confederate cause, as evidenced by his painting Holding the Line at All Hazards. *Though often associated with Tennessee, Gaul in reality spent less than a quarter of his life in the state. (Birmingham Museum of Art, Alabama, gift of John Meyer)*

Alexander Simplot painted this scene of the Union ironclad Monarch *sinking the Confederate*
Beauregard *on the Mississippi near Memphis in June of 1862. It was patterned after sketches
he made as an artist correspondent during the Civil War. (Chicago Historical Society)*

longer. This anomaly heightened the vicious behind-the-lines conflict between
civilians, guerrillas, bushwhackers, and outlaws of differing loyalties. Violence and
pillage were common.

The military campaigns consisted mostly of Federal thrusts south and Confederate attempts to stop them. The major battles of Fort Donelson, Shiloh, Stones
River, Chickamauga, and Chattanooga, and the less violent but important Tullahoma Campaign, all fit this pattern. Two exceptions were the Confederate advance
on Knoxville in late 1863 and the Confederate army's brief return to Middle Tennessee in late 1864.

Tennessee contributed 187,000 soldiers to the Confederacy, though no Tennessean ever commanded a Confederate army and no Tennessean served in high
political office in the Confederacy. Tennessee contributed 51,000 men to the
Union cause, 40 percent of whom were African Americans. The rest were mostly
East Tennesseans.

HISTORY:
CIVIL WAR

CIVIL WAR IN TENNESSEE

A TIMELINE OF MAJOR EVENTS

1860

> *November* Abraham Lincoln elected president.

1861

> *February* A referendum on secession shows East Tennessee against, Middle against, West for secession.

> *April* Tennessee refuses to answer Lincoln's call for volunteers.

> *June* By more than two to one, Tennessee votes for secession.

1862

> *February* Fort Donelson surrenders unconditionally to U.S General Ulysses S. Grant.

> *April* Battle of Shiloh.

> *June* Naval battle at Memphis.

> *December* Battle of Stones River (Murfreesboro).

1863

> *September* Battle of Chickamauga.

> *November* Battle of Chattanooga.

1864

> *November—December* Battles of Franklin and Nashville.

1865

> *April 9* Confederate General Robert E. Lee surrenders to Union General Ulysses S. Grant.

> *April 15* President Lincoln assassinated.

> *April 16* Tennessee war-governor Andrew Johnson becomes president.

CIVIL WAR TENNESSEE

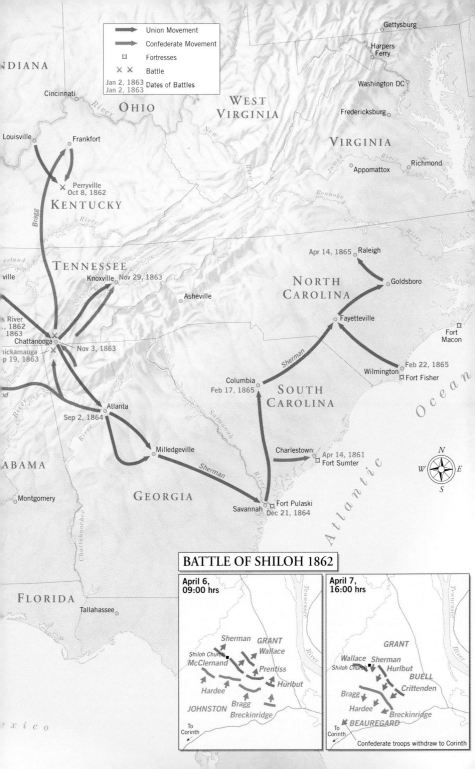

Union Movement
Confederate Movement
Fortresses
Battle
Jan 2, 1863
Jan 2, 1863 Dates of Battles

INDIANA
Cincinnati
OHIO
Louisville Frankfort
Perryville
Oct 8, 1862
KENTUCKY
TENNESSEE
Knoxville   Nov 29, 1863
Nov 3, 1863
Chattanooga
Chickamauga
Sep 19, 1863
Atlanta
Sep 2, 1864
Milledgeville
ALABAMA
Montgomery
GEORGIA
Savannah   Fort Pulaski
Dec 21, 1864
FLORIDA
Tallahassee

WEST
VIRGINIA

Gettysburg
Harpers
Ferry
Washington DC
Fredericksburg
VIRGINIA
Appomattox Richmond
Asheville
NORTH
CAROLINA
Apr 14, 1865   Raleigh
Goldsboro
Fayetteville
Fort
Macon
Wilmington
Feb 22, 1865
Fort Fisher
Columbia
Feb 17, 1865
SOUTH
CAROLINA
Charlestown   Apr 14, 1861
Fort Sumter

N
W   E
S

Atlantic Ocean

BATTLE OF SHILOH 1862

April 6,
09:00 hrs

Sherman   GRANT
Wallace
Shiloh Church
McClernand
Prentiss
Hurlbut
Hardee
Bragg
Breckinridge
JOHNSTON
To
Corinth

April 7,
16:00 hrs

GRANT
Wallace Sherman
Shiloh Church   Hurlbut
BUELL
Bragg   Crittenden
Hardee   Breckinridge
BEAUREGARD
To
Corinth
Confederate troops withdraw to Corinth

1862   FORT DONELSON

February 6-16, Cumberland River, near Dover.

USA: Gen. Ulysses S. Grant with Generals McClernand, Smith, and Wallace; also Adm. Foote of the US Navy.

CSA: Gen. John B. Floyd with Generals Buckner, Forrest, and Pillow.

Result: Buckner surrenders Fort Donelson.

Casualties*: US: 2,624; **CS:** 1,500 plus 2,200 soldiers surrendered.

Effect on war: A critical Federal victory that pierces the heart of the South. A relatively obscure Union general, Ulysses S. Grant, earns the *nom de guerre* "Unconditionial Surrender" and is promoted to major general.

Events: Re-enactments by local citizens and volunteers each February.

Fort Donelson National Battlefield: West edge of Dover on US-79; 931-232-5706; www.nps.gov/fodo.

USA: Ulysses S. Grant   (1822-1885)
A tanner's son from Ohio, Grant fought valiantly in the Mexican War but was unable to adjust to civilian life—at one time he sold firewood for a living. A relative unknown at Fort Donelson, he rose to become commander of the Federal armies and later, president of the United States.

CSA: Simon Bolivar Buckner (1823-1914)
A Kentuckian and a West Point graduate, Buckner opposed secession but eventually joined the Confederate army. He had the misfortune of being abandoned at Fort Donelson by two ranking officers and was forced to surrender to his old friend Ulysses S. Grant. Held captive until August and freed in a prisoner exchange, Buckner remained friends with Grant and was a pall bearer at his funeral.

***Casualty records** vary widely for individual Civil War battles. Some figures reflect the inclusion of casualties from skirmishes connected to battles, others do not. In general, Union casualty figures are more reliable than Confederate. These are the publisher's best estimates based on a variety of sources.

1862 SHILOH (PITTSBURGH LANDING)

April 4-6, 1862 at Tennessee River, near border of Mississippi.

USA: Gen. Ulysses S. Grant (Army of the Tennessee) with Generals Buell (Army of the Ohio), Prentiss, Sherman, and Wallace.

CSA: Gen. Albert Sydney Johnston with Gen. P. G. T. Beauregard (Army of Mississippi).

Result: Confederate attack repulsed. General Johnston killed.

Casualties: US: 13,047; **CS:** 10,694

Effect on war: An equivocal victory for the Union with enormous losses on both sides including that of Confederate General Johnston. Timely Union reinforcements from generals Crittenden, Nelson, and Wallace, and the lack of same from Confederate General Van Dorn, help turn the tide in Grant's favor. The death of Johnston is deeply mourned by Confederate President Jefferson Davis, as it is throughout the South. Beauregard's retreat to Corinth, Mississippi, further cements the Union's dominance in Tennessee.

Events: Exhibits, anniversary re-enactments, Memorial Day Services.

Shiloh National Military Park: About nine miles south of Savannah, TN; 731-689-5696; www.nps.gov/shil.

CSA: Albert Sidney Johnston   (1803-1862)
A Kentuckian and West Point graduate, Johnston was a charismatic leader who fought in the Black Hawk War and the Mexican War. Confederate President Jefferson Davis considered him "the greatest soldier… then living." Johnston died of a leg wound sustained at Shiloh.

CSA: Pierre Gustave Toutant Beauregard (1818-1893)
Beauregard ordered his men to fire the first shots of the Civil War—on Fort Sumter (South Carolina), April 12, 1861. Courtly and of soldierly bearing, he was the son of an old Louisiana Creole family. Beauregard assumed command at Shiloh after General Johnston was killed.

1863   STONES RIVER (MURFREESBORO)

December 31, 1862 to January 2, 1863 at Stones River northwest of Murfreesboro.

USA: Gen. William S. Rosecrans (Army of the Cumberland).

CSA: Gen. Braxton Bragg (Army of Tennessee); Generals Breckinridge and Hardee.

Result: The Federals repulse Bragg's army, which retreats.

Casualties: US: 13,249; CS: 11,739

Effect on war: A crucial Federal victory after the crushing defeat at Fredericksburg, Virginia. Wrote Lincoln to Rosecrans after the victory: "I can never forget ... you gave us a hard-earned victory, which had there been a defeat instead, the nation could scarcely have lived over." Technically considered a military draw, Bragg's order to retreat is roundly criticized by his military advisors.

Events: Re-enactments on anniversary; major service on Sunday before Memorial Day.

Stones River National Battlefield: From I-24, take exit 78B. Follow TN-96 to its junction with US-41/70. Take US-41/70S north to Thompson Lane; turn left at Thompson Lane to Old Nashville Hwy.; follow signs to visitor center. 615-893-9501; www.nps.gov/stri.

*USA: **William S. Rosecrans**
(1819-1898)
Born in Ohio, "Old Rosy" graduated from West Point in 1842. A gifted strategist, he led the Union Army at Stones River. An error in his battle instructions at Chickamauga cost the Federals the battle, and he lost his command.*

1863   TULLAHOMA CAMPAIGN

June–July along Duck and Elk Rivers.

Effect on war: In just 11 days General Rosecrans maneuvers the Confederates out of Middle Tennessee, setting the stage for the battles of Chickamagua and Chattanooga. Though overshadowed by subsequent and current events (Gettysburg and Vicksburg), the campaign is a turning point in the Civil War.

> **Note:** As a rule, the Union named its armies after rivers—Army of the Tennessee (River)—and named the battle sites after the closest landmark—Battle of Stones River. The Confederacy, however, named its armies after states—Army of Tennessee—and named the battle sites after the nearest town—Battle of Murfreesboro.

1863   CHICKAMAUGA & CHATTANOOGA

September 19 to November 25, 1863 at Chickamauga (GA) and Chattanooga.

USA: Gen. William S. Rosecrans (Army of the Cumberland); then Gen. Grant with Generals Hooker, Sherman, and Thomas.

CSA: Gen. Braxton Bragg (Army of Tennessee) with Generals Longstreet and Wheeler.

Result: The Federals defeat Bragg's army forcing him to retreat.

Combined casualties: US: 21,993, **CS:** 24,941

Effect on war: Having regrouped from the Battle of Murfreesboro, Bragg's army lures Rosecrans on September 19 into a trap at Chickamauga Creek just south of Chattanooga. Longstreet, finding a hole in Rosecrans's line, routs the Federals until Gen. George H. Thomas stands firm on Snodgrass Hill, earning him the sobriquet "Rock of Chickamauga."

Nevertheless, the defeated Federals retreat into Chattanooga. There, blockaded by Bragg, Rosecrans's army faces either surrender or starvation. Alarmed, Gen. Ulysses S. Grant joins Rosecrans (whom he removes from command), bringing with him 36,000 men under generals Sherman and Hooker. Foiling the blockade with a pontoon "Cracker Line" across the Tennessee River at Brown's Ferry, Grant is able to ferry Hooker's forces (and rations) into Chattanooga. Bragg (at Davis' order) sends Longstreet and Wheeler to Knoxville, a dangerous decision, but one based on the impregnability of the Confederate positions on the high ground—Missionary Ridge, Lookout Mountain, and Orchard Knob. Grant decides to attack immediately.

On November 23, Thomas's men rout the Confederates from Orchard Knob. On the 24th Hooker's soldiers push the Confederates off Lookout Mountain, the fabled "Battle Above the Clouds." With Bragg's forces now concentrated on Missionary Ridge, Grant orders Thomas to attack. His men, disobeying orders, pursue the Confederates up the mountainside, staying so close to the fleeing enemy that the riflemen above shoot high in order to avoid hitting their own men. That night the Confederates retreat into Georgia; the result leaves the Union in control of nearly all of Tennessee.   *(continues)*

USA: *Joseph Hooker:* *(1814-1879)*
Fine looking and contentious, Hooker was the grandson of an officer in George Washington's army. A West Point graduate, his style was autocratic, yet he was known for improving conditions for his troops and raising their morale. He lost badly to Robert E. Lee at Chancellorsville but regained his reputation at Chattanooga, when he captured Lookout Mountain and joined the decisive assault at Missionary Ridge.

Events: Exhibits, re-enactments during anniversary days; a major service on the Sunday before Memorial Day.

Chickamauga & Chattanooga National Military Park. Chickamauga, Georgia, is on US-27 just south of Chattanooga. The Chattanooga sites are scattered throughout the city; information: 706-866-9241; www.nps.gov/chch/.

1864 FRANKLIN & NASHVILLE
November–December, 1864 at Franklin.

USA: Gen. George Thomas (Army of the Cumberland) with Generals Smith, Schofield, Cox, Wilson, Steedman.

CSA: Gen. John Bell Hood (Army of Tennessee) with Generals Forrest and Stephen Lee.

Result: Although Grant has received reluctant support from President Lincoln to replace Thomas for lack of action, Thomas leads the Federals in two battles that vanquish Hood and the Confederate Army of Tennessee, effectively removing them from the rest of the war.

Casualties: US: 5,387; **CS:** 7,752

Effect on war: On November 29, 1864, General Hood outflanks Schofield's Federals and has them trapped. But that night, while the Confederates sleep, the entire Union army sneaks past the Confederate lines. Having escaped the trap, Schofield deploys his troops on a long arc in a bend of the Harpeth River at Franklin.

USA: George Henry Thomas
(1816-1870)
A graduate of West Point, Thomas fought in the Mexican War and in Texas with the 2nd Cavalry. Though a Virginian, he remained loyal to the Union. Big and deliberate, he was greatly admired by his men who called him "Slow Trot." At Chickamauga he held off a Confederate attack long enough to allow Rosecrans to retreat to Chattanooga. At Chattanooga he stormed Missionary Ridge routing Bragg, and at the battle of Nashville he crushed Hood's army.

Hood's attack is repulsed and Schofield is able to join Thomas in Nashville. Bad weather limits the armies to occasional skirmishes until December 15 when Thomas attacks Hood, who retreats but re-establishes a line south of Nashville. On the 16th, with General Steedman holding the Confederate right flank, Thomas sends Schofield and the bulk of the Union army at Hood's left flank. The Confederate center collapses and even though Forrest's calvary wages a devastating rear-guard action against the Federals, Hood's Army of Tennessee is vanquished. Hood retreats to Tupelo, Mississippi, where he relinquishes his command.

Franklin. Battle sites are in and near the town of Franklin and are described on pages 208-209 and 212.

CSA: Nathan Bedford Forrest
(1821-1877)
The son of a blacksmith on the Tennessee frontier, Forrest was a tall, fierce man and a slave trader before the onset of the Civil War. One of the Confederacy's greatest cavalrymen and raiders, in 1862, at Murfreesboro, he took a thousand Federals prisoner and captured a million dollars worth of supplies. After arguing with Braxton Bragg at Chickamauga, he was transferred.

CSA: John Bell Hood
(1831-1879)
A native of Kentucky and a graduate of West Point, Hood led Confederate forces valiantly at Second Manassas, Antietam, Fredericksburg, and Gettysburg. He lost a leg at Chickamauga and thereafter rode into battle strapped to his horse. Hood was held responsible for the Confederate disaster at Franklin and was relieved of his command at his own request.

— by Pennfield Jensen

William Cooper painted this portrait of Andrew Johnson in 1856. Johnson, an opponent of secession, was the only Southern member of the U.S. Senate during the Civil War. Johnson became President on April 15, 1865, upon Lincoln's assassination. He served until 1868, when he was nearly impeached for what was perceived to be excessive sympathy for the defeated South. Johnson lost the Democratic presidential nomination in 1868, but returned to the Senate briefly in 1874. He died in July of 1875. (Tennessee Historical Society)

■ RECONSTRUCTION AND THE NEW SOUTH

The drive to bring divided Tennessee back into the Union began well before the Confederacy collapsed, when early in 1862 Lincoln appointed former governor and staunch East Tennessee Unionist Andrew Johnson as military governor. When Johnson went to Washington in 1865 as Lincoln's vice president, the governorship passed to Knoxville's William G. "Parson" Brownlow, a passionately pro-Union minister-turned-newspaper publisher. He soon implemented punitive policies against former Confederates. The next five years saw political turmoil that some said was worse than the war.

Brownlow was no abolitionist, but he found it expedient to promote civil rights for newly freed slaves to keep his Radical Republicans in power. He pushed through legislation abolishing slavery, granting blacks the right to vote, and

(opposite) Published in an 1866 Harper's Weekly, *this Thomas Nast cartoon depicts Andrew Johnson as Iago of Shakespeare's* Othello, *in which the deceitful Iago betrays the dark-skinned Othello. The portrayal satirizes Johnson as an enemy of the newly freed slaves, whose economic position deteriorated during his administration. (Library of Congress)*

ratifying the Fourteenth Amendment. With that, Tennessee, the last state to leave the Union, became the first state to return.

Former Confederates were in the majority in Tennessee, and a backlash was inevitable. Resistance was both clandestine, as in the case of the Ku Klux Klan, and more overtly political. When Brownlow left for the U. S. Senate in 1869, his successor took a more conciliatory approach to former Confederates. When the convention met in Nashville in 1870 to write a new state constitution, former Rebels were firmly in control. This marked the end of Tennessee's unique Reconstruction. One-time Confederate general John C. Brown was elected governor, and within two decades, conservative Democrats were in complete control of state government.

In the aftermath of the Civil War, landowners found it necessary to give newly freed slaves and landless whites a stake in the land to keep them working on it. A form of tenancy called "sharecropping" evolved in which former plantations were subdivided and portions rented to laborers who paid a share of their crop as rent. The number of farm units in Tennessee doubled between 1860 and 1880. Many blacks migrated to the cities where they became craftsmen and successful business owners. Schools and colleges for blacks opened. The freedmen organized their own churches. Blacks elected their numbers to political office.

The new freedom proved illusory, however. As time passed, sharecropping trapped tenants in cycles of debt, dependence, and poverty. The conservatives who controlled Tennessee's government imposed a new racial order of legally mandated segregation. The new poll tax made it difficult, impossible in some cases, for blacks to vote. Violence against blacks grew. Lynchings became more common. The high hopes of emancipation evaporated in the hot Tennessee sun.

Tennessee's elites embraced the post-Reconstruction "New South" push toward industrialization. As in everything else, the movement's results varied by Grand Division, with East Tennessee becoming the most industrialized. Capital investment in Chattanooga in the 1870s grew by 450 percent as the city became a major center for iron and steel manufacturing. Textile mills sprung up in nearly every East Tennessee town. Much of the industry was extractive, exploitive, and colonial in nature, especially in the Cumberland Plateau coal fields. Low wages and cheap natural resources created wealth for a few, but they did little to relieve the poverty that prevailed in much of Tennessee. The dream of making Tennessee an industrial powerhouse hadn't been realized by the dawn of the 20th century.

TVA photographer Lewis Hine took this photograph of a homestead in Stooksbury, near Andersonville, in 1933. The construction of the Norris Dam caused the flooding of this 350-acre estate. (Tennessee Valley Authority Collection)

■ THE NEW DEAL

President Franklin D. Roosevelt promised the nation a "New Deal" after his 1932 election. He committed the resources of the Federal government as never before to lift the country out of the Great Depression. Politicians in many states resented federal intrusion, and resisted the new programs. Not in Tennessee. The political leadership welcomed it with enthusiasm. The New Deal had a greater impact on Tennessee than on any other state, as a host of "alphabet" agencies altered the landscape. The WPA built schools, hospitals, roads, parks, post offices, courthouses, and public housing. The CCC developed the Great Smoky Mountains National Park and state parks and forests. The government built model communities like Norris and the Cumberland Homesteads.

The New Deal agency generating the most profound impact was the Tennessee Valley Authority. Established by Congress in the first hundred days of Roosevelt's administration, TVA used a multifaceted approach to transform the region. TVA built dams that created a series of huge lakes up and down the Tennessee River and its tributaries and instituted progressive programs in agriculture, soil conservation, reforestation, navigation, and flood control. The most momentous changes in ordinary life came about after electricity arrived in rural homes and villages. Only three percent of rural residents had electricity in 1933. Electric irons, pumps for indoor plumbing, refrigerators, stoves, radios, and lights were almost unknown

outside the cities, but by 1940, nearly everyone had them. TVA was by 1945 the nation's largest producer of electricity. Regional per capita income rose from 44 percent of the national average to 61 percent by 1953.

■ WORLD WAR II AND AFTERWARDS

The impact of World War II on Tennessee was not unique, but it was profound. Components for the atomic bomb were built at Oak Ridge, and army and air corps fields were built across the state. When soldiers returned from war, they were in no mood to tolerate subjugation. Fed up with what they perceived as a corrupt political system, veterans in McMinn County in 1946 formed a political party. When it looked like the old machine was stealing the election, the veterans armed themselves and retrieved the ballot boxes in what came to be called "The Battle of Athens." The same year in Columbia armed black veterans protected their community from a mob.

A soon-to-be soldier bids goodbye to his sweetheart and family at Nashville's Union Station in the early days of World War II. (Tennessee State Library and Archives, photograph by Ed Clark)

U.S. Senator Albert Gore joins his wife and son in a victory salute after winning the Democratic primary race in 1958. (Bettmann/CORBIS)

In postwar elections, Estes Kefauver, Albert Gore Sr., and Frank Clement defeated established candidates, and, though by no means allies, they became the dominant forces in Tennessee politics. Kefauver and Gore, along with Lyndon Johnson, were the only U. S. senators from the former Confederacy who refused to sign the "Southern Manifesto" opposing school desegregation after the Supreme Court ordered it in 1954. Other than at Clinton, where in 1956 Governor Clement deployed the Highway Patrol and the National Guard to quell the anti-integration mob, and in Nashville, where a school was blown up, school desegregation was mostly peaceful. Oddly enough, the instigator of violence in both places was a man who traveled to Tennessee from New Jersey, John Kasper.

Tennessee abolished the onerous poll tax in 1953. Intimidation of black voters was not pervasive in Tennessee, but it did exist in the West Tennessee counties of Fayette and Haywood. When a black World War II veteran, John McFerrin, and his wife, Viola, helped launch a voter registration drive in 1959, white landowners retaliated by evicting black tenants—who then moved onto black-owned land in what came to be called "Tent City." The stalemate ended with a court consent decree in 1962 that guaranteed the right to vote. In 1960, Nashville became the first Southern city to voluntarily desegregate its public accommodations—four years before the civil rights act required it. It was not without a struggle, however, as it followed four months of sit-ins by courageous students led by James Lawson, Diane Nash, and future U. S. Congressman John Lewis.

A civil rights protestor is forcibly removed from a Nashville restaurant during a 1963 sit-in.
(Nashville Public Library, The Nashville Room)
(above, right) FedEx employs 30,000 workers at its Memphis headquarters.
(FedEx Service Marks, used by permission)

■ "THREE STATES" IN THE LATE 20TH CENTURY

The lay of the land's grip on Tennessee's culture loosened in the last quarter of the 20th century, but not altogether. Manufacturing and services replaced agriculture as the dominant sectors of the economy. Places like Vonore, Morrison, Decherd, Spring Hill, and Union City became home to enormous plants that helped make Tennessee fourth in the nation in automotive manufacturing and 16th in overall manufacturing. The service sector fueled explosive suburban growth around the big cities. Nashville is now the center of the world's proprietary health care industry. Memphis is a major distribution center, where one employer alone, the FedEx Corporation, employs 30,000 workers. Tennesseans can crisscross the state on interstate highways unaware of the "Grand Divisions." And, too, the same forces homogenizing the rest of America are at work in Tennessee—the same chain stores, same fast food joints, same TV shows.

Still, regional differences remain. Once you get away from the interstates and the strip malls, it's much as it's always been in the "three states of Tennessee." When the Houston Oilers moved to Nashville in the late 1990s to be the "Tennessee" whatever, the team adopted a logo with three stars, one for each Grand Division. They renamed themselves the "Titans" because it sounded good. They had wanted a name that would be distinctly Tennessee, one that would unify the whole state, one everyone could identify with. They couldn't come up with one.

NOTABLE TENNESSEANS (BORN OR SETTLED HERE)

Andrew Jackson   1767–1845
The ever-popular "Old Hickory" defeated the British at New Orleans and became seventh president of the United States. He and wife Rachel lived at The Hermitage in Nashville.

David ("Davy") Crockett   1786–1836
A frontier legend and cultural icon, he served three terms in Congress, and died defending the Alamo.

Sam Houston   1793–1863
Called "Black Raven" by the Cherokee with whom he grew up, Houston became governor of Tennessee in 1827. He is perhaps more famous as president of the Republic of Texas. Later, as a senator from the state of Texas, he was expelled for refusing to support secession.

James K. Polk   1795–1849
Eleventh president of the United States, Polk was variously dubbed "The Dark Horse," "Napoleon of the Stump," and "Young Hickory." Polk oversaw the acquisition of California and the Southwest during a tumultuous tenure. He died at home in Nashville three months after leaving office.

David Glasgow Farragut   1801–1870
The outstanding naval officer of the Civil War. "Damn the torpedoes!" became his hallmark phrase. First U.S. officer to attain the rank of admiral (1866).

Andrew Johnson   1808–1875
Staunchly opposed to secession, Senator Andrew Johnson was appointed military governor of Tennessee by President Lincoln. Later he ran for vice president with Lincoln. Upon Lincoln's assassination, Johnson became the 17th president.

Nathan Bedford Forrest   1821–1877
Commander of all the cavalry under John Bell Hood's Army of Tennessee, Forrest was the Confederacy's greatest cavalryman. He was known for his lightning strikes deep into enemy territory and may have been responsible for the massacre at Fort Pillow.

Cordell Hull   1871–1955
A renowned American statesman, Hull served as secretary of state under FDR and was awarded the 1945 Nobel Peace Prize. His legacies? Both the IRS and the United Nations.

Alvin York   1887–1964
During World War I, York—formerly a conscientious objector—led eight men in a raid on a German machine gun nest, killing 17 Germans with 17 rifle shots and eight more with eight pistol shots. The 132 remaining Germans surrendered their position, and "Sergeant York" became known as one of great heroes of World War I.

Bessie Smith   1894–1937

Extolled as "Empress of the Blues," she is still considered by many to be the finest female blues vocalist ever.

Robert Penn Warren   1905–1989

American novelist, poet, and critic who won the Pulitzer Prize for his novel *All The King's Men* and later became the nation's first poet laureate.

James Agee   1909–1955

Author of *A Death in the Family* and, with photographer Walker Evans, *Let Us Now Praise Famous Men*. Screenplays include *The African Queen* and *Night of The Hunter.*

Alex Haley   1921–1992

Author of the worldwide best seller and Pulitzer Prize–winning *Roots,* as well as of the critically acclaimed *Autobiography of Malcolm X.*

Patricia Neal   1926–

A popular actress whose early successes include *The Day The Earth Stood Still* and an Oscar-winning performance in *Hud*. She later overcame both family tragedy and a paralyzing stroke to be nominated for a second Oscar in *The Subject Was Roses.*

Carl Perkins   1932–1998

A seminal rockabilly musician whose *Blue Suede Shoes* became a classic and who strongly influenced Johnny Cash, Willie Nelson, Jerry Lee Lewis, and the Beatles.

Red Grooms   1937–

One of the earliest practitioners of the "happening," the artist is best known for his satirical and cartoon-like pop-art constructions.

Tina Turner   1938–

Powerhouse rock and R&B singer who began as a backup singer to Ike Turner, and later, on her own, became a film and music legend.

Elvis Presley   1935–1977

America's greatest rock and roller moved to Memphis in 1948 and got his first chance at Sun Studios. *(See pages 287-291.)*

Wilma Rudolph   1940–1994

The 20th of 22 children, she overcame childhood polio to become one of the premiere athletes of her time, winning medals at the 1960 Olympics as well as the James E. Sullivan Memorial Award in 1961.

Dolly Parton 1946–

(See page 191.)

Al Gore Jr.   1948–

Vice President of the United States (1993-2001) and Democratic candidate for president in 2000. Son of Albert Gore, Sr., 1907-98, Democratic senator from Tennessee (1953-71).

Kathy Bates   1948–

This gifted actress has enlivened such films as *Misery, Fried Green Tomatoes, Primary Colors, Titanic,* and *A Civil Action.*

THE MOUNTAINS

MOUNTAINS

◆ **AREA OVERVIEW**

Travel Basics: The high mountains rising like a giant blue wall above the eastern margin of the Tennessee Valley embrace some the most inviting and most visited places in America. Known locally by different names—Great Smokies, Balds, Unakas, Unicois—they're the western edge of the part of the Appalachians geologists call the Blue Ridge Province that stretches from Pennsylvania to Georgia. You'll see on the official Tennessee highway map that Tennessee's eastern border is marked with a ragged swath of green denoting public lands. The mountains lie within the boundaries of either the Great Smoky Mountains National Park or the Cherokee National Forest. Together they offer a million-plus acres of unparalleled beauty and unlimited outdoor recreational opportunities.

Getting Around: The best way to get around Tennessee's mountains is on your own power, hiking on the 1,400 miles of trails, and canoeing, kayaking, or rafting the scenic rivers. The Appalachian Trail (AT) climbs up and down 284 miles along Tennessee's crests and gaps on its 2,140-mile, 14-state journey from Maine to Georgia. The trail stretches in Tennessee along the Roan Highlands and the Smokies are the highest on the entire Appalachian Trail. For AT information, call the AT Conservancy at 304-535-6331.

Driving the mountain roads can seem like heaven or hell depending on the time and place. Roads crossing Tennessee's mountains into North Carolina offer spectacular views. That goes for routes through river gorges—US-70 along the French Broad, I-40 along the Pigeon, and US-64 along the Ocoee—and those that climb over the mountains—TN-143 across the Roan Highlands, the Newfound Gap Road over the Smokies, and the Cherohala Skyway.

Around the Smokies during summer and on autumn and holiday weekends, traffic backs up for miles around Gatlinburg and Pigeon Forge and on the Newfound Gap and the Cades Cove Roads. The GSMNP is, after all, the most visited national park in the country. Nearly 10 million visitors a year. Still, you can beat the crowds. Stay away from the tourist towns. Be at Newfound Gap to witness the pink and golden sunrise over the distant Balsam Mountains. Arrive at Cades Cove at first light as the deer graze along meadow's edge.

Climate: There is no best season to visit the mountains. Each has its own special beauty. Keep in mind that the higher you go, the colder, wetter, and windier it will be. The lowlands may be sweltering in the 90s in summer, while the highest mountains never get above 80. Winters are fickle, with temperatures in the high country sometimes quickly falling from the 40s to the teens or colder. Spring and fall temperatures are mostly moderate, and even winter has spring-like interludes. High elevation ice and snow are common from November through April. Mountain weather shouldn't keep you from doing anything you want. Just be prepared for it.

Food & Lodging: The Great Smoky Mountains are big-time tourist country, so there is no shortage of places to eat and sleep outside the park. Food and lodging are harder to find around the Cherokee National Forest. With the exception of a few inns near the Smokies, food and lodging are only adequate, nothing more; cabin rentals are nice alternatives.

MOUNTAINS

■ THE SETTING

The mountains are like a wrinkled quilt draped over the Appalachian crest, with half falling into Tennessee and the other half into North Carolina, a patchwork of distinct parts. Up high, above 5,000 feet, where the ridges often disappear into the clouds, a dense, dark forest of spruce and fir covers the crest, and below that, down to 4,500 feet, is a Canadian-type forest of northern hardwoods like birch, beech, and red maple. Oak-hickory forests blanket the lower ridges, except the dry southern exposures that are covered with pine. Coves and valleys are filled with majestic hardwoods like tulip poplar and sugar maple and are carpeted with wildflowers. Dark groves of towering hemlock dot the whole area.

Mountain-crest forests are broken by openings called "balds," heath balds and grassy balds. Locals call the heath balds "laurel slicks," but they're actually tangles of Catawba rhododendron. In June, they look like patches of pink and purple painted on the peaks. Grassy balds are meadows in deep green or bright tan, depending on the season, fringed in rhododendron, laurel, azalea, and blackberry.

Flaming azalea blooms on Gregory Bald Mountain in Great Smoky Mountains National Park.

*Moss forms a dense carpet on rocks in Little Santeetlah Creek in
Joyce Kilmer–Slickrock Wilderness Area.*

The heavens pour nearly 100 inches of rain on the highest ridges—more than any other place in the contiguous 48 states outside the Northwest—creating an environment of staggering diversity. In the Smokies, there are 130 species of trees. That's more than are found on the continent of Europe. There are 1,500 kinds of blooming plants and 2,500 species of mosses, lichens, and fungi.

Roaring rivers breach Tennessee's mountains through steep-sided gorges—the Nolichucky, the French Broad, the Pigeon, the Tellico, the Hiwassee, and the Ocoee. Other rivers—the South Holston, the Watauga, and the Little Tennessee —have been dammed to form lakes whose cool, clear waters lap against steep, green ridges. Streams starting as trickles high on the Tennessee side tumble down the mountains on some of the world's steepest gradients, providing miles of icy trout water.

(following pages) Sunrise as seen from Cherohala Skyway.

MOUNTAINS

Evidence of human activity is scant in parts of the mountains, apparent in others. Settlers in the 19th century cleared most of the coves for farming. Some are still in farms. Cades Cove in the Smokies is the one most people know about. Shady Valley in the state's northeastern corner is another. Forests have reclaimed some of the coves. Greenbrier in the Smokies is a good example. Cut-and-run timber barons swept through the mountains in the first two decades of the 20th century, leaving only the trees they couldn't reach. Second growth covers most of the mountains. But not all of it. There is still virgin timber, more than any other place east of the Rockies. And the second growth is getting older all the time. It'll soon be a century since much of it felt the sting of an ax.

■ THE APPALACHIAN TRAIL

The Appalachian Trail (AT) is a continuous marked footpath meandering 2,140 miles from Maine to Georgia through Tennessee and 13 other states. Tramping along the trail's 284 miles on Tennessee's eastern border takes you through some of the AT's finest scenery. The stretch across the open balds of the Roan Highlands in the Cherokee National Forest is considered by many to be best on the entire trail.

A lone hiker makes his way across a bald along a section of the Appalacian Trail.

Rhododendron in bloom on Roan Mountain.

ROAN MOUNTAIN

I had come to relish hiking and the feeling of physical prowess that accompanied it, but it wasn't until the day in late May when we ascended Roan Mountain, a hulking six-thousand-footer in northwestern Tennessee, that I first experienced the sheer bliss of foot travel. The ascent to the top led up two thousand vertical feet, which would have destroyed me a month earlier. A freak snowstorm had blown in the previous day, layering the entire wilderness in a crystal glaze, and I remember the climb as a continuum of fairy tale scenes and vistas: the surrounding snow-clad peaks, pink rhododendron and delicate mountain laurel blossoms frozen in full flower, and ice-laden spruce boughs shimmering in the sun. Along the steep ascent, utter fascination supplanted any concern I might have had over distance or altitude. As I reached the open, sun-drenched alpine meadows at the top, I realized that I would gladly have scaled four thousand more feet just for the opportunity to see it.

—David Brill, *As Far as the Eye Can See,* 1979

The AT reaches its highest point (over 6,500 feet) in Tennessee as it penetrates the dark, damp spruce-fir forest atop Clingmans Dome in the Great Smoky Mountains National Park.

Stretch your legs on the AT in the beautiful Tennessee spring, and you're sure to encounter a "thru hiker"—AT jargon for someone who hikes it all at once. Once it was rare for someone to make the four-to-six-month trek, but hundreds do it each year these days. Most folks, though, are on the AT for day hikes or for shorter backpacks, "section hiking" in AT language. Primitive shelters are spaced at intervals along the trail at dependable water sources.

The idea for the trail started with Benton MacKaye of Massachusetts who first proposed it in a 1921 issue of the *Journal* published by the American Institute of Architects. The Appalachian Trail Conservancy (ATC) was formed in 1925 and coordinated planning and building the trail, which was completed in 1937 (though the AT is constantly being relocated and improved).

If you plan to hike, call the ATC at 304-535-6331 or review their website *www.atconf.org* for up-to-date information.

■ GREAT SMOKY MOUNTAINS NATIONAL PARK *maps pages 53 and 58*

◆ DRIVES

The Smokies offer an intimate, sensual experience. Most visitors miss it. That's because they never get far from their cars. There are some magnificent drives, to be sure. The **Newfound Gap Road** makes a spectacular 5,000-foot climb up the steep gradient of the West Prong of the Little Pigeon River before falling off into North Carolina. The road from the gap to Clingmans Dome climbs even higher to Tennessee's highest point (6,643), just 41 feet shy of Mount Mitchell, North Carolina—the highest point in the East (6,684). The **Little River Road** twists and turns along one of the world's most beautiful streams. And the drive around **Cades Cove** offers breathtaking views of verdant, peaceful fields hemmed in by tall mountains.

◆ HIKES

But to really feel the Smokies, to sense their special flavor, to become infected as millions do with the longing to return, you'll have to leave your car. You don't have to be a big-time hiker. Pick a road into the mountains, any road, drive to its end, and start walking. You'll be on the gentle grade of a pre-park logging railroad, in a

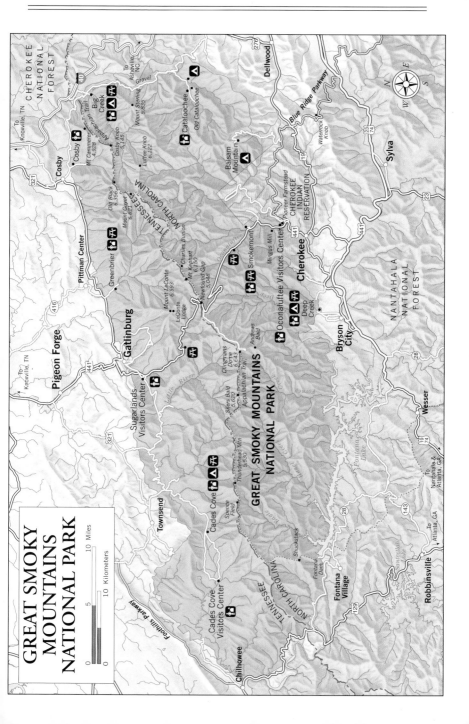

GREAT SMOKY
MOUNTAINS
NATIONAL PARK

forest dominated by matchstick-straight tulip poplars standing tall over a thick understory of rosebay rhododendron and dog hobble. The soothing sound of a stream cascading through rounded rocks fills the air. This pattern is repeated at Cosby, Greenbrier, Elkmont, Tremont, Cades Cove, Big Creek, Cataloochee, Smokemont, Deep Creek, and Twentymile.

There is no finer way to enjoy the Smokies than to hike up one of the five trails to the summit of **Mount LeConte** (6,593 feet), the distinctive three-peaked mountain standing apart from the main Smokies ridge and dominating the views for miles around. Walking up to the top of LeConte, you'll encounter the same successive changes in habitat that you would traveling 1,200 miles north into Canada, only here it's compressed into about six miles. And there is no need to lug along a backpack. **LeConte Lodge** offers room and board by reservation. 865-429-5704.

Other hikes on most people's list of favorites are to the 360-degree panorama from the craggy top of **Mount Cammerer** (4,928 feet); through the virgin forest to **Ramsay Cascade** where the creek tumbles down a hundred feet of ledges; and to **Spence Field,** the long meadow stretching below celebrated Rocky Top on Thunderhead Mountain.

The park's **main visitor center** is at Sugarlands near Gatlinburg; others are in Cades Cove and at Oconaluftee near Cherokee. Information: 865-436-1200.

Franklin D. Roosevelt dedicates Great Smoky Mountains National Park in 1940. Behind him sit Anne M. Davis, Cordell Hull, Prentice Cooper, Kenneth McKellar, and Eleanor Roosevelt. (Tennessee State Library and Archives)

Dawn along Sparks Lane, Cades Cove, in Great Smoky Mountains National Park.

■ GATLINBURG   *map page 58, right center*

It's like coming out of a dark theater on a bright June afternoon, entering Gatlinburg from the national park. A blinding assortment of gaudy attractions, tacky souvenir shops, wedding chapels, hotels, and restaurants are crammed into the narrow valley. The place is either an abomination or paradise depending on your perspective. Judging from the hoards who waddle endlessly up and down the main drag, there is no shortage of those who believe it the latter.

Gatlinburg does have a certain charm, though, particularly when it's not so crowded. With a little effort you can find shops and galleries worth a stop. The best ones feature local arts and crafts. Back before mountain folk could hop in the pickup and head for the nearest Wal-Mart, their isolation required them to be largely self-sufficient. This tradition lives on in Gatlinburg's lively arts and crafts scene.

MOUNTAINS

The Arrowcraft Shop offers products of the highest quality from the Southern Highland Craft Guild and is housed in a lovely 1939 building constructed of native stone and wood; 576 Parkway; 865-436-4604.

East of town off US-321 is the **Great Smoky Arts and Crafts Community,** a collection of close to a hundred roadside shops offering every conceivable kind of craft. Some, such as brooms, candles, pottery, and leather goods serve utilitarian purposes. Others, such as watercolors, oil paintings, photographs, wood carvings, and stained glass, are purely decorative.

Burning Bush makes a credible stab at fine dining in this town packed with tourist restaurants. Come for breakfast and you won't need to eat again all day; 1151 Parkway. Nearby, at 1110 Parkway, is the **Park Grill,** built of massive wood beams and reminiscent of a lodge in a Western national park.

(above) Richard Whaley and Charles Huskey build a drop-leaf table at Gatlinburg's Shop of the Woodcrafters and Carvers, in 1933. (Tennessee Valley Authority)

(opposite) Potter James Coffeit throws a pot at First Impressions Gallery on Glades Road in Gatlinburg.

MOUNTAINS

◆ FOUR MOUNTAIN INNS

If you come to stay, pick an inn that will give you time to savor the smells and colors of the mountains. The best known and best loved Smokies lodging is in Gatlinburg. It's the **Buckhorn Inn,** built in 1938 of native stone and wood on 25 quiet acres with sweeping views of Mount LeConte; 2140 Tudor Mountain Road; 865-436-4668.

Nearby, quiet Wear Valley is the location of a remote entrance to Great Smoky Mountains National Park. **Little Greenbrier Lodge,** a refurbished 1930s mountainside lodge with pine-paneled rooms and valley views will give you the time you need to appreciate the surrounding beauty; 3685 Lyon Springs Road in Wear Valley; 800-837-7022. **The Wonderland Hotel** in Wear Valley is a rustic down-home lodge with views of Cove Mountain; 3889 Wonderland Way, Wear Valley; 865-428-0779.

Above Wear Valley sits comfortable **Von Bryan Mountaintop Inn** with broad views of the Smokies. 2402 Hatcher Mountain Road; 800-633-1459.

See Tennessee Valley map pages 70-71 for sites in this area

11E   40   Dandridge

Knoxville   66   *Douglas Lake*   411

441   Newell Station

129   Sevierville

140   Dollywood   **Pigeon Forge**   32

Fort Loudoun Lake   **Alcoa**

Loudon   321   **Maryville**   321   *Parkway*   **Wear Valley**   **Gatlinburg**

The Arrowcraft Shop

72   *Tellico Lake*   411   *Foothills*   **Townsend**   Sugarlands Visitors Center   Mt LeConte 6,593 ▲

Newfound Gap Road   Newfound

Sweetwater   **Vonore**   Fort Loudoun State Historic Area   Great Smoky Mountains   *Appalachian*   ▲ Clingmans Dome   44

68   See Great Smoky Mountains Nat'l Park map page 53   Oconaluft Visitors Cen

Sequoyah Birthplace Museum   **Tallassee**   129   **National Park**   Blue Ridge Parkw

Madisonville   **Calderwood**   **Cherokee**

Cherokee National Forest South   *Fontana Lake*   **Bryson City**

Englewood   UNICOI MOUNTAINS   *Lake Santeetlah*

30   19 74

11   **Etowah**   68   **Robbinsville**   129

To Chattanooga

75

Delano   **Coker Creek**   *River*   *Apalachia Lake*   **NORTH CAROLINA**   **Andrews**

411   **Benton**   **Farner**   *Lake Hiwassee*   64 74

Hiwassee

Ocoee   64   **Harbuck**   294   **Murphy**   64

Lake Ocoee   *Ocoee*

Conasauga   Ocoee State Rec Area   **Copperhill**   64 74   **Ranger**   19 129   64

McCaysville   **GEORGIA**

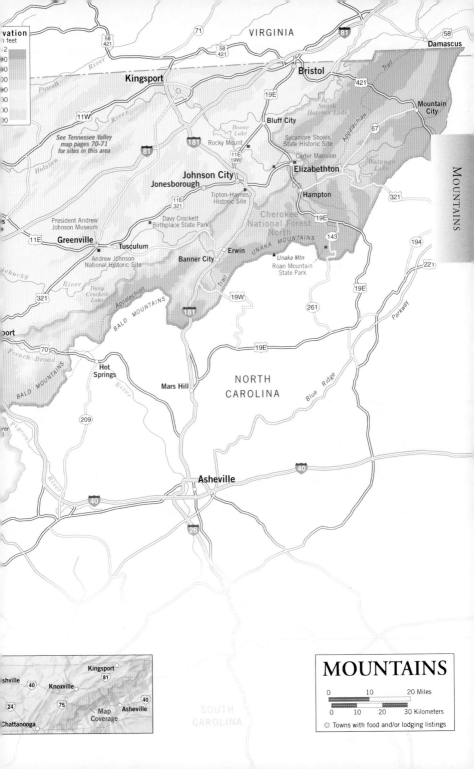

MOUNTAINS

■ PIGEON FORGE   *maps pages 53, top, and 58, right center*

Don't fight Pigeon Forge. If you're offended by six lanes of asphalt lined with corny attractions and glitzy hotels and theaters, travel to the Smokies by another route. But if you go to Pigeon Forge, throw yourself into it. Play miniature golf among live bunnies and stuffed hillbillies. Speed around in go-carts. Hop into the indoor skydive simulator. Spend good money to see the car where legendary sheriff Buford Pusser died. Load up on things you don't need at more than two hundred outlets. And by all means enjoy the music, arts and crafts, and rides at **Dollywood** (you can't miss it), the surprisingly tasteful theme park based on the talented, versatile, and generous native, Dolly Parton; 865-428-9488.

Pigeon Forge connects with the surrounding mountains at least once a year during January's **Wilderness Wildlife Week.** More than 10,000 visitors come to learn everything there is to learn about the mountains—bears, photography, fly-fishing, hiking—you name it—from experts who lead field trips and give lectures. For information, call 865-429-7350.

(above) A miniature golf course in Pigeon Forge.

(opposite) Dreamland Forest in Dollywood.

MOUNTAINS

■ TOWNSEND   *maps pages 53, left center, and 58, center*

Townsend calls itself "the peaceful side of the Smokies." Sitting at an entrance to the national park in Tuckaleechee Cove, it's a nice place for visitors who want to avoid the hustle and bustle of Gatlinburg. Be prepared, though, during warm weather to muscle your way through the throngs crowding the park entrance to bounce in inner tubes down the frigid Little River.

Blackberry Farm, an inn set on 1,100 acres on the edge of the Great Smoky Mountains Park is a luxurious place to soak up mountain beauty. Near Foothills Parkway at 1471 W. Millers Cove Road, Walland; 865-380-2260.

Built in the style of a Southern Appalachian cantilever barn, and overlooking Rich Mountain, **Richmont Inn** offers rooms furnished with antiques; 220 Winterberry Lane; 865-448-6751.

Dogwoods in their springtime finery—a roadside scene outside Elizabethton.

Round Bald in Northern Cherokee National Forest.

■ CHEROKEE NATIONAL FOREST

The Great Smoky Mountains National Park divides the Cherokee National Forest in two parts which makes it like two separate forests. Though not as pristine as the park, the national forest is much like it. And much less crowded. For CNF information, call 423-476-9700.

◆ NORTHERN CHEROKEE   *map page 59*

The northern CNF is sprinkled with 13 wilderness, scenic, and primitive areas. They range from the high, flower-filled meadows atop Rogers Ridge to the gorge holding Laurel Falls, a frothy 50-foot-wide cascade of horsetails tumbling down 55 feet of stair-step rocks.

The highlight of the northern Cherokee is the massif known as the **Roan Highlands.** It includes 6,285-foot Roan High Knob and lesser peaks like Big and Little Hump Mountains.

HONEYMOON IN THE UNAKA

*T*he road was even narrower than he remembered. It lurched and bucked through the granite spines of the Unaka Mountains, cutting through tilting pastures and scrub forest like the dusty tongue of a coon dog lapping the Nolichucky River a few miles farther on. They weren't going that far, though. The trail to the old homeplace should lie past a few more bends in the road. There would be a mark on an outcrop of limestone, his cousin Whilden had told him, and a little turnoff where he could park the four-wheel drive. They would have to walk the rest of the way.

"Course you can't drive up there," Whilden had warned him. "It's purt near straight up. We couldn't hardly get a mule up there to clear timber."

That was fine with Carl. He would welcome the isolation, but he'd had a hard time convincing Whilden of that. "A-lord, Carl-Stuart," his cousin kept saying. "You don't want to spend your honeymoon in that old place. Why, there ain't no lights nor running water." He had even offered the newlyweds his own room, reckoning he could bunk on the sofa if they were so dead set on coming for their honeymoon.

⋘ ⋙

*W*hy had he been so insistent on coming back here? he hadn't been back to Tennessee in years. Perhaps it was some sort of familial instinct—this urge to bring his bride back to the family seat, as if the ghosts would look on her and approve. Anyway, he had wanted Elissa to see the hills.

⋘ ⋙

"So theses are your precious Appalachians." Elissa smiled, nodding at a not-too-distant skyline. "They don't seem like mountains."

"I know." He had thought about that when he realized that the Rockies were different from his mountains. The Appalachians don't stand back and pose for you, he finally decided. They come up close and hold you, so they don't seem so big and imposing.

—Sharyn McCrumb, "Telling the Bees,"
in *Foggy Mountain Breakdown,* 1997

This painting by John Stokes (1872) depicts a Smoky Mountain "shivaree," an old mountain custom in which the bride and groom are pursued by wedding celebrants who pester them with noise—the blowing of horns, the clanging of pots and pans, the ringing of bells—until the newlywed couple provides them with food and drink. (Tennessee State Museum)

Starting low in the valley of the Doe River, TN-143 makes a long, gradual climb to Carvers Gap, on the border with North Carolina, where the constant wind whistles through the split-rail fences lining the road. Up from the gap on one side is the world's best display of Catawba rhododendron, 600 acres of natural "gardens" that light up the mountain in June. Up from the gap on the other side is **Round Bald,** the first in a string of the grassy balds that are unique to the southern Appalachians. The 13-mile stretch of the Appalachian Trail from Carvers Gap across these balds is regarded as the most exceptional on its entire 2,140-mile length, bestowing vast panoramas from the waves of sedges, grasses, and wildflowers rippling in the breeze.

The highway up to the gap weaves through **Roan Mountain State Park,** the only park in Tennessee's system with cross-country ski trails; 800-250-8620 or 423-772-0190.

The Roan's landscape of dark stands of spruce and fir, patches of rhododendron, and grassy balds is repeated at slightly lower elevations on **Unaka Mountain.**

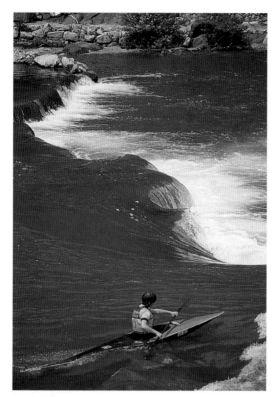

A competitor paddles pre-waterfall in the Ocoee World Cup 2000, a whitewater kayaking race held on the Ocoee River.

It's reached from Erwin on a loop made up of TN-395, TN-107, and Forest Service Road 230. When you get to the high grassy bald at Beauty Spot, you'll see how it got its name. Wildflowers grow all around, and there are stunning views of the Roan and of the distant Black Mountains.

◆ SOUTHERN CHEROKEE   *map page 58*

A tourism brochure proclaims this to be "the land of oohs & aahs." If you're looking for a raucous thrill, you'll find it in the southern Cherokee. If you're looking for solitude, you'll find it, too. But not on the **Ocoee River** in the summertime. Thanks to the 1996 Olympic canoe and kayak slalom competition, the Ocoee is one of nation's best-known stretches of whitewater. It often feels more like a theme park than a river in a national forest, as weekend crowds jam the gorge that's only wide enough for the river and a thin ribbon of asphalt. If the thought of paddling your own boat through violent rapids doesn't appeal to you, sign on for a raft trip with one of the many outfitters.

The **Hiwassee River** is gentler, less crowded, and more scenic. Like the Ocoee, its water is released from an upstream dam, so there is big water even in the dry months of summer and fall. When the flow is low on the Hiwassee, waders tiptoe through its cool water enjoying some of the best trout fishing in the Southern Appalachians. For information about the rivers and outfitters, call the Ocoee Whitewater Center, 877-OWC-6050 or 423-496-5197.

Now for the "aahs." The two largest national forest wilderness areas in the East are two the Cherokee share with adjoining forests in Georgia and North Carolina, the combined Big Frog and Cohutta and the combined Citico Creek and Joyce Kilmer-Slickrock. They're laced with tempting trails. You might encounter another hiker in the old growth forest on the way to the waterfall on Falls Branch, or a fly fisherman trying for a wily brown trout on Slickrock Creek, or a hunter calling a wild turkey on the slopes of Big Frog Mountain. Then again, you might not. You might not see anyone for days.

Whatever you fancy in the outdoors, you'll find it in the popular **Tellico District.** The Tellico River Road follows the swift river for miles and miles, and passes the 100-foot falls where the Bald River thunders into the Tellico. The Cherohala Skyway is a miniature version of the Blue Ridge Parkway ("Chero" for the Cherokee National Forest and "hala" for the Nantahala National Forest). It'll get you over the mountains to Robbinsville, North Carolina. But that's not the point. The point is the scenery. The road starts low, at less than 1,000 feet, and climbs to 5,390 feet.

Autumn color reflected in the Tellico River at Cherokee National Forest.

TENNESSEE VALLEY

Map
pages 70-71
Jonesborough
Davy Crockett Birthplace
Nashville
Knoxville
Chattanooga
Map page 112

◆ HIGHLIGHTS

◆ AREA OVERVIEW

Travel Basics: The Tennessee Valley is a segment of the Great Valley of the Appalachians stretching from Pennsylvania to Alabama. It gets its name in East Tennessee because it encompasses the eastern watershed of the Tennessee River. The valley's rivers and reservoirs offer a myriad of outdoor pursuits, and its rural countryside, surrounded as it is by mountains, is some of the prettiest in the nation. The valley is the gateway to the mountains. Sites of ancient Cherokee villages, reconstructed colonial forts, frontier-era houses, historic towns, and engaging museums—all are here. Chattanooga is a major destination in its own right, particularly its Civil War battlegrounds.

The Tennessee Valley is actually a series of parallel valleys and ridges, which accounts for the name geologists give it, Valley and Ridge Province. Tennesseans from the Middle and the West tend to view all of East Tennessee as mountainous and its people as mountaineers. Some valley residents—city folks in particular—don't like it, but there is some truth to the perception. Aside from a few urban enclaves, the valley's culture is distinctly Southern Appalachian.

A view of the Tennessee River and Chattanooga from Lookout Mountain.

Getting Around: Knoxville's motorized trolleys offer convenient transport to all but the most out-of-the-way places. Downtown Chattanooga is pedestrian friendly, intentionally so, but if you tire of walking, you can hop aboard the electric-powered shuttles. A car is a must elsewhere. Except in the Tri-Cities area (Bristol-Kingsport-Johnson City), most main highways run up and down the parallel valleys. Only a few cut across the grain. The narrow valleys can be choked with commercial clutter as towns slowly but inevitably sprawl towards each other, rendering travel painfully slow at times. But turn away from the congestion, cross the nearest ridge, and the beauty of the East Tennessee countryside reveals itself.

Climate: January highs average in the 40s, lows in the upper 20s. July is humid and highs reach the 90s. As in the rest of Tennessee, the long springs and autumns are the best times to visit. Be prepared for cold weather as late as April and as early as October. It's cooler the farther up the valley you go, and snow and ice are more common on the ridges and in the upper valley.

Food & Lodging: Knoxville, Chattanooga, and the Tri-Cities have a smattering of sophisticated restaurants, but for the most part, the pickings are slim. East Tennessee is not a region known for gourmet food. Aside from a handful of interesting hotels and inns, you're mostly limited to chains, and most of them are out along the interstates.

■ UPPER EAST TENNESSEE

"Upper East Tennessee" is the handle Tennesseans use for the sliver of the state that's squeezed between Virginia and North Carolina. It was here during the mid-1700s, along the Watauga, Holston, and Nolichucky Rivers, that the settlement of Tennessee began. The region harbors a few scattered but surprisingly well preserved remnants of life on that early frontier, some fascinating reproductions, and a handful of charming old towns that grew up along the Great Stage Road.

The sprawling Tri-Cities of Bristol, Kingsport, and Johnson City form a delta-shaped frame that supports Tennessee's fifth largest metropolitan area. The three cities grew up around smokestack industries, and their historic cores look a bit rusty today. The cities themselves are thin on places of interest to visitors. Put their congestion in your rear-view mirror, and you'll find yourself rambling down back roads that twist and turn through knobby pastures, ease through valleys sheltering swift streams, and climb over gaps in the wooded ridges.

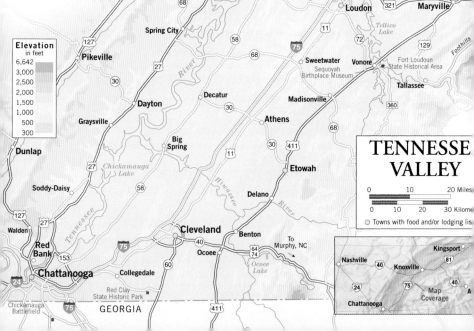

Pineville KENTUCKY 421 Pennington Gap

Cumberland Gap National Historic Park 58 71

Jonesville VIRGINIA 58 421

Middlesboro 58 70 Weber City Bristol

land River Sneedville River Eidson Church Hill Kingsport 11W

25E 33 70 11W Warriors Path State Park 19E

Tazewell Clinch Surgoinsville Holston River 11E 19W

33 25E 11W Rogersville 93 Rocky Mount Carter Mansion Elizabethton

Bean Station 66 Sycamore Shoals St Hist Site Johnson City

rris ake 11W Cherokee Lake Jonesborough 321 Tipton-Haynes Historic Site

Rutledge Bulls Gap President Andrew Johnson Museum Davy Crockett Birthplace State Park 181

ardville Great Stage Road Morristown 81 11E Greenville 321 Embreeville

11E Andrew Johnson National Historic Site Tusculum Tusculum College 107

Jefferson City White Pine Nolichucky River

Great Stage Road 92 321

Dandridge 25E

40 Newport

66 Douglas Lake 411 70 French Broad To Asheville, NC

Springs well Station Sevierville 321

Pigeon Forge 66

arkway 441

Up here, in the headwaters of the Tennessee, in what boosters call the Mountain Empire, it's tough to distinguish between the valley and the mountains.

In most places, it's obvious where the mountains end and the valley begins. Valley ridges are not called mountains and none are tall enough to look like one. Not so in the Upper East. There, many valley ridges are called mountains, as in Clinch Mountain and Bays Mountain—but geologically these are part of the Ridge and Valley Province, not the mountains (Blue Ridge Province). Without a geologic map, it would be hard to say whether you were in the mountains or the valley.

◆ THE "FIRST FRONTIER" REGION

Historians cite "push-pull" forces that prompted the first permanent settlement outside the original 13 colonies. The settlers were pushed by conditions under unpopular colonial governments in North Carolina and Virginia and pulled by the promise of abundant land and a fresh start. It was probably 1770 when the first group of any size arrived. They were led by a 27-year-old North Carolinian named James Robertson and his bride, Charlotte. Isolated as they were, the pioneers needed some type of government. In 1772, four years before the Declaration of

Independence, they formed the Watauga Association—one of America's first democratic governments. Lord Dunsmore, the British governor of Virginia, was not impressed. He reported to London that the association set a "dangerous example to the people of America, of forming governments distinct from and independent of his majesty's authority."

❖   **Sycamore Shoals State Historic Area**   *map page 71, top right*

East from Johnson City at Elizabethton, the Sycamore Shoals Historic Area sits on the Watauga River. When you follow the path to this reconstructed fort, keep in mind that you're where Tennessee as it exists today got its start. This is the valley the Robertsons and their friends settled in 1770, where in 1772 the Watauga Association was formed, and where in 1775 land speculator Richard Henderson negotiated the Transylvania Purchase that led to the settlement of distant Nashville and Middle Tennessee. Sustained hostilities between the Cherokees and the settlers erupted here in 1776, with devastating consequences for the Cherokees. They were eventually forced out of Tennessee in 1838. It was here, too, in 1780, that more than a thousand "Overmountain Men" gathered to start their arduous journey to find and defeat the British at Kings Mountain, South Carolina, during the American Revolution.

This painting by Lloyd Branson depicts the muster of the Overmountain Men at Sycamore Shoals a week before their victory over the British at Kings Mountain on October 7, 1780. (Tennessee State Museum, Nashville)

This engraving from the early 19th century is a fanciful rendition of a Cherokee attack on a frontier Tennessee fort.

The fort, rebuilt based on archaeological and historical data (and located on a new site), wouldn't provide much protection today, but the original was secure enough to withstand the British-supported Cherokee attack in July 1776. Some women were milking outside the fort when the attack came—the settlers had been warned and were gathered at the fort—and all but one made it inside safely. Catherine "Bonny Kate" Sherrill was saved from certain death—or worse—when she high-jumped next to the stockade and was pulled over by a young John Sevier. Four years later, they married, and twenty years later, Sevier became Tennessee's first governor.

The path along the Watauga makes for a delightful walk. On a crisp autumn morning mist rises gently from the river, and the roar of gin-clear water tumbling over rocks signals that the shoals are not far. Before long, they'll come into view through the yellow, crimson, and orange foliage.

Sycamore Shoals hosts a year-round lineup of events, including Revolutionary War re-enactments, colonial encampments, and, in July, "The Wataugans," an outdoor drama depicting the 18th-century settlement. For park information call 423-543-5808.

❖ **Rocky Mount**   *map page 71, top right*

This imposing, two-and-a half-story log house atop a small rise is believed to be the oldest house in Tennessee. It's difficult to see how another could be older. William Cobb started building it around 1770 as soon as the first settlers planted themselves within the borders of today's Volunteer State. William Blount, governor during Tennessee's 1790-96 territorial period, used it as the seat of government from the time of his appointment by President George Washington until he moved the capital to a more centrally located place, which Blount named Knoxville in 1792. (Tennessee's nickname, Volunteer State, by the way, comes from the call for troops issued by Blount's half brother, Willie Blount, who was the state's governor during the War of 1812. The number of volunteers far exceeded the number Blount requested.)

Entering the house from the modern museum, you'll be greeted by none other than William Cobb. He'll explain how he and his family managed to include such

Rocky Mount Historic Home is believed to be the oldest home still standing in Tennessee.

In this photograph (circa 1890), Mrs. R. A. Marcum uses chairs to support a rack of spools from which she spins yarn onto skeins. (Tennessee State Library and Archives)

finery as glass windows and sawed lumber. He'll show you to the room Blount used as his office, and he'll lead you upstairs to see how cramped the quarters were in those days, even for the elite. You'll meet the Cobb women, who'll demonstrate how they spun yarn, made cloth, and dyed it. The smell of smoke and the aroma of cooking draw you to the detached kitchen, where you'll see how food was preserved and cooked. The sound of metal striking metal will draw you to the blacksmith. Special events at this living history museum include the popular candlelight tours on December weekends.

Off US-11E/19W near Piney Flats between Johnson City and Bristol; 423-538-7396.

❖

In Elizabethton, not too far from Sycamore Shoals, is the **Carter Mansion,** Tennessee's oldest frame house, dating from 1775. It has an amazingly decorative interior considering the time and place of its construction. US-321, Elizabethton *(map page 71, upper right);* 423-543-5808.

◆ **BRISTOL**   *map page 71, upper right*

This city that Tennessee shares with Virginia boasts that it's the "birthplace of country music." That's a stretch, but Bristol is the site of what one authority terms the "epochal event" in early country music. For two weeks in 1927, Ralph Peer of the Victor Talking Machine Company set up shop on Bristol's State Street and recorded, among others, the Carter Family and Jimmie Rodgers. They became the first commercially successful recording artists in the genre we now call country. The "Bristol Sessions" are memorialized in a mural painted on the side of a building on State Street, Bristol's struggling main drag that's half in Tennessee and half in Virginia.

Bristol's boast that it's a big-time stock car racing place is no stretch, for each April and August, more than 150,000 NASCAR fans pack the Bristol Motor Speedway on US-11E out toward Johnson City; 423-764-1161.

◆ **KINGSPORT**   *map page 71, upper right*

This city at the meeting of the forks of the Holston River is best known as home to Eastman Chemical Company, the massive enterprise started in the 1920s to supply photographic chemicals for Eastman Kodak. It was once Tennessee's largest private employer, but has been eclipsed by FedEx in Memphis at the opposite end of the state.

The mountain dominating the view around Kingsport is Bays Mountain, just over 2,000 feet. Bays stays green because it's in **Bays Mountain Park,** a 3000-acre preserve that features a planetarium, a mountain-top lake, and 25 miles of hiking trails; 853 Bays Mountain Road off I-181.

Exchange Place is a pioneer homestead of cabins and barns where re-enactors in period dress demonstrate household activities of the frontier. Exchange Place was a relay station on the Great Stage Road *(see page 78).* Located at 4812 Orebank Road off TN-93; 423-288-6071.

Another Great Stage Road stop, the **Netherland Inn,** dates back to 1802 and is in Kingsport's Boatyard District, so named because William King, who gave his name to the city, built boats here in the early 1800s. He also built a boarding house which was enlarged in 1818 and operated as an inn by Richard and Margaret Netherland. It welcomed guests until 1841. The three-story inn, which occupies a lovely site along a riverside greenway at 2144 Netherland Inn Road is open to the public; 423-247-3211. It was from nearby Fort Patrick Henry on December 22, 1779 that John Donelson and his party shoved their makeshift fleet of 30 boats into the Holston's swift current to start the incredible thousand-mile voyage to the Cumberland country that led to the founding of Nashville *(see page 154).*

Warrior's Path State Park, just outside of Kingsport on I-81, is described on page 306.

◆ JOHNSON CITY   *map page 71, upper right*

The rusty look of the industrial Tri-Cities is softened in Johnson City by the campus of East Tennessee State University and the spacious grounds and distinctive architecture of the nearby Mountain Home Veterans Hospital. It was started in 1903 on 450 acres as a home for Union Civil War veterans. It feels more like a college campus than the real one across the road, and in fact, part of **Mountain Home** is now the university's medical school, one of the nation's top-rated for training rural doctors. If you'd like a nice place to stretch your legs, you won't do better than to wander Mountain Home's quiet lanes lined with massive sugar maples that are a sight to behold in October. State of Franklin Road (TN-381).

In Johnson City, **Dixie Barbeque** at 3301 N. Roan Street offers a varied supply of pork and beef barbecue, plus chicken and ribs. Equally good is the Texas-style barbecue offered at the **Firehouse** at 627 Walnut Street. The building is a converted 1930s fire hall, decorated with fire-fighting memorabilia, including a 1925 Seagraves fire truck.

❖   **Tipton-Haynes Historic Site**   *map page 71, upper right*

Resting quietly in the shadow of Buffalo Mountain, resplendent with brilliant colors in the fall, this collection of buildings has led several lives. In 1784 John Tipton built the substantial log house facing the ancient path that became the stage road to Jonesborough. After Landon Carter Haynes acquired it in 1839, it was made over in the Greek Revival style. The log outbuildings between the house and the fine new visitor center are left over from several periods.

Controversy found a home here. Tipton was an opponent of the short-lived State of Franklin. John Sevier was Franklin's governor. Fighting between their two factions broke out here in February 1788 in what came to be called the "Battle of the Lost State of Franklin." Landon Carter Haynes was something of an oddity in these parts. He was pro-Confederate. In fact, he served as senator from Tennessee in the Confederate Congress. He moved to more friendly territory after the Civil War, to faraway Memphis. 2620 S. Roan Street, Johnson City; 423-926-3631.

This painting (artist anonymous) shows the Great Stage Road between Johnson City and Knoxville as it appeared about 1890. (First Tennessee Heritage Collection)

■ DOWN THE GREAT STAGE ROAD *map page 71, center left*

The Great Valley of the Appalachians has been a pathway for trade and migration for centuries. The Great Indian Warpath became the Great Trading Path when colonists started using it in the late 1600s. The Great Stage Road followed roughly the same north-south route after the postmaster-general awarded the first contract to haul mail down from Abington, Virginia, as early as 1805. One branch ran along the west side of the Holston River Valley, the other up the valley's east side. The first route roughly follows today's US-11W and the second route US-11E. East Tennessee's early towns grew up along the stage routes, which were the main paths of commerce until the railroad arrived in the late 1850s.

Several inns that welcomed weary travelers along the muddy routes still stand in Jonesborough, Rogersville, and elsewhere. Although none operate as inns today, they all have one thing in common. Each claims to have hosted Tennessee's three 19th-century presidents, Andrew Jackson, James K. Polk, and Andrew Johnson. Blountville's 18-room Deery Inn dates from 1785. Kingsport's elegant three-story Netherland Inn, beautifully sited along the South Holston River, was completed in 1808 (see Kingsport, page 76). Dandridge has two inns, the 1820 Shepard's Inn and the 1845 Hickman Tavern, now City Hall.

(opposite) A prize-winning quilt from Jonesborough.

◆ **JONESBOROUGH** *map page 71, top right*

If you could visit only one Tennessee town, Jonesborough, the oldest, should be your choice. The tidy red-brick 19th-century storefronts house the state's best collection of arts and crafts galleries, and the town has a nice selection of inns and eating places. Jonesborough was chartered in 1779 by the state of North Carolina, which included Tennessee in those days, and grew in importance as a stop on the Great Stage Road. It remained Upper East Tennessee's preeminent town until the railroad brought industry to other places. The **Chester Inn,** dating from 1797, is the finest along the Great Stage Road, with fancy Victorian detailing and a broad porch added in the 1880s. Now the headquarters of the Storytelling Foundation International, it is open to the public and worth seeing—and you'll see it on Main Street as you walk through town.

Come to Jonesborough the first week in October, and you'll sense an air of excitement. The **National Storytelling Festival** is held here the first weekend in October, bringing in the world's best English-language storytellers. It's hard to believe

in this day and time that there are entertainers who make their living by their wits alone. And it's hard to believe that 10,000 eager listeners come each year to be entertained by them at what has evolved into one of the nation's premier folk culture events. For details, call 800-952-8392 or 423-753-2171.

You might be surprised to know that this Tennessee town was prominent in the early anti-slavery movement. *The Emancipator,* the nation's first anti-slavery publication, was started here by Elihu Embree in 1820.

Two lodgings are intertwined with the town's history. One is the **Eureka Hotel,** in heart of the historic district, a restored building dating from 1797. It provides elegant accommodations and is furnished with antiques and period reproductions; 127 W. Main Street; 877-734-6100. **Hawley House** at 114 E. Woodrow Avenue is a small, welcoming, antique-furnished B&B in a 1793 log-and-frame dwelling, the oldest in town; 800-753-8869. Stop by the **Main Street Café** to enjoy simple food in a homey atmosphere at 117 W. Main.

This painting, by an anonymous artist circa 1810, is the earliest known view of Jonesborough. (*Tennessee State Museum, Nashville*)

Today Jonesborough is home to fine arts and crafts galleries, historic inns, and homey cafes.

◆ **DAVY CROCKETT BIRTHPLACE STATE PARK** *map page 71, right*

The road to the park from US-11E twists through rolling pastures, tobacco patches, and rich farms set against the backdrop of the Bald Mountains. Classic East Tennessee scenery. Pulling into the park, you'll see right away that Crockett wasn't "born on a mountaintop in Tennessee" as proclaimed in the wildly popular 1950s song. The reconstructed pioneer cabin marking the spot where David or "Davy" Crockett was born in 1786 overlooks the sycamore-draped Nolichucky River. The cabin is a typical frontier home, one room with a sleeping loft and fitted with crude homemade furnishings.

So which was it, David or Davy? Both. David was a real person, born here in East Tennessee, who lived for a time in Middle Tennessee where he began his political career, moved to West Tennessee where he was elected to Congress, and went to Texas after being defeated for reelection. He was killed defending the

DAVY CROCKETT REMEMBERS

1786-1836
Born in a cabin in Tennessee, Davy Crockett became a great legend of the American frontier. He died at the battle of the Alamo.

An early portrait of Davy Crockett. (University of Tennessee Library)

I had remained for some short time at home with my father, when he informed me that he owed a man, whose name was Abraham Wilson, the sum of thirty-six dollars, and that if I would set in and work out the note, so as to lift it for him, he would discharge me from his service, and I might go free. I agreed to do this and went immediately to the man who held my father's note, and contracted with him to work six months for it. I set in, and worked with all my might, not losing a single day in the six months. When my time was out, I got my father's note and then declined working with the man any longer, though he wanted to hire me mighty bad. The reason was, it was a place where a heap of bad company met to drink and gamble, and I wanted to get away from them, for I know'd very well if I staid there, I should get a bad name, as nobody could be respectable that would live there. I therefore returned to my father, and gave him up his paper, which seemed to please him mightily, for though he was poor, he was an honest man and always tried might hard to pay off his debts.

I next went to the house of an honest old Quaker, by the name of John Kennedy, who had removed from North Carolina, and proposed to hire myself to him, at two shillings a day. He agreed to take me a week on trial; at the end of which he appeared pleased with my work, and informed me that he held a note on my father for forty dollars, and that he would give me that note if I would work for him six months. I was certain enough that I should never get any part of the note; but then I remembered it was my father that owed it, and I concluded it was my duty as a child to help him along, and ease his lot as much as I could. I told the Quaker I would take him up at his offer, and immediately went to work. I never visited my father's house during the whole time of this engagement, though he lived only fifteen miles off. But when it was finished and I had got the note, I borrowed one of my employer's horses, and, on a Sunday evening, went to pay my parents a visit. Some time after I got there, I pulled out the note and handed it to my father, who supposed Mr. Kennedy had sent it for collection. The old man looked mighty sorry, and said to me he had not the money to pay it, and didn't know what he should do. I then told him I had paid it for him, and it was then his own; that it was not presented for collection, but as a present from me. At this, he shed a heap of tears; and as soon as he got a little over it, he said he was sorry he couldn't give me any thing, but he was not able, he was too poor.

The next day, I went back to my old friend, the Quaker, and set in to work for him for some clothes; for I had now worked a year without getting any money at all, and my clothes were nearly all worn out, and what few I had left were mighty indifferent. I worked in this way for about two months; and in that time a young woman from North Carolina, who was the Quaker's niece, came on a visit to his house. And now I am just getting on a part of my history that I know I never can forget. For though I have heard people talk about hard loving, yet I reckon no poor devil in this world was ever cursed with such hard love as mine has always been, when it came on me. I soon found myself head over heels in love with this girl, whose name the public could make no use of; and I thought that if all the hills about there were pure chink, and all belonged to me, I would give them if I could just talk to her as I wanted to; but I was afraid to begin, for when I would think of saying any thing to say to her, my heart would begin to flutter like a duck in a puddle; and if I tried to outdo it and speak, it would get right smack up in my throat, and choak me like a cold potatoe. It bore on my mind in this way, till at last I concluded I must die if I didn't broach the subject; and so I determined to begin and hang on a trying to speak, till my heart would get out of my throat one way or t'other. And so one day at it I went, and after several trials I could say a little. I told her how well I loved her; that she was the darling object of my soul and body; and I must have her, or else I should pine down to nothing, and just die away with the consumption.

I found my talk was not disagreeable to her; but she was an honest girl, and didn't want to deceive nobody. She told me she was engaged to her cousin, a son of the old Quaker. This news was worse to me than war, pestilence, or famine....

—Davy Crockett, *A Narrative of the Life
of David Crockett,* 1834

Alamo in 1836. Davy is a legendary figure, a frontier hero who performed outrageously heroic deeds. "Killed him a bear when he was only three." The legend of Davy was enhanced by a popular 1835–56 periodical called the *Crockett Almanac* that told tall tales about Crockett, and by the 1950s Disney TV show romanticizing the "King of the Wild Frontier" that spawned worldwide Crockett-mania.

The park is off US-11E near Limestone; 423-257-2167.

◆ **GREENEVILLE** *map page 71, center right*

Greeneville is an old town, dating to the post–Revolutionary War period, and is named for Nathanael Greene, the Rhode Islander who commanded America's troops in North Carolina in the battle for independence from Britain. The two people who get most of the attention around here are Andrew Johnson and John Hunt Morgan. Johnson is of interest because he became president of the United States and Greeneville was his home. Morgan, a Confederate cavalry raider, captures the imagination because he slipped into this Union-controlled town in September of 1864 to visit his mistress and ended up surprised by his enemy. Caught in Mrs. William's house by Federal soldiers, he was killed as he tried to escape through her garden. In the excitement, Yankees lodged a cannonball in the brick facade of the Cumberland Presbyterian Church. It's still there.

Greeneville's rich if somewhat sad political history comes to life as you meander its brick sidewalks on the self-guided walking tour (available from the National Park Service Visitor Center on Depot Street) that shows off houses, churches, and commercial buildings as old as the 1790s. Greeneville is where Unionists gathered in 1861 following Tennessee's secession and tried in vain to make East Tennessee a separate state; and Greeneville was the home of Johnson, who until 1998, had the dubious distinction of being the only American president to be impeached.

The walking tour takes you past a log cabin that doesn't look much like a capitol building. But it is, or at least it's a replica of one, the capital of the "Lost State of Franklin," the ill-fated attempt to create a 14th state in the complex period following the American Revolution. The desire of Congress to raise funds by having southern states cede their trans-Appalachian lands to the U.S., the "Great Land Grab" of 1783, North Carolina's cession of its western lands the next year, and the settlers' complaints of the remote North Carolina government's inattention to their needs all contributed to the creation of Franklin, named for Benjamin Franklin. The new state, made up of today's Upper East Tennessee, was organized in 1784, but its attempt to be admitted as the 14th state failed. North Carolina repealed its act of cession and took back what is now Tennessee. Then a bitter and sometimes violent rivalry erupted between leaders John Sevier and John Tipton. The Franklin movement fizzled. North Carolina gave up Tennessee again, this time for good, and it became a U.S. territory in 1790 and the 16th state in 1796.

The town today has a companionable modern beat. In the historic 1904 tannery, just up the street from Andrew Johnson NHS visitor center you'll find the **Tannery,** which serves homemade soups and sandwiches.

Several 19th-century railroad hotels have been combined and completely made over, at a cost of $15 million, to form the **General Morgan Inn**. The fabulous interior design is by Joyce Von Graven. Hotel dining is at Brumley's, which includes a stunning mahogany bar; 111 N. Main Street; 423-787-1000.

Everyone goes to **Stan's** for the best barbecue pork, beef, and chicken around. It's at 2620 E. Andrew Johnson Highway (US-11E).

❖ **Andrew Johnson Historic Sites**   *map page 71, center*

The oft-used description of Andrew Johnson as having "humble origins" is an understatement if there ever was one. Johnson arrived in Greeneville in 1826 at age eighteen with his mother and stepfather in a little wagon carrying everything they owned, pulled by a blind pony. Though Johnson had never attended a day of school, he had considerable knowledge of classic literature and oratory. Back in North Carolina, where he had been an apprentice tailor since age ten, his boss had someone read to him while he worked. Johnson continued that practice when he set up his own tailor shop, learning the classics and great speeches. He used his knowledge in a political career that saw him elected Tennessee's governor and senator in the turbulent decade before the Civil War.

Andrew Johnson was a staunch Unionist—he was the only senator from a secessionist state to remain in Congress—when President Lincoln made him military governor of Tennessee early in the Civil War. And in 1864, Lincoln put him on the ticket as vice president. Johnson feuded with the North's Radical Republicans after the Civil War because he believed compromise with ex-Confederates was both sensible and politic. After Lincoln was assassinated and Johnson became president, his effort to implement lenient post-war policies led to his impeachment. The May 16, 1868, polling of the Senate fell one vote short of the two-thirds quorum needed for conviction and removal from office.

Johnson is buried beneath a towering monument at the national cemetery, part of the **Andrew Johnson National Historic Site** that includes the informative visitor center at his preserved tailor shop and the comfortable if plain family home a few blocks away. You'll notice that Johnson always seems to have such a sour look.

"Did he ever smile?" The young ranger leading the tour is ready with the answer. She's obviously been asked before. "It's said that children made him smile. That's the one time we know of when he smiled, when he was around children." 423-638-3551.

Just east of Greeneville, on the graceful campus of **Tusculum College,** with its stunning mountain views, the "Old College" building that Johnson's contributions help build in 1841, is now the **President Andrew Johnson Museum and Library**. On TN-107 in Tusculum; 423-636-7348.

(above) The parlor in the Andrew Johnson home and (opposite, top) the Andrew Johnson National Historic Site in Greeneville.

◆　ROGERSVILLE　*map page 71, center*

You can't get to Rogersville except by a pretty drive, especially coming up the valley from Knoxville on US-11W paralleling imposing Clinch Mountain or cutting across the valley's grain on TN-66 from its intersection with US-11E at Bulls Gap near Greeneville.

Squeezed tightly into the corrugated landscape between the Holston River and Clinch Mountain, Rogersville is one of Tennessee's most charming towns. The grassy square laid out in 1796 is adorned with dogwoods to brighten it in April and sugar maples to do the same in October. Facing the square is the columned 1836 Courthouse, Tennessee's oldest courthouse still in use. An 1824 lodging built for travelers on the Great Stage Road, Hale Springs Inn, still stands.

The folks in Rogersville intend for you to take your time seeing their lovely town. The pamphlet you can pick up at the 1890 railroad depot, now a museum showcasing Rogersville as an early printing center, is titled "A Strolling Tour." After walking about, stop by **Oh Henry's** in the middle of the historic district to enjoy Tennessee home cooking; 201 E. Main Street.

■ KNOXVILLE   *map page 70, center right*

Knoxville is the largest city in the Southern Appalachians and is the economic and
cultural capital of East Tennessee. Aside from being home to the football-crazed
University of Tennessee, it's best known for what it's near—the mountains, a host
of beautiful lakes and scenic rivers, and high-tech Oak Ridge. Knoxville doesn't
seem to mind that image. The fabulous interactive visitor center is called the **Gateway Regional Visitor Center** to showcase Knoxville's role as a gateway to other
places; 900 Volunteer Landing Lane off TN-158, which intersects with I-40; 800-
727-8045 or 865-523-7623.

But Knoxville itself is worthy of a stop. The city has a great zoo, interesting museums, and a lively arts scene. April's **Dogwood Arts Festival** is a grand time to
visit. You can follow several "trails"—on your own or on a bus—through quiet
neighborhoods lush with blooming trees, as well as delight in a host of performing

The Women's Basketball Hall of Fame with the skyline of Knoxville in the background.

Pink dogwood accents the simple white clapboard of the Blount Mansion.

and visual arts activities; 865-523-7263. Be sure to visit **Old City,** the neighborhood of restaurants, coffee houses, galleries, and antique dealers in late 19th- and early 20th-century buildings that has managed to dodge the theme restaurants and trendy chain stores that tend to colonize such places.

◆ Volunteer Landing

The Gateway Center is part of the Volunteer Landing urban revival overlooking the Tennessee River a few miles from where it is formed by the meeting of the French Broad and Holston Rivers. The landing offers stunning views of Knoxville's beautiful arched bridges, and while there, you can hop aboard a boat for a river tour or take a train out to the forks of the river.

Volunteer Landing features Knoxville's oldest and its newest. **James White's Fort** is a restoration based upon White's original 1786 house that started the settlement of Knoxville.

TENNESSEE
VALLEY

The Cumberland University women's basketball team, Wilson County, 1909.
(Tennessee State Library and Archives)

Over on the next hill—Old Knoxville rests on hills separated by three creeks—
is **Blount Mansion.** "It doesn't seem like a mansion." You're sure to hear this if
you tour the plain, white frame house with a school group. You'll be thinking the
same. Consider, though, the circumstances under which this national historic
landmark was built. It was 1792 and this was the wild frontier, when shelter for
most families consisted of dirt-floored, windowless cabins made of rough-hewn
logs. William Blount selected James White's fort for his second capital after President George Washington named him governor of the Southwest Territory. 200 W.
Hill Avenue; 865-525-2375.

Walk back past the fort and fast-forward more than two hundred years to the
National Women's Basketball Hall of Fame. It's hard to miss, as it's topped by a
giant basketball. If you're a woman, or a sports fan of any gender, you'll be moved
by the exhibits tracing the history of women's basketball from the first game
played at Smith College in 1893 to today's WNBA, and along the way, the game's

admission to the Olympics, and its emergence as a big-time college sport. Of particular interest is Elizabeth MacQueen's 17-foot three-figure bronze representing the past, present, and future of women's basketball, and the exhibits on the All American Red Heads, the team of natural and dyed redheads that barnstormed the nation starting in the 1930s. If you keep up with basketball, you know why the Hall of Fame is in Knoxville. It's where University of Tennessee Lady Vols coach Pat Head Summitt established herself as the most successful college women's coach in history, winning, as of 2000, six national titles. She coached the U.S. team to a gold medal in the 1984 Olympics and played for a silver in the 1976 Olympics. She is in the inaugural class of Hall of Fame inductees. The museum is located at 700 Hall of Fame Drive; 865-633-9000.

The University of Tennessee's second football team sits for a photograph in 1892.
(University of Tennessee)

◆ **University of Tennessee**   *map page 70, right center*

Roaming this sprawling campus along Peyton Manning Pass, named for a quarter-back ("Pass." Get it?), Phil Fulmer Way, named for a coach, and Johnny Majors Drive—he was a player and a coach—you can see that, to borrow an old East Tennessee expression, "They's kinley eat up with it 'round here." We're talking about UT football. The Vols' Neyland Stadium, rising next to the river, seats 104,000, barely losing to Michigan's as the nation's largest. If you were to get the impression that football is about all there is at UT, you'd be wrong. As Tennessee's flagship public university, with an enrollment of 26,000, there has to be more.

This painting by Flavius James Fisher depicts Knoxville as it appeared in 1871 when viewed from the cupola of Old College. Today that building is near Ayers Hall, and it stands on the campus of the University of Tennessee.
(Hunter Museum of American Art, Chattanooga, gift of Mr. and Mrs. Norman Hirschl)

TENNESSEE
VALLEY

The oldest part of the campus, "The Hill," is topped by splendid **Ayers Hall.** Just outside it is a botanical garden simulating several of Tennessee's distinct environments, where students experiment with plants used by prehistoric cultures.

The Frank H. McClung Museum shows off a permanent exhibit called Archaeology and Native Peoples of Tennessee, chronicling 12,000 years of human life in the state. You can spend quite a while learning how people lived in 1450, before Europeans arrived in America, studying the life-size mural depicting the prehistoric town of Toqua as UT archaeologists believe it appeared. The whole exhibit is fascinating. The museum also has a permanent collection on Ancient Egypt, featuring fabulous pieces loaned by New York's Metropolitan Museum. The Mc-Clung Museum is located at 1327 Circle Park Drive; 865-974-2144.

TENNESSEE VALLEY

AUTHOR'S CHOICE:
KNOXVILLE INNS AND RESTAURANTS

LODGINGS

Hotel St. Oliver
Intimate downtown location on historic market square. 407 Union Avenue; 865-521-0050.

Maplehurst Inn
Delightful lodgings in 1917 home in historic, Tudor-revival Maplehurst Park district downtown. 800 W. Hill Avenue; 800-451-1562 or 865-523-7773.

RESTAURANTS

Calhoun's
Pleasing riverside version of popular local chain serving ribs, burgers, salads, steak, and chicken. 400 Neyland Drive, Volunteer Landing; 865-673-3355.

Chesapeake's
Downtown seafood place voted Knoxville's best year in and year out. 500 Henley Street; 865-673-3433.

Copper Cellar
Long-standing university-area favorite, specializing in beef and seafood. 1807 Cumberland Avenue. Also at 7316 Kingston Pike.

Manhattan's Bistro
Old City. Fun, casual bar and grill serving a varied menu, ranging from meat loaf to jambalaya. 101 S. Central Street; 865-525-2333.

Orangery
Knoxville's premier restaurant for decades, with a French-slanted menu. 5412 Kingston Pike; 865-588-2964.

Patrick Sullivan's Saloon
Historic 1888 building makes it worth a visit, a richly detailed saloon started by the real Patrick Sullivan. Pub grub, casual dining fare, and great beer selection. 100 N. Central Street, Old City; 865-637-4255.

Riverside Tavern
Gorgeous new building, with an arched steel-frame roof to match the nearby arched bridges. Outstanding grilled fish, chicken, and steaks, and wood-burning oven pizza from the Regas family, Knoxville's leading restaurateurs for generations. 950 Volunteer Landing; 865-637-0303.

Sam & Andy's West
This popular family establishment has been serving great grilled burgers and steamed deli sandwiches to UT students and grads since 1946. 11110 Kingston Pike; 865-675-4242.

◆ FAR FLUNG KNOXVILLE

Outside Knoxville are three historic sites that form a half-moon southeast of town if you connect them on a map.

Sam Houston Schoolhouse
map page 70, right center
This schoolhouse, the oldest in the state, rests where it was built in 1794, in the shadow of Chilhowee Mountain. The flags of Tennessee and Texas fly here. Houston is the only American who served as governor of two states.

He taught in this one-room log structure in 1812 when he was 18, taking his pay in corn, calico, and cash. School was in session during the growing season, between spring planting and fall harvest. Old Sam Houston School Road, off TN-33 south of Knoxville; 865-983-1550.

TENNESSEE VALLEY

W. B. Cooper painted this portrait of Samuel Houston in 1845.
(Tennessee Historical Society)

Marble quarrying was once a mainstay of Knoxville's economy, as this Lloyd Branson painting, Hauling Marble, *circa 1910, suggests. (Frank H. McClung Museum, Knoxville)*

Marble Springs

This farmstead belonged to Tennessee's first governor, John Sevier, and his wife, Bonny Kate. It's marked by the stark two-story log house the Seviers made their home from 1790 until his death in 1815. Sevier was governor of two states, too, sort of. He was chief executive of Franklin, the would-be 14th state in what is now Upper East Tennessee. 1220 Gov. John Sevier Highway (TN-168); 865-573-5508.

Ramsey House

The Ramsey House was "the most costly and admired building in Tennessee" says the 1800 census. Compare it to the other frontier houses in East Tennessee, even fine ones like Rocky Mount and Blount Mansion, and you'll agree. English native and Charleston builder Thomas Hope spared no effort when he constructed it for Francis Alexander Ramsey in 1795–97. The two-story, Georgian-style structure of pink marble and blue limestone has fancy details unheard of on the frontier. The house has been impeccably furnished using the estate inventory taken at Ramsey's death in 1820. 2614 Thorngrove Pike, off Gov. John Sevier Highway (TN-168); 865-546-0745.

■ CLINCH RIVER COUNTRY

The Clinch, a major Tennessee River tributary, ranks as one of the most ecologically rich rivers on earth. But humans just can't resist tampering with it. Three TVA dams trap much of its water. And along its banks during World War II, the ingredients were produced for the most destructive man-made force on earth, the atomic bomb.

◆ NORRIS AREA   *map page 70, top right*

The New Deal's strong legacy in Tennessee is strongest around Norris, the town TVA built in the 1930s as a model planned community. You sense the town's uniqueness the minute you turn into it from the clutter I-75 is depositing on its doorstep. With its forested greenbelt, village greens, patches of woods, meandering

The first dam to be built by the TVA, the Norris Dam was completed in 1936 and was named after U.S. Senator George W. Norris, often referred to as the "Father of the TVA." Here the senator poses in front of his namesake. (Tennessee Valley Authority)

A BETTER LIFE WITH TVA

*T*his is an entirely different region from what it was ten years ago. You can see the change almost everywhere you go. You can see it in the copper lines strung along back country roads, in the fresh paint on the houses those electric lines were built to serve. You can see it in new electric water pumps in the farmyards, in the community refrigerators at the crossroads, in the feed grinders in the woodsheds. You can see the factories that stand today where there were worn-out cotton fields and rows of tenant shacks a few years ago. You can see new houses, by the thousands, on the edges of the towns—new houses of the men who take away as much cash from a few trips to the payroll window as they used to earn in a year.

You can see the change best of all if you have flown down the valley from time to time, as I have done so frequently during these past ten years. From five thousand feet the great change is unmistakable. There it is, stretching out before your eyes, a moving and exciting picture. You can see the undulation of neatly terraced hillsides, newly contrived to make the beating rains "walk, not run, to the nearest exit"; you can see the grey bulk of the dams, stout marks across the river now deep blue, no longer red and murky with its hoard of soil washed from the eroding land. You can see the barges with their double rows of goods to be unloaded at new river terminals. And marching toward every point on the horizon you can see the steel crisscross of electric transmission towers, a twentieth-century tower standing in a cove beside an eighteenth-century mountain cabin, a symbol and a summary of the change. These are among the things you can see as you travel through the Tennessee Valley today. And on every hand you will also see the dimensions of the job yet to be done, the problem and the promise of the valley's future.

—David E. Lilienthal, Chairman, Tennessee Valley Authority,
TVA, Democracy on the March, 1944

footpaths, serpentine roads, hand-laid stone bridges and curbs, and handsome red-brick Georgian-style school, Norris remains one of America's prettiest towns. TVA completed **Norris Dam,** its first major construction project, in 1936. The dam's pleasing art deco style fits so nicely into the verdant landscape that it looks as if it grew there. The deep blue lake extends up countless coves and valleys, creating 800 miles of shoreline. The town and dam are named for Nebraska Senator George Norris, who during the 1920s, attempted to enact legislation creating something similar to the TVA, only to have it blocked by Republican presidents. He found a willing ally in Franklin D. Roosevelt, who secured passage of the TVA act in 1933 during his first hundred days in office.

Just below Norris Dam and Norris Dam State Park on US-441 is the 3.1-mile **River Bluff Trail.** Located on TVA property along the Clinch River, it is noted for lavish displays of spring wildflowers.

TENNESSEE VALLEY

An exhibit of Pentecostal signs at the Museum of Appalachia near Norris.

❖ **Lenoir Museum** *map page 70, top right*

Maybe it's something in the water at Norris. Folks can't seem to resist collecting things. Will G. Lenoir's eclectic collection of artifacts, tagged a "mini-Smithsonian," is crammed into the Lenoir Museum below the dam. Next to it, gathering its power from the cool waters of Clear Creek, is the **18th Century Grist Mill** whose intricate wooden workings are fascinating to behold. On US-441 below Norris Dam; 865-494-9688.

❖ **Museum of Appalachia** *map page 70, top right*

Lenoir's collection pales in comparison to that of John Rice Irwin, a descendant of the family that owned the 1796 mill. His collection of more than 250,000 items is displayed at the Museum of Appalachia. When he was a boy, Irwin chose to take an oldtime coffee grinder as pay for some farm work, and from then on, he took his collecting seriously. He eventually abandoned his chosen profession as a teacher and opened the museum, now a 65-acre functioning Appalachian village with dozens of log structures and with geese, ducks, chickens, peacocks and sheep

John Rice Irwin is a descendant of the family that in the 18th century operated a mill near the Museum of Appalachia.

CHILDHOOD BY NORRIS DAM

I used to ponder why I have such a passion for the outdoors. Being surrounded by nature feels like my natural state. I can't go for more than a few days without getting into the woods or into the rural countryside. It is nourishment that sustains me as much as the water I drink and the food I eat. It dawned on me fairly late in life that growing up in the idyllic East Tennessee town of Norris is the likely source of my love of the outdoors.

Norris was conceived and developed as a model community where the natural and built environments blend so harmoniously that it's often difficult to distinguish one from the other. The town is bordered by rugged, forested hills sliced by the trout-filled Clinch River and rightly named Clear Creek. The woods are public lands, acquired by TVA when it built the town and mighty Norris Dam, the New Deal agency's first big project. Three camps of the Civilian Conservation Corps set up around Norris, and the "CCC boys" built trails all through the area. This was my playground when I was growing up in the 1940–50s. Back in those days, before TV and computers, kids didn't play indoors and most of the year, when we weren't in school, we literally lived in the woods.

We had our favorite places, like the Bear Hole (we knew bears lived there, though we never saw one), Alligator Log (it reminded someone of an alligator), and the Giant Pine (a lone white pine in the hardwood forest). We gave names to places no one else ever thought about, such as a jumble of rocks we could hide in that we called "Fort Little Rock" and a shimmering little rivulet we named "Silver Creek." The woods farthest away, out by the dam, we called the "North Woods." We were forever laying plans for the construction of a fort, and started several, but never finished a single one.

In summer, there were briars to contend with, it was hot, and there was a fear of snakes, though I never saw a poisonous one. So we shifted our outdoor pursuits to beautiful Norris Lake. We could walk or ride our bikes—it was only a mile or two—and had the whole place to ourselves on weekdays. We assembled a collection of logs that we kept on the shore at our "yacht club" which we called "Sheridan Oaks," a name one us of thought was the name of a real one somewhere. (Obviously not in the South, with a name like that.) We would drift for hours lazily around the lake. I recall falling asleep once and rolling off my log.

I remember with pleasure the spontaneous, imaginative, good times we had, and I'm happy that the love of the outdoors is so deeply imbedded in me. I can't conceive of my life without it.

—by author of this book

TENNESSEE
VALLEY

The Daniel Boone Cabin at the Museum of Appalachia.

all mingling about. The place can feel a bit overwhelming, so don't plan on rushing through it. It takes time to absorb it all. Each October, the museum hosts the five-day **Tennessee Fall Homecoming,** one of the nations' largest and most authentic mountain music and craft festivals. The Museum of Appalachia is just west of Norris on TN-61; 865-494-7680.

◆ OAK RIDGE   *map page 70, top center*

On the surface, it looks like an ordinary small city. The usual collection of strip malls and franchised businesses. But Oak Ridge is no ordinary city. It was built overnight, in 1942–43 when the U.S. Army acquired 60,000 acres as part of the Manhattan Project. Its goal: to build an atomic bomb before the Germans. The goal was met. The bomb was dropped on Hiroshima on August 5, 1945. In just over a week, Japan surrendered, ending World War II. With a population less than half its 75,000 war-time high, Oak Ridge is still a major research center.

The **American Museum of Science and Energy** features hands-on exhibits on energy and technology. Most interesting for adults, though, are the exhibits on Oak Ridge during the war years—the phenomenal construction project, everyday life behind the fence in a secret city, and the mission to build the bomb. 300 S. Tulane Avenue; 865-576-3200.

❖ Oak Ridge National Laboratory

On the grounds is the 1924 **New Bethel Church,** which has an interpretative exhibit describing the lab's mission during the war. (It's also a good sample of a rural Tennessee church.) Just up the road is the **Graphite Reactor** that began operation in 1943 to study the feasibility of producing plutonium from uranium. The story of this national historic landmark is a little hard to grasp on your own, unless you're into nuclear physics, so you might want to arrange a tour. ORNL: New Bethel Road between TN-60 and TN-95; 865-574-4160.

The fissionable material for the atomic bomb was manufactured at Oak Ridge. Despite the purpose of what was being created here, civilian life went along as usual. Here is a wartime photograph of the local Girl Scout troop of the "City Behind a Fence." (Department of Energy)

◆ KINGSTON   *map page 70, center*

Kingston, founded in 1799, was Tennessee's capital. But only for one day, on September 21, 1807, to fulfill a treaty with the Cherokees in which they gave up all the land between the Tennessee and Duck Rivers—7,000 square miles. Partially reconstructed **Fort Southwest Point** occupies the dramatic heights above the confluence of the Clinch and Tennessee Rivers. Using data from archaeological investigations, a blockhouse, stockade, and barracks have been reconstructed where the originals were built in 1797. Troops were garrisoned here to keep peace between the settlers and the Cherokees, and the fort served as headquarters for Connecticut native Return Jonathan Meigs, the U.S. government's agent to the Cherokees. 1226 S. Kentucky Street (TN-58); 865-376-3641.

Drop by the **Old Roan County Courthouse,** completed in 1856, and visit the museum. There are artifacts as old as the Early Archaic Period, 8000-6000 BCE, as well as items from the fort and an exhibit on the Confederate company that organized in the historic building; 119 Court Street; 865-376-9211.

To stay awhile to enjoy the beauty of the area, try the **Whitestone Country Inn,** an elegant lakeside inn on 360 acres with stunning views of valley and mountains. 1200 Paint Rock Road; 888-247-2464.

■ OVERHILL COUNTRY

It's called "Overhill" because it is just that. The Cherokee towns along the Little Tennessee and Hiwassee Rivers were over the mountains from the other Cherokee towns. Hardly a trace of them remains, but there is still lots to see—reconstructions, memorials, and museums—all set against the backdrop of the mountains. It's a stunningly beautiful area. Tourism boosters formed the **Tennessee Overhill Heritage Association** and do a first-class job interpreting the area and giving guidance to visitors. The office is located in Etowah at 727 Tennessee Avenue in the L&N Depot; 423-263-7232.

In the town of **Loudon,** a historic, well-preserved Tennessee River town, you can stay in a grand Civil War–era mansion that serves today as an inn: **Mason Place** at 600 Commerce Street; 865-458-3921.

OVERHILL CHEROKEES

Some historians believe that the Cherokees came down into the Appalachian Mountains from the eastern Great Lakes not long before Europeans arrived in North America, a theory supported by the Cherokee language—it's of the Iroquois family—and their own creation legends. Archaeological evidence leads others to conclude that the Cherokees are descendants of the Mississippian "mound builders" culture that had vanished by the time the Europeans came. Most likely Cherokee arrived and absorbed some of the original culture into their own.

When English colonists took their first timid steps over the mountains in the late 1600s, the Cherokees were the main native group living permanently in present-day Tennessee. They were linked by culture and language to clusters of natives in the Carolinas and Georgia, but there was no Cherokee central government. Each town was politically autonomous, though each cluster of towns had a mother town such as the Overhill town of Chota.

Village life centered around a large octagonal council house surrounded by a plaza, with households spread as much as a mile along the river. Men and women had distinct roles, with the men serving as hunters and fighters and the women as farmers and homemakers. Each household had a summer and a winter house.

Only men served on the village council, but women were allowed to speak, and exalted "Beloved Women" wielded considerable authority, including deciding whether prisoners were killed or adopted into a clan. Each village had a "White Chief" who presided in the warm season when the focus was on domestic affairs, and a "Red Chief," who presided in the cold season, the time for hunting and for war.

The seven clans were the most important Cherokee social institutions. They were matrilineal, so that children became members of their mother's clan. Each clan had regulations, enforced by the women. Marriage and sex within a clan was forbidden, as it was considered incest, even though there might be no blood relation. A wrong committed against one member was treated as a wrong against the whole clan. A Cherokee could count on being welcomed by his or her clan at any Cherokee settlement.

◆ **ALONG THE LITTLE "T"**

The story of white-Cherokee relations is a long and sad one, full of misunderstandings and violence and of greed and treachery. Sustained contact between the races started in 1673 when Gabriel Arthur and James Needham, traders from the colony of Virginia, wandered into the Overhill Towns. Interaction continued until 1838 when the Cherokees were forcefully removed to today's Oklahoma. The Cherokees lost their struggle against the whites' greed for land through a succession of treaties from 1684 (with South Carolina) to 1835.

Cherokee towns were mainly clustered along the fertile banks of the Little Tennessee River, enlarged now as the lake created by TVA's controversial 1970s Tellico Dam, which has wiped out most traces of the towns.

❖ **Sequoyah Birthplace Museum**   *map page 70, center right*

This enterprise of the Eastern Band of Cherokees honors the gifted tribesman who, around 1820, created a syllabary for the Cherokee language. The museum is devoted to pre-removal Cherokee history and culture. East of Venore on TN-360; 423-884-6246.

❖ **Fort Loudoun State Historic Area**   *map page 70, center right*

Located near the Sequoyah museum, this area covers a green peninsula jutting into Tellico Lake. The park has an informative visitor center, but its main feature, aside from its awesome setting, is the reconstruction of the fort the British erected in 1756–57, during the French and Indian War. It looks as you'd expect a frontier fort to look, a rough-hewn stockade surrounding crude cabins. The fragile British-Cherokee alliance broke down in 1760 with tragic consequences. The Cherokees slaughtered or enslaved most of the fort's men, women, and children. Visitors today can hear the boom of muskets at one of the **Garrison Weekends** and at September's **18th Century Trade Faire.** 423-884-6217.

❖ **Tellico Blockhouse**

Across the lake, in an equally stunning setting, is the site of the Tellico Blockhouse. This fort dates to a later period when the new American nation sought to promote trade between the Indians and the settlers. Cherokees traded pelts of bear, deer, wolf, elk, and otter for axes, plows, buttons, beads, rifles, dishes, and combs. The fort was occupied from 1794 until 1806 when the Cherokees gave up their Little Tennessee homeland. The stone foundations have been uncovered and restored. Off US-411 across from Fort Loudoun State Historic Area (found on map page 70, center right).

The trading carried on at the Tellico Blockhouse was part of the deerskin trade that was important to Cherokee life for the better part of two centuries. The trade contributed to the tribe's undoing. The British used the trade to win the Cherokees' loyalty in the long, violent struggle with the French for control of the frontier. When the American colonies revolted, the Cherokees remained loyal to the Crown, further alienating them from the fiercely independent trans-Appalachian settlers who craved their hunting grounds. Exhaustion of game through over-hunting drove native hunters further from home, which put the Cherokees in conflict with other tribes, conflict exploited by land speculators. And the trade made the Cherokees dependent on trade goods, rifles and lead in particular, which put them at the mercy of the often unscrupulous white traders and eroded their traditional way of life.

❖ **Chota**

Chota in the early 1700s emerged as the largest and most important Overhill town, the de facto capital of the Cherokees. Visiting the Chota memorial early on a summer's morning is a mystical experience. Wisps of fog rise from the lake. The marsh lining the narrow peninsula is alive with birds. The rustling of some unidentified creature makes you want to stop and investigate. The stillness is broken by a flock of geese overhead and the slurp of a fish taking an unsuspecting bug from the glass-smooth water. At the point of land rise seven stone pillars, each carved with the symbol of one of the clans that were so essential to Cherokee life. Oconastota's grave is here. He was the great war chief of the 1700s. As the road to Chota curves around the lake, it passes the imposing monument bearing the seals of the state of Tennessee and the Cherokee Nation. It marks the site of **Tanasi,** the village that gave its name to the nation's 16th state.

To get to Chota and Tanasi, follow TN-360 south beyond the Sequoya Museum. Where the highway turns sharply right to cross an arm of Tellico Lake, go straight and follow the county road as it snakes over the ridges to the main body of the lake. The Chota memorial is at the end of a peninsula, reached by a foot path that leads from the dead end of the road.

(following pages) On the shores of Tellico Lake stands a reconstruction of Fort Loudoun,
built by the British during the French and Indian War.

TENNESSEE VALLEY

◆ **ETOWAH**   *map page 70, lower right*

Etowah was built in the first decade of the 1900s when the Louisville & Nashville Railroad opened its new Cincinnati-Atlanta main line and needed a division headquarters and shops. **The L&N Depot and Railroad Museum** on Tennessee Avenue not only preserves the magnificent 1906 depot, with its fabulous wood-paneled interior, it also tells the story of life and work in a railroad town that at its peak employed 2,250 workers. **Tennessee Overhill Heritage Association** is also in the depot and provides excellence guidance to visitors; 423-263-7232.

◆ **CLEVELAND AREA**   *map page 70, lower center*

Standing atop a small hill near where US-411 crosses the Ocoee River is the **Nancy Ward Grave.** Born Nanye'hi at Chota in 1738, she achieved the exalted Cherokee status as Ghighau, a "Beloved Woman." In a battle with the Creeks in 1755, she took up the weapon of her slain husband and rallied the Cherokees to victory. From then on, she was influential in Cherokee affairs. She later married English trader Brian Ward. Nancy Ward tried to negotiate peace with the white settlers, from whom she learned to make cheese and butter. She introduced dairy cattle to the Cherokees. When the Cherokees ceded their lands along the Little Tennessee, Nancy Ward moved to the Ocoee, where she operated an inn until she died in 1822. She became a legend in her own time among both her own people and the whites whom she befriended. The stone pyramid beneath the tall cedar was erected on the 100th anniversary of her death by the Nancy Ward Chapter of the Daughters of the American Revolution.

Red Clay State Historic Park, located off TN-60 south of Cleveland, preserves the site of the last Cherokee capital in the East. It's a quiet and peaceful spot, a field in a narrow valley watched over by tall pines and oaks, at its center the sacred Blue Hole. The spring issues 352 gallons of blue water every minute. Most Cherokees lived in Georgia by 1830. The reconstructed homestead shows how the Cherokees had adopted the white man's way of living, abandoning the native tradition of common land in favor of profit-driven private ownership. The Cherokees hoped that by following the white man's path, they would be left alone to live in peace.

They were wrong. Georgians coveted their land. To make life difficult for the Cherokees, the state outlawed national assemblies, or councils; the council ground

A spring-fed creek winds through Red Clay State Historic Park, the last Cherokee capital in the East.

was relocated just over the border here in Tennessee. It served in that capacity until the 1838 removal. Annual events at Red Clay include August's **Cherokee Days of Recognition**, which draws Cherokees from across the country; 423-478-0339.

Another Cherokee heritage event takes place each February at the Hiwassee Wildlife Refuge off TN-60 north of Cleveland, the **Cherokee Indian Heritage & Sandhill Crane Viewing Days.** The birds are the main attraction. They're impressive creatures, with wingspans up to seven feet and standing as tall as 48 inches. Each winter, more than 30,000 of them stop by on their journey to Florida from the upper Midwest and Canada. It's quite a sight. For details, call 423-334-5850.

■ CHATTANOOGA *map page 70, lower left; and below*

With the mountains of the Cumberland Plateau escarpment forming green walls that rise more than a thousand feet above it, Chattanooga is one of the most dramatically situated cities in America. Its name is said to be Cherokee for "rock that comes to a point," a reference to towering Lookout Mountain. This was still Cherokee country in 1838 when the tribe was herded west to Oklahoma on what

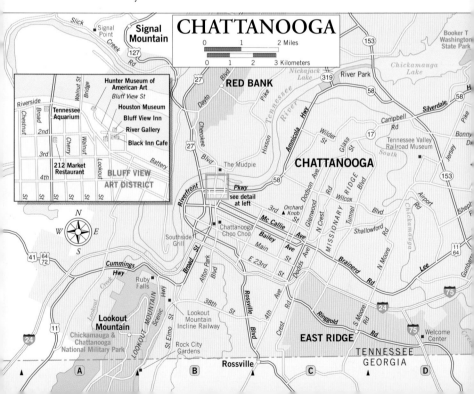

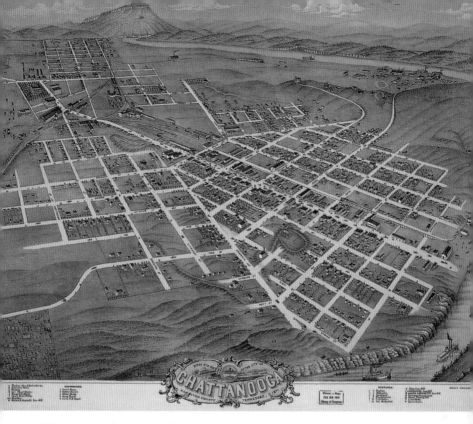

This 1871 map shows a view of Chattanooga as seen from the north. Lookout Mountain rises in the distance. (Library of Congress)

came to be known as the "Trail of Tears." Sitting where the Tennessee River cuts a path through the ramparts of the Cumberland Plateau, Chattanooga was naturally suited as a railroad junction. The first line, the one from Atlanta, reached it 12 years after the Cherokee removal. Chattanooga has been a vital rail hub ever since.

There was a time when Chattanooga didn't get much respect. To most travelers it was a mere obstacle, a rusty bottleneck on the way to someplace else. Now Chattanooga is the envy of other cities. A city-wide "visioning" process developed a model for resolving competing interests and taking advantage of the city's surroundings (which are splendid) and railroad heritage. Chattanooga is now cleaned up, fixed up, added on, and rebuilt—transformed into a major visitor destination. Its formerly lifeless downtown is anchored at one end by the dignified 1909 Beaux-Arts Terminal Station, converted into a hotel and shopping complex named for Glenn Miller's 1941 classic "Chattanooga Choo Choo," and at the other end

by the fabulous Tennessee Aquarium. It's surrounded by Ross's Landing Plaza, named for Cherokee Chief John Ross, creatively designed to reflect the region's natural environment, history, and culture in public art and native plants. It's the site for Chattanooga's biggest event, June's **Riverbend Festival,** nine days of music and celebration.

Add to all this sites of Civil War battles that altered the course of history, miles of riverside greenways and parks, upmarket outlets in restored warehouses, and one of the nation's premier railroad museums, and it's easy to see why *Family Life* and *Vacations* magazines list Chattanooga as a top family vacation destination.

Tennessee Aquarium

map page 112, A-1

Everyone who visits the world's largest freshwater aquarium at Ross's Landing comes away impressed. Visitors ride a long escalator to the top of the uniquely designed structure, then follow the water from the headwaters in the Great Smoky Mountains, into the Tennessee River, through manmade lakes, down the mighty Mississippi past a Louisiana cypress bayou, and into the Gulf of Mexico, all the while gazing at aquatic life in amazingly realistic simulated habitats. You'll see giant turtles in the Gulf, 'gators in the swamp, and enough trout in the mountain stream to cause a fly fisherman's heart to palpitate. The Rivers of the World section puts you face to face with giant sturgeon of the Volga, piranhas of the Amazon, and crocodiles of the Congo. Ross's Landing at end of Broad Street; 800-262-0695.

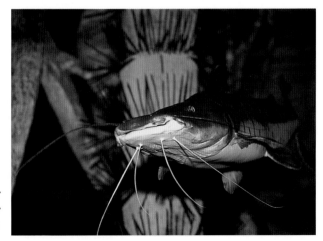

A catfish at the Tennessee Aquarium.

Bluff View Art District

map page 112, A/B-2

This captivating little neighborhood atop a sheer river bluff is where Chattanooga's late 19th- and early 20th-century industrialists built their sumptuous homes. Today they're filled with museums, galleries, inns, and restaurants. They include the following:

Hunter Museum of American Art.

Hunter Museum of American Art: This elegant 1904 Classical Revival mansion (something to see in its own right) is complemented by an award-winning contemporary addition. The permanent collection of 1,500 works is one of the best in the Southeast. 10 Bluff View; 423-267-0968.

Houston Museum: This fine Victorian house across from the Hunter is where the eccentric Anna Safley "Antique Annie" Houston's astounding collection of glass, china, furniture, and other items is displayed. She reportedly owned 15,000 pitchers at one time. The woman who lived most of her life in poverty collected husbands, too, nine in all. 201 High Street; 423-267- 7176.

River Gallery Sculpture Garden: Walk over to the sculpture garden to see the unique pieces spread out in a little park on the edge of the bluff.

From Ross's Landing, you can easily walk to Bluff View via the inviting **River Walk,** part of the 20-mile Tennessee Riverpark.

Coolidge Park/Walnut Street Bridge

map page 112, A-1

Chattanooga has had a love affair with this venerable truss bridge ever since it was built in 1891. It's been converted to a pedestrian walkway, which makes it, at nearly a half-mile in length, the world's longest pedestrian bridge over water. Tromp across the wooden decking high above the river to Coolidge Park with the kids, and they'll think they've gone to heaven. The fountain surrounded by eight statues of water-sprouting animals is cleverly designed to lure children into its spray. But first, join the youngsters for a ride on the century-old antique carousel—wet clothes are not allowed. The park surrounds the memorial to Sgt. Charles A. Coolidge, who was awarded the Congressional Medal of Honor for heroism in France during World War II.

The fountain in Coolidge Park.

Chattanooga Choo Choo
map page 112, B-2

Pardon me boy, that is the Chattanooga Choo Choo. Not the train described in the 1941 Glenn Miller hit, but the magnificent early 20th century railroad station befitting of Chattanooga's status as a railroad hub. Terminal Station at its peak had 14 tracks with 68 trains arriving and departing daily. The restoration as a hotel includes antique steam locomotives, a model train layout, and a 1924 New Orleans trolley standing by to take you on a ride. 1400 Market Street; 800-TRACK-29 or 423-266-5000.

Lookout Mountain Incline Railway
map page 112, B-3

Its billing as "America's Most Amazing Mile" isn't off the mark. The world's steepest railroad has been hauling passengers nearly straight up and down Lookout's es-

carpment since 1895. It's a short walk from the mountaintop station to the Point Park unit of the national military park. 3917 Saint Elmo Avenue; 423-821-9056.

Rock City Gardens
map page 112, B-3

They were regarded as tacky in their heyday, the barns painted with "See Rock City." Now they're hip. So are "See Rock City" birdhouses. They advertise the Depression-era tourist attraction atop Lookout Mountain that features spectacular natural rock formations and more than 400 species of native plants. Can you really "see seven states" from Lovers Leap as promised? Have a look for yourself. 1400 Patten Road, Lookout Mountain, Georgia; 706-820-2531.

Chattanooga's Terminal Station once served as a major railroad hub, with 14 tracks and 68 trains arriving and departing daily.

TENNESSEE VALLEY

Ruby Falls

map page 112, B-3

An elevator takes visitors deep into a Lookout Mountain cavern to a 145-foot natural waterfall that delivers 300 gallons per minute into a clear plunge pool. A tourist trap or a worthwhile natural wonder? Only one way to find out. 1720 S. Scenic Highway; 423-821-2544.

Tennessee Valley Railroad

map page 112, D-2

Chattanooga's railroad heritage is alive and well at the South's largest operating railroad museum. Steam- and diesel-powered trains travel former Southern Railway lines that include the Civil War–era line through the 1858 tunnel under the Missionary Ridge battleground. The museum also operates rail excursions to Chickamauga. 4119 Cromwell Road; 423-894-8028.

■ CIVIL WAR CHATTANOOGA

We're fortunate that in the 1890s, veterans and politicians had the foresight to start preserving Civil War battlefields. Chickamauga & Chattanooga was the first and is the largest. Back in those days, the landscape was pretty much as it had been in 1863 when it was a battleground. Not so today. The widely dispersed units of the **Chickamauga & Chattanooga National Military Park** are surrounded by the growth of Tennessee's fourth largest city. So in addition to preserving hallowed ground, the park bestows some luscious green space amidst urban sprawl. For general park information contact Point Park Visitors Center, 1116 East Brow Road, Lookout Mountain; 423-821-7786.

◆ CHICKAMAUGA BATTLEFIELD

Chickamauga is said to mean "river of death" in some native dialect. The steep-banked creek lived up to its name for two days in September 1863, as the two principal western armies fought the battle that ranks in casualties second only to Gettysburg's three days. Quiet roads wander through thick woods of cedar, dogwood, oak, and hickory interspersed with fields, past 1,400 markers and heroic monuments—more than any other battlefield—and to pivotal sites like the place where Longstreet's men charged through the unexpected gap in the Union line and Snodgrass Hill where General Thomas earned honors as the "Rock of Chickamauga." The visitor center features a gripping multimedia presentation, the Fuller gun collection of 355 weapons, and one of the best selections of Civil War books anywhere. Fort Oglethorpe, Georgia, South of Chattanooga off US-27; 706-866-9241.

AUTHOR'S CHOICE: CHATTANOOGA INNS AND RESTAURANTS

LODGING

Adams Hilborne Mansion Inn
Dramatic 1889 Romanesque mansion at the entrance to the Fort Wood Historic District serves as an elegant inn, complete with 16-foot coffered ceilings, hand-cut stained and beveled glass, inlaid floors, and decorative wood moldings. Lodging and restaurant. 801 Vine Street; 423-265-5000.

Bluff View Inn
Bed-and-breakfast accommodations in three 19th-century mansions overlooking Tennessee River in fabulous Bluff View Art District. 411 E. Second Street; 800-725-8338 ext. 2, or 423-265-5033.

Chattanooga Choo Choo
Sleep in remade rail cars or in a conventional hotel at the restored Terminal Station. A destination in itself now run by Holiday Inn. 1400 Market Street; 423-266-5000.

Read House Hotel
On the site of the Crutchfield House hotel, important in the Civil War, Chattanooga's grandest hotel applies a Civil War theme to each floor. Dining in the Green Room is an elegant Chattanooga tradition. 827 Broad Street; 423-266-4121.

RESTAURANTS

Back Inn Café
Bistro with Italian flavor and fabulous views in the Bluff View Art District. 412 E. Second Street; 423-265-5033, ext 1.

Big River Grille & Brewing Works
Lively, casual dining next to Ross's Landing featuring sandwiches, salads, fish, pasta, and outstanding beer and ale. 222 Broad Street; 423-267-2739.

Mount Vernon Restaurant
The best in Southern cooking and rich desserts at this Chattanooga institution at foot of Lookout Mountain. 3509 Broad Street; 423-266-6591.

Rembrandt's Coffee House
European-style cafe with fresh-baked pastries, sandwiches on homemade bread, soups, and, of course, gourmet coffee. 204 High Street, Bluff View; 423-265-5033, ext 3.

Southside Grill
Made-over meat packing plant near Choo Choo is setting for contemporary dining billed as "creative regional." Whatever, it's a hit with locals and visitors alike. 1400 Cowart Street; 423-266-9211.

Tony's Pasta Shop and Trattoria
No secret what's served in this first-class Bluff View eatery, but it's no ordinary spaghetti. 212-B High Street; 423-265-5033, ext.6.

212 Market
Creative, popular, upscale dining next to Ross's Landing featuring pasta, lamb, and beef. 212 Market Street; 423-265-1212.

♦ LOOKOUT MOUNTAIN   *map page 112, A/B-3*

The November 23, 1863, fighting on Lookout Mountain is romantically called the "Battle Above the Clouds." Low-hanging clouds did shroud the mountain that day, but in truth the fighting was beneath them on the slopes, not on the summit. Lookout's fiercest fighting took place on a small plateau about halfway up the mountain. It's marked by the reconstructed **Cravens House** and several monuments. Off Scenic Highway, TN-148.

From the summit at **Point Park,** you can spot the battle sites from the **Ochs Museum and Overlook,** named for the Chattanooga newspaper man who, in 1896, purchased the near-bankrupt *New York Times* and built it into one of the world's great papers. Up here, 1,500 feet above the hum of the city, on a clear day you can make out the blue ridges of the mountains on the far side of the Tennessee Valley. Observing Lookout from down below, you'll see the top of a monument poking above the trees. The **New York Peace Monument** is even more imposing up close, for you can clearly see the massive statues of Federal and Confederate soldiers shaking hands underneath an American flag.

This 1864 painting by James Walker illustrates why the Battle of Lookout Mountain was called the "Battle above the Clouds." (U.S. Army Center for Military History, Washington, D.C.)

TENNESSEE VALLEY

Next to the entrance to Point Park is the private **Battles for Chattanooga Museum,** where a three-dimensional electronic map featuring 5,000 miniature soldiers and 650 lights explains the fighting of November 1863. For information call 423-821-2812.

◆ ORCHARD KNOB   *map page 112, C-2*

This little hill, covered now in monuments and markers, was taken by the Federals on November 23, 1863, the first of three days' fighting to lift the Confederate siege of Chattanooga. Grant stood here two days later and watched in disbelief as Federal troops did the seemingly impossible: They fought their way up the near-vertical heights of heavily fortified Missionary Ridge. Orchard Knob Avenue off McCallie Avenue (US-11/64).

◆ MISSIONARY RIDGE   *map page 112, C-2*

The long ridge rising as much as 600 feet served as the eastern wall of the Confederates' perimeter around Chattanooga. Federal troops defied all odds and forced

CHATTANOOGA AND THE CIVIL WAR

It worked once for Maj. Gen. William S. Rosecrans. He divided his Federal Army of the Cumberland into three parts in June 1863 and maneuvered the Confederate army nearly out of Tennessee, all the way to Chattanooga. Rosecrans tried it again in August. He sent his army over the mountains in three different places with the intent of getting between Atlanta and the Confederates at Chattanooga. The tactic worked. At least at first. On September 8, fearing that he was about to be trapped in Chattanooga, Confederate General Braxton Bragg marched his Army of Tennessee 25 miles south toward Atlanta.

When Bragg realized that the Federal army was divided, he halted, and sent "deserters" to spread tales of an army fleeing in panic toward Atlanta. Emboldened by these false reports, Rosecrans kept his army dangerously divided. Bragg devised a sound plan to pick off the three parts one at a time, but bungling and insubordination by his lieutenants delayed the attack long enough for Rosecrans to gather his scattered army. Without a moment to spare, the three corps of the Union army rejoined just as Bragg's men slammed into them on the morning of September 19, 1863 south of Chattanooga along the banks of Chickamauga Creek. In desperate fighting in thick woods along a four-mile front, the Confederates pushed the Federals back to the road to Chattanooga. Bragg's goal was to wheel them around, block the road, and trap them in a Lookout Mountain cove. But it didn't turn out that way.

Lt. Gen. James Longstreet was headed west with two divisions from Robert E. Lee's army. Confederates from the east heard the first guns of Chickamauga as the trains carrying them from Virginia chugged into nearby Ringgold. The next day, September 20, a communication lapse caused a gap in the Union line at the same time and place that Longstreet's new arrivals were attacking. Rosecrans and half his army were routed and fled to Chattanooga. Maj. Gen. George Thomas, a Virginian who had stayed in the Federal army, took command of the remaining forces and led a heroic stand that held off until dark wave after wave of Confederates. Chickamauga was a Confederate victory. But only in the sense that the Southerners controlled the bloody woods at the end of the day. Nearly 30 percent of the Confederates were killed, wounded, or missing.

Bragg's army occupied the heights around Chattanooga and tried to starve the

Federals into surrender. Conditions in Chattanooga grew desperate. Men were reduced to feeding off the 10,000 dead mules and horses. In October, President Lincoln named Ulysses S. Grant, the hero of Fort Donelson, Shiloh, and Vicksburg, commander of all Federal troops in the West. Grant set out for Chattanooga. One of his first acts was to replace Rosecrans with Thomas. In the meantime, just as Longstreet had brought Confederate reinforcements from Virginia, "Fighting Joe" Hooker brought 20,000 Federals from the East to help rescue Chattanooga. Grant reached the town below Lookout Mountain on October 23, "wet, dirty, and tired" as it was reported to Washington. He immediately started planning relief of the siege, planning that included opening the "Cracker Line" to bring in food and supplies and that included a forced march from faraway Mississippi by Grant's former army, now commanded by his trusted lieutenant, William T. Sherman.

In stark contrast to Grant's decisive leadership, Bragg's command was in disarray. Confederate President Jefferson Davis came to mediate the endless bickering between Bragg and his generals, but left having done little more than approving a foolish plan to send Longstreet's corps to Knoxville, thus reducing Bragg's force by more than a third.

When Sherman's ragged men trudged in from their long march, Grant wasted no time in ordering a breakout. Thomas's troops took Orchard Knob on November 23, 1863, and the next day, Hooker's men swept the Southerners off Lookout Mountain. On November 25, Grant ordered Thomas's men to take the rifle pits at the foot of Missionary Ridge. This was to be a distraction to enable Sherman's army to sweep down the crest of the ridge from the north. In one of the most dramatic fights of the Civil War, the men from the Army of the Cumberland, still stinging from their defeat at Chickamauga, and without any orders to do so, passed through the rifle pits, fought their way up the near-vertical heights of the ridge, and threw off the Confederate defenders. The Army of Tennessee retreated to Georgia where Bragg ended his stormy career as its commander.

Grant was effusive in his praise for his men. "By your noble heroism and determined courage, you have most effectually defeated the plans of the enemy for regaining possession of the states of Kentucky and Tennessee. You have secured positions from which no rebellious power can drive or dislodge you." The door was ajar to Atlanta and to the Deep South.

A view of Chattanooga from Point Park on Lookout Mountain.

their way over it on November 25, 1863, ending the Army of Tennessee's tenure in its namesake state—except for a brief period a year later—and ending Confederate Gen. Braxton Bragg's controversial tenure as a field commander. Crest Road curves and climbs the entire length of the Confederate line, passing countless reservations, monuments, and tablets that explain the battle. Parking is next to impossible, so you might want to park at the DeLong Reservation and walk south. (Reservations are small parks preserving certain areas from development.)

◆   **SIGNAL POINT**   *map page 112, A-1*

This tiny unit of the park marks the Federal signal station on the tip of Walden's Ridge, the eastern escarpment of the Cumberland Plateau, overlooking the start of the river's curving path through the Tennessee River Gorge. It's also the terminus of the **Cumberland Trail,** the footpath that will someday cross the state to the Cumberland Gap. Town of Signal Mountain, off US-127.

◆ CHATTANOOGA NATIONAL CEMETERY   *map page 112, B-1*

The bulky oaks shading this spacious burying ground reveal that it's been here a while. Since 1863, in fact, shortly after the battles. The remains of more than 12,000 Union soldiers, half of them unknown, were reinterred here after the battles here and elsewhere. This is the final resting place for some of Andrews's Raiders, the 22 Union soldiers led by civilian James Andrews, whose commandeering of the locomotive "General" near Atlanta in April 1862 led to "The Great Locomotive Chase." The raiders were the first Americans to receive the Congressional Medal of Honor. Their graves are marked by the replica of the "General" you'll see as you enter the cemetery. The stone arch, erected to honor the Civil War dead, is impressive as well. Holtzclaw Avenue between Bailey Avenue (US-11/64) and Main Street (US-41/76); 423-855-6590.

TENNESSEE VALLEY

This photo of Major General Ulysses S. Grant (left) standing on Lookout Mountain was taken after the battle there in 1863. (Library of Congress)

CUMBERLAND PLATEAU

Map
pages 130-131

Big South Fork
Nashville
Rugby
Cumberland Gap
Nat'l Historic Park

Falls Creek Falls SP
South Cumberland Rec Area
Sewanee

CUMBERLAND
PLATEAU

◆ **AREA OVERVIEW**

Travel Basics: The Cumberland Plateau is a high, rolling, forested tableland where rushing mountain streams have carved out rugged gorges. It is part of the larger Appalachian Plateau that runs from near Lake Ontario in New York all the way to middle Alabama. Rivers plunging through boulder-strewn gorges draw paddlers with their canoes and kayaks. Hikers and horseback riders follow trails through the oaks and the pines to laurel-fringed bluff overlooks, to waterfalls in every imaginable shape and size, and to rock pinnacles and natural arches. Anglers try their luck in waters ranging from the sheltered coves of deep reservoirs to tiny streams draped in rhododendron. Hunters stalk the deer and wild turkey that have rebounded from near extinction in the region.

Getting Around: Though much of the plateau is remote, road access is perfectly adequate. Interstates 24, 40, and 75 cross it. Except for a few places where roads meet the gorges at the Big South Fork, the Obed and its tributaries, and Fall Creek Falls, the plateau's most scenic drives are those along the adjacent lowlands that offer views of the escarpment. TN-63 from LaFollete to Cumberland Gap, TN-111 from Sparta to

Buzzard's Roost in Fall Creek Falls State Park.

Spencer, TN-56 from McMinnville to Beersheba Springs, US-41 between Manchester and Monteagle, and US-64 from I-24 past Winchester all fit this category. The most spectacular plateau drive is along US-127 through the Sequatchie Valley, the narrow, fertile rift that slices the plateau in half between Crossville and Jasper. Outdoor recreation is the main draw on the plateau, however, not windshield sightseeing. The real fun starts where the pavement ends, at the trailheads and the boat ramps.

Climate: Spring arrives in late March up here, and can be glorious. In mid-summer, the heat (low 90s) and humidity can make this area quite uncomfortable. Fall arrives by late September and is an especially fine time to visit. Wintry weather can blow in between October and April when low-hanging clouds frequently shroud the plateau in fog. Nashville's forecasts are usually indicative of plateau weather, except that the plateau is a few degrees cooler than the city center, a significant difference in winter when rain at lower elevations often turns to snow and ice.

Food & Lodging: This is not the place for fancy dining and charming inns, except for the Sewanee-Monteagle area, which has a fair supply of both. Cabins in half a dozen state parks make convenient bases. Fall Creek Falls State Park has a hotel.

■ TENNESSEE'S OTHER MOUNTAINS

To early Tennesseans, the Cumberland Plateau was nothing but an obstacle on the way west to more fertile lands. That attitude changed in the late 1800s as heavy industry needed natural resources to fuel its engines. Absentee landowners with huge holdings hired local men to cut the trees and dig the coal. These activities provided jobs in a poor region. But it also trapped the few inhabitants in cycles of boom and bust typical of extractive economies, and it laid waste to the land.

The land stared to heal with the arrival of New Deal land conservation programs in the 1930s. Some of the most scenic places—which were also some of the most abused—were set aside at Fall Creek Falls, Pickett, Standing Stone, and other parks. The environmental movement of the 1970s brought another wave of protection. The Big South Fork, the Obed, and the South Cumberland were added to the list of preserves. The unregulated strip mining ravaging the mountains was brought under control. Streams that had been polluted for generations began to cleanse themselves. Forests were allowed to mature.

The Cumberlands are still a poor region. And there are still threats to the land. But in most places, the healing continues. The plateau is one part of our world that is getting better with time.

Coal miners pose for a group photo in Anderson County around the end of the 19th century.
(Tennessee State Library and Archives)

George Caleb Bingham painted Daniel Boone Escorting Settlers Through the Cumberland Gap *in the 1850s—almost a century after the event.*
(Mildred Lane Kemper Art Museum, Washington University in St. Louis.
Gift of Nathaniel Phillips, 1890)

■ CUMBERLAND GAP   *map page 131, top*

It doesn't seem like a big deal now, getting over the green wall west of the Tennessee Valley. But if you were on foot or on a horse, the Cumberland escarpment would present a formidable barrier. You'd search for a passage. The Cherokees and Shawnees found this one. So did the hunters and the explorers. And the land speculators and the pioneers. Daniel Boone first passed through the gap in 1769. Then in 1775 he led a crew of axmen that built the Wilderness Road through the gap. It was the main pathway west until steamboats, canals, and railroads provided better alternatives.

A comfortable lodging here is the **Cumberland Gap Inn** in Cumberland Gap, the Victorian village below the famous passage through the mountains. It's located at 630 Brooklyn Street; 423-869-9172.

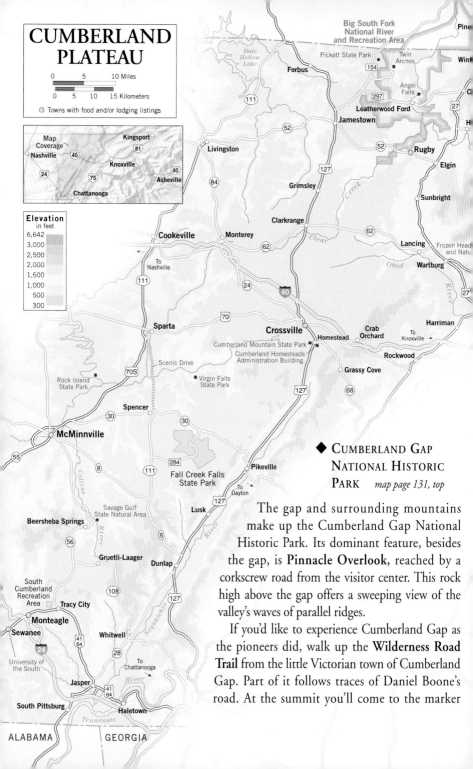

CUMBERLAND PLATEAU

0   5   10 Miles

0   5   10   15 Kilometers

○ Towns with food and/or lodging listings

Map Coverage

Nashville   Kingsport   81
40   Knoxville
24   75   40   Asheville
        Chattanooga

Elevation
in feet

6,642
3,000
2,500
2,000
1,500
1,000
500
300

Big South Fork
National River
and Recreation Area   Pine

Dale   Pickett State Park   Twin
Hollow   154   Arches   Win
Lake   Angel
Forbus   Falls
                         297   27
                    Leatherwood Ford
111   Jamestown   H

52   52   Rugby

Livingston   127   Elgin

                    Grimsley   Sunbright

                Clarkrange   Creek

To   Clear   62   Lancing
Nashville   Cookeville   Monterey   Frozen Head
111   62   Obed   and Natu
                         24   40   Wartburg
                                                        27
                    70
Sparta   Crossville   Homestead   Crab
               Cumberland Mountain State Park   Orchard   To
               Cumberland Homesteads   Knoxville
               Administration Building   Rockwood
        Scenic Drive
70S   Virgin Falls   Grassy Cove
               State Park
Rock Island
State Park   127   68
Spencer
30
McMinnville   30

55   8   Pikeville
          111   284
               Fall Creek Falls
               State Park   ◆ CUMBERLAND GAP
          To   NATIONAL HISTORIC
          Dayton   PARK   *map page 131, top*
               Lusk
Beersheba Springs   127
               Savage Gulf   The gap and surrounding mountains
56   State Natural Area   make up the Cumberland Gap National
          8   Dunlap   Historic Park. Its dominant feature, besides
     Gruetli-Laager   the gap, is **Pinnacle Overlook**, reached by a
South   corkscrew road from the visitor center. This rock
Cumberland   108   high above the gap offers a sweeping view of the
Recreation   valley's waves of parallel ridges.
Area   Tracy City   127
Monteagle   If you'd like to experience Cumberland Gap as
Sewanee   41   the pioneers did, walk up the **Wilderness Road**
          64   Whitwell   **Trail** from the little Victorian town of Cumberland
University   24   28   Gap. Part of it follows traces of Daniel Boone's
of the South   To   road. At the summit you'll come to the marker
          Chattanooga
Jasper   41
         64
South Pittsburg
          Haletown
     Tennessee

ALABAMA   GEORGIA

To
Lexington, KY
JCKY
Jellico
75
25W
Scenic Drive
63
LaFollette
25W
ryville
Cumberland Gap
National Historic Park
Middlesboro
Cumberland
Gap
Lincoln Memorial University
Harrogate
25E

with plaques from each of the three states that hold the gap. The actual junction of Tennessee, Kentucky, and Virginia is a short climb up a trail that is the start of the Cumberland Trail. Other trails and historic sites straddle the Kentucky-Virginia border northeast of the gap.

◆ LINCOLN MEMORIAL UNIVERSITY   *map page 131, top*

Lincoln Memorial University is in the shadow of Cumberland Mountain, at Harrogate. You'll know it by the imposing statue of the Great Emancipator facing the highway. The school was started here in 1897 and named for Lincoln in honor of his concern for pro-Union East Tennessee during the Civil War. The college's **Abraham Lincoln Museum** is regarded as one of the best in the nation honoring our 16th president. Among the artifacts is the cane the president had with him at Ford's Theater the night John Wilkes Booth put a bullet in the back of his head. Museum information: 423-869-6235.

A view of Cumberland Gap as seen from Pinnacle Rock.

■ BIG SOUTH FORK *map page 130, top*

When you hear someone say they're headed for the Big South Fork, they could be going to the remote seven-county area on the Tennessee-Kentucky line that's drained by the Cumberland River's south fork. Or they could be headed for some whitewater fun on the river itself as it flows north to join the Cumberland's main stem. Most likely they're on their way to the 125,000-acre national recreation area that takes its name from the river.

WAVING MOUNTAIN BEAUTY

John Muir, at the age of 29, decided to pursue his passion for "botanizing" by walking from Kentucky to the Gulf of Mexico. In 1867, two years after the Civil War ended, he crossed the Cumberland Plateau, noting its great beauty, as well as recording an encounter with Confederate guerrillas: "All were mounted on rather scrawny horses, and all wore long hair hanging down on their shoulders." (They let him pass thinking him to be a country herb doctor.) As we might expect from Muir, he saw in the natural beauty of Tennessee proof of the grace and munificence of God.

September 18

U p the mountain on the state line. The scenery is far grander than any I ever before beheld. The view extends from the Cumberland Mountains on the north far into Georgia and North Carolina to the south, an area of about five thousand square miles. Such an ocean of wooded, waving, swelling mountain beauty and grandeur is not to be described. Countless forest-clad hills, side by side in rows and groups, seemed to be enjoying the rich sunshine and remaining motionless only because they were so eagerly absorbing it. All were united by curves and slopes of inimitable softness and beauty. Oh, these forest gardens of our Father! What perfection, what divinity, in their architecture! What simplicity and mysterious complexity of detail! Who shall read the teaching of these sylvan pages, the glad brotherhood of rills that sing in the valleys, and all the happy creatures that dwell in them under the tender keeping of a Father's care?

—John Muir (1838–1914), *A Thousand-Mile Walk to the Gulf,* 1867

(opposite) Morning fog clears over Angel Falls in Big South Fork National River and Recreation Area. (following pages) A hiker enjoys fall scenery along a trail in the Big South Fork National River and Recreation Area.

A view from the Angel Falls overlook in Big South Fork National River and Recreation Area.

◆ BIG SOUTH FORK NATIONAL RIVER
AND RECREATION AREA   *map page 130, top*

There doesn't seem to be much of interest along the Leatherwood Ford Road (TN-297) leading into the park from Jamestown through a second-growth forest of mostly small trees. All of a sudden, wham! A steep descent, a hairpin curve, an even steeper descent, and another tight curve. Before you know it, you're gazing up at multihued sandstone bluffs in one of the deepest canyons in the eastern United States. The water is so powerful in late winter and early spring that you'll have to shout to be heard above the roar. This is one of the few natural wonders easily accessible to even car-bound tourists. **Leatherwood Ford** is the only place where a paved road penetrates a gorge. An easy trail meanders downstream to **Angel Falls,** a jumbled rapids that challenges the most experienced paddler. On the park's western edge, **Twin Arches** are a pair of gigantic sandstone natural bridges standing in tandem high above the headwaters of Station Camp Creek.

The trails in adjacent **Pickett State Park** are perfect for a family outing. The Civilian Conservation Corps boys must have had children in mind when they built them in the 1930s. Big South Fork NR&RA; 423-569-9778.

◆ RUGBY   *map page 130, top right*

Tennessee in the 1800s was a magnet for Utopian communities. Hardly a trace of them remains, except at Rugby. Twenty of the 70 Victorian buildings are still in use on the point of land between the gorges of Clear Fork and Whiteoak Creek. Lovely little **Christ Church** has held Episcopal services since 1887. The 1882 library holds 7,000 volumes, the oldest printed in 1687 and the newest in 1899. At its peak, close to 400 people lived at Rugby.

So who were they? Many were British. Author and social reformer Thomas Hughes conceived Rugby as a place for younger sons of Britain's landed aristocracy to live in a cooperative community free of class distinctions. It would be a cultured, intellectual environment where they would earn an honest living from the land. The plateau's shallow sandy soil didn't produce much. The railroad never built the promised spur from the main line. The winters were severe. And there

was a typhoid epidemic. The enterprise that started in 1880 was largely over by 1900. But Rugby lived on as a little village. It's a popular destination, complete with food, lodging, and annual events like May's **Festival of British & Appalachian Culture.** Tours are offered daily; 423-628-2441.

In the historic English colony adjacent to the Big South Fork NR&RA is a mansard-roofed inn from the 1880s. It's the moderately priced **Newbury House Inn,** on TN-52; 423-628-2441. Another nearby and comfortable small inn is the **Wildwood Lodge** on TN-154 just east of Jamestown; 931-879-9454.

A demonstration of soap making in historic Rugby.

■ AROUND CROSSVILLE   *map page 130, upper center*

It's always been a crossroads. That's how Crossville got its name. Travelers in the late 1700s started passing through here headed for the rich country around Nashville. Crossville is today a mecca for "halfbacks," retired Midwesterners tired of Florida who have moved halfway back home. Golf course–intensive development is straining the resources, but it's also helping support amenities that are rare in this part of Appalachia. One is the **Cumberland County Playhouse,** a superb theater company that's in its third decade of providing first-class entertainment. 221 Tennessee Avenue; 931-484-5000.

◆ CUMBERLAND HOMESTEADS   *map page 130, center right*

Observant travelers on US-127 south of Crossville will notice the similarity between the evenly spaced houses. They're reminiscent of cottages you might see in the English countryside, except that local Crab Orchard stone is used in the construction. They're the Cumberland Homesteads, the 1930s resettlement community designed to provide jobs and a decent place to live in this area hit hard by the Great Depression. About 250 houses were built, each surrounded by enough land for a small farm. The homesteads now comprise a national historic district.

The homesteads administration building, with its lighthouse-inspired tower, sits in the fork where TN-68 splits from US-127. It's a charming structure, covered on the outside with native stone and on the inside with native pine. It's now a museum telling the story of the often tense relationship between the mountaineers and the idealistic New Deal social planners. A photo of one of the most idealistic of them all greets visitors at the entrance. On a hot summer day in 1934, Eleanor Roosevelt stood on the bed of a logging truck and gave a pep talk to the nascent homesteaders. A comfortable lodging near the headquarters of the Cumberland Homesteads (where you can soak up the spirit of the place) is the **Homestead B&B** at 1165 TN-68; 931-456-6355.

The park the CCC built in the middle of the homesteads is **Cumberland Mountain State Park.**

◆ GRASSY COVE   *map page 130, center right*

After it passes the last of the distinctive homestead houses, Highway 68 curves through a gap and descends into Grassy Cove, where the forests on the surrounding mountains come down to brilliant green pastures. The cove is dotted with

Sheep graze in Grassy Cove, an area known for the radiant green of its meadows.

CUMBERLAND PLATEAU

neatly painted steeple-topped red barns kept up by descendants of the original German settlers. If you'd like to catch a spectacular view of the cove, hike from the gap along the **Cumberland Trail** to the bluff on Brady Mountain. When it's all done, the state scenic trail will be a continuous marked footpath extending 280 miles across Tennessee from Cumberland Gap to Chattanooga. For information, call 931-456-6259.

■ OBED WILD AND SCENIC RIVER   *map page 130-131, center*

They're named "Widow Maker," "90 Right–90 Left," and "Ohmigod!"

The names of the rapids in the deep gorges of the Obed River, Clear Creek, and Daddys Creek are proof enough that this is some of the nation's most exciting whitewater. But it's not all life-threatening. There are miles of peaceful water suitable for wading, swimming, and fishing. If you prefer dry land for your thrills, you can hike a stretch of the Cumberland Trail. Information: 423-346- 6294.

■ FROZEN HEAD STATE PARK
AND NATURAL AREA   *map page 131, center left*

A big chunk of the mountains that make up the northeast corner of the Cumberland Plateau is preserved at Frozen Head, named for the 3,324-foot peak that's often covered with snow in winter. Fifty miles of trails wander through the undisturbed forest past waterfalls, rock bluffs, and shows of wildflowers (especially trillium) that many consider second only to the Great Smokies—which, by the way, you can see on a clear day from the top of Frozen Head. Information: 423-346-3318.

■ BOWATER WILDERNESS AREAS

From its hundreds of thousands of acres of plateau timberland that feed its massive paper mill, Bowater has set aside extraordinarily scenic places as "pocket wilderness" areas and invited the public to hike the trials. At **Virgin Falls** near Sparta *(map page 130, center left)*, a creek pours out of a cave, drops over a 110-

CUMBERLAND PLATEAU

(above) Dwarf-crested iris, the state flower, in bloom in Virgin Falls Pocket Wilderness.
(opposite) A wintry scene in Cumberland Mountain State Park.

foot cliff, then disappears into a deep sink. And it's only one of four magnificent falls at this pocket wilderness. Other Bowater areas are **North Chickamauga** near Chattanooga, **Laurel-Snow** near Dayton, and **Stinging Fork, Piney River,** and **Twin Rocks** near Spring City. For maps, call 423-336-7205.

■ FALL CREEK FALLS STATE PARK   *map page 130, lower center*

The combination of beautiful scenery, diverse recreational options, and comfortable lodgings make this Tennessee's flagship state park. You can start the morning with a bike ride to Fall Creek Falls (at 256 feet the highest east of the Rockies), play a midday round of golf, rent a boat for fishing as things quiet down in the late afternoon, and still be at the inn's dining room as the sun sets over the lake. Two-thirds of the park's 19,000 acres is a designated natural area, where Fall Creek is only one of several waterfalls that plunge into deep gorges filled with hemlock and rhododendron. There are panoramic views from overlooks on the trails and from the scenic drive hugging the rim of Cane Creek Gorge. Information: 423-881-3297.

A spotted eft in camouflage among autumn leaves.

CUMBERLAND PLATEAU

Lower Greeter Falls in Savage Gulf State Natural Area.

To stay a few days and enjoy this beautiful park, try **Fall Creek Falls Inn,** a spacious hotel with a lakeside restaurant; 800-250-8610 or 423-881-5241. **Fall Creek Falls B&B** is a pleasant, small inn with cabins just outside the park on TN-284; 423-881-5494.

■ SOUTH CUMBERLAND RECREATION AREA   *map page 130, lower left*

The ten distinct preserves that make up this state-managed area provide some of the Southeast's most intriguing and challenging outdoor recreation.

Savage Gulf State Natural Area is the largest and most spectacular. More than 50 miles of trails wind through three 800-foot-deep gorges, or "gulfs," that come together like a giant crow's foot. The Stone Door entrance to Savage Gulf is at Beersheba Springs, an intriguing, private, bluff-top resort since the days before the Civil War.

BEERSHEBA SPRINGS

*I*n July, Mother and Father went up to Beersheba Springs, on the Cumberland Plateau, for a few days' relief from the hot weather. Beersheba was an old-fashioned watering place, the resort in past time of Episcopal bishops, Louisiana planters, and the gentry of Middle Tennessee. By the 1920s only a select few from the Nashville Basin kept cottages there and held sway at the old hotel. It was the kind of summer spot my parents felt most comfortable in. It had never had the dash of Tate Springs or the homey atmosphere of Monteagle, but it was older than either of those places and had had since its beginning gambling tables, horses, and dancing. Behind the porticoed hotel on the bluff's edge the old slave quarters were still standing, as was also the two-story brick garçonniere, reached by a covered walkway from the hotel. There was an old graveyard overgrown with box and red cedar, enclosed by a rock wall and containing old gravestones leaning at precarious angles but still bearing good Tennessee–Virginia names like Burwell and Armistead. Farther along the bluff and farther back on the plateau were substantial cottages and summer houses, a good number of them built of squared chestnut logs and flanked by handsome limestone end-chimneys.

—Peter Taylor, *In the Miro District and Other Stories,* 1974

Grundy Forest State Natural Area packs more dramatic scenery per acre than just about any place you'll find. Cascading streams, waterfalls, rock pinnacles, natural arches, virgin hemlock groves, and a wide assortment of wildflowers lie along Big and Little Fiery Gizzard Creeks. The two-mile trail at **Carter State Natural Area** leads to the opening of Lost Cove Cave. It's quite a sight: 100 feet wide and 80 feet high beneath a 150-foot cliff with a crystal clear stream gushing out of it. **The South Cumberland visitor center** on US-41 near Monteagle is the place to get information and see exhibits about the area's natural and cultural history.

■ SEWANEE AND MONTEAGLE   *map page 130, lower left*

Where I-24 crosses it, the Cumberland Plateau narrows to just a few miles, barely wide enough to hold two towns that owe their existence to the Mountain Goat. Not the four-legged kind, but the steep rail branch that connected with the main line at the foot of the mountain. When the Sewanee Mining Co. built it before the Civil War, it offered 10,000 acres to the Episcopal bishops who were looking for a place to build a university "above the malaria line."

The University of the South at Sewanee offers a delightful taste of Oxford in the Tennessee mountains. The library started in 1868 with a donation of books from Oxford and Cambridge. Some of the Gothic-style buildings are modeled after ones at Oxford. It's a treat to wander among them beneath towering, century-old white pines. The Gothic architecture climaxes at All Saints Chapel, with its English stained glass and flags hanging high in the interior. For tours call 800-367-1179 or 931-598-1286. Summer on the mountain brings the music festival and the **Sewanee Writers' Conference,** funded through the estate of the late Tennessee Williams; 800-367-1179.

All Saints Chapel on the campus of the University of the South in Sewanee.

Students maintain the 20-mile Sewanee Perimeter Trail that circles the 10,000-acre campus. A 1.4-mile stretch leads through wildflower- and waterfall-filled Shakerag Hollow from Green's View to University Gate. A mile-long hike leads along the bluff from University View to Morgan's Steep.

❖

If you're in Sewanee and want to eat with local people, try **Pearl's Foggy Mountain Café** at 15344 Sewanee Highway (US-41A). The cooking is inventive with a Southern touch. Or stop by **Shenanigan's** at 12595 Sollace Freeman Highway (US-41A). This restaurant is located in a tilting old store in what passes for Sewanee's downtown and serves up what people like: hearty homemade soups, salads, quiche, sandwiches, draft beer, and good times.

The **Monteagle Sunday School Assembly** spreads out on the edge of the town Canadian founder John Moffat named for his friend Lord Mounteagle. The assembly started in 1882 as the "Chautauqua of the South," a combination religious training-arts-vacation center patterned after the one in upstate New York. The assembly is today a summer resort colony, distinguished by dozens of colorful Victorian cottages. Don't despair if you're not fortunate enough to own one. There are two delightful inns. One is the **Adams Edgeworth Inn,** a restored Victorian decorated with antiques and fine art. Its wrap-around porch is a fine place to relax after a hike in the South Cumberland's trails; 931-924-4000. In town, at 204 W. Main Street you'll find the elegant **Monteagle Inn**, which serves a delicious breakfast; 931-924-3869.

The Mountain Goat connected with the main railroad line down at Cowan, the squeaky clean Victorian town in sight of Sewanee's bluffs. To breach the Cumberland Plateau, the railroad in the 1850s built what was then, at 2,220 feet, the nation's longest tunnel. Locomotives based at Cowan still push trains through it. The classic 1904 depot is now the **Cowan Railroad Museum,** right in the middle of town; 931-967-3078.

The Sewanee and Monteagle Mountain Goat train climbs the mountain over a mainline train emerging from the Cowan railroad tunnel, circa 1940. (Tennessee State Library and Archives)

CLARENCE DARROW AND THE MONKEY TRIAL

Many a visitor traveled to the town of Dayton, Tennessee, in the heat of the summer of 1925 for what some still consider the trial of the 20th century.

Fundamentalists had persuaded the Tennessee legislature to enact a law making the teaching of evolution a crime. A young and attractive teacher, John Scopes, was persuaded to make a test case out of it. He was a popular figure with his high school students and probably didn't realize his name would live in history as a man who was prosecuted by William Jennings Bryan, sometimes known as the Great Commoner, and defended by no less than Clarence Darrow, sometimes called the Attorney for the Damned.

A carnival atmosphere erupted in the little town of Dayton with a population of 3,000. Lemonade and hot dog stands were everywhere. A storekeeper whose last name was Darwin hung up a sign, "Darwin is Right—Here." Bryan offered a reward of $100 to any scientist who would admit he was descended from an ape. Reporters came from all over the country, including H. L. Mencken.

The courtroom was the theater of the day. One thousand people could be accommodated inside the courtroom, seven hundred sitting and three hundred standing. But in the unbearable heat with fans in hand and jackets off, the judge adjourned to the courthouse lawn. Darrow insisted a sign be taken down which read, "Read your Bible," as being prejudicial.

The great crisis of the trial came when the judge, a courteous, Bible-reading man, ruled that all the biologists, geologists, and other experts for the defense would not be allowed to testify. Darrow protested bitterly. The judge said he hoped Mr. Darrow did not mean to reflect on the court. Darrow retorted, "Your Honor can hope." The judge retaliated, "I can do more than that." There was an order for Darrow to show why he shouldn't be held in contempt. Darrow eventually apologized. And the judge replied that the Man whom he believed came to save humankind had taught forgiveness. Therefore, "Colonel" Darrow should also be forgiven.

A compromise on experts was reached. Bryan was to take the stand as an expert on religion. Darrow was to cross-examine him. Bryan (a famed orator who had run unsuccessfully three times for the U.S. presidency) was the leader of a campaign to impose anti-evolutionary laws throughout the United States. He was also a strong supporter of temperance, that is, in all things but food. He could down a breakfast of a cantaloupe, two quails, and battercakes swimming in butter—and still want more.

Darrow was famous as organized labor's chief lawyer until 1912 when he stood trial himself in Los Angeles for bribing jurors in his defense of the McNamara brothers, union leaders. The first jury acquitted on one charge. The second jury couldn't agree on the next charge. Nevertheless, Darrow's reputation continued to grow. Motivated by a disdain for those who would hold back knowledge, he volunteered to represent John Scopes without charge.

Darrow's cross examination challenged Bryan's literal interpretation of the Bible: "You say Jonah was swallowed by a whale? You say Joshua made the earth stand still? You say Eve was made from a rib of Adam? Ever figure out where Cain got his wife?" Bryan replied, "No. I leave that to the agnostics." Quite a show. Bryan made a fatal admission, shocking to the faithful, that the creation might have taken a million years. This was a little longer than the Biblical seven days. Some felt Bryan left the stand a broken man.

The next morning, the judge stopped the cross-examination. Darrow told the jury to find Scopes guilty so he could get on with the appeal. The judge found Mr. Scopes guilty, fining him $100. The Tennessee Supreme Court reversed the conviction on the grounds that in Tennessee only a jury could impose a fine more than $50.

After the trail, Bryan wanted to deliver the summation he never got to give. A few days later, during a hot midday of the Tennessee summer, Bryan ate one of his gargantuan meals and died shortly thereafter.

Although the people of Dayton, Tennessee profoundly disagreed with Darrow's ideas, Darrow always admitted he had been treated with rare and great courtesy by most of the town folks. And between them, there was much affection.

—by Henry G. Miller, a lawyer and writer
who has spoken extensively on Clarence Darrow

You can visit the courtroom where John Scopes was tried in the restored 1891 Rhea County Courthouse in Dayton (map page 70, lower left). It's outfitted with the same furnishings that were used then. A museum in the courtroom has exhibits on the "Monkey Trial."

John T. Scopes meets Clarence Darrow upon the lawyer's arrival in Dayton, July 1925. (Tennessee State Library and Archives)

N A S H V I L L E

Map page 159, page 183
●Nashville

◆ **AREA OVERVIEW**

Travel Basics: Nashville is a city people love to visit. They come for the music, mostly, but soon discover that there is much more to Nashville than country music. Tennessee's capital city is what it's always been, a city of contrasts. Contradictions, some would say. "Music City, U.S.A." and "The Athens of the South," headquarters of the country music industry and a higher education and publishing center. It's a city noted for classical architecture, imposing plantation mansions, and a pleasing natural setting. You can stroll through ancient forests, wander the grounds of Andrew Jackson's Hermitage, take in a performance of the Grand Ole Opry, or see a major league football or hockey game, all within a few miles of each other.

Getting Around: Most places visitors like to go are conveniently served by the faux trolleys. Downtown is pedestrian friendly, but much of the rest of town is downright hostile to people on foot. Nashville can be tricky to find your way around by car, as its main arteries follow the meanderings of ancient buffalo paths, streets change names, and there is a curious absence of directional signs. Nashville is a town that thrives on visitors, though, and its residents, many of whom came from someplace else, will most always help you when you ask, and often when you don't ask.

Climate: Spring is glorious, arriving as early as late February and lingering until mid-May. Fall is especially nice too, lasting from early October until Thanksgiving, sometimes Christmas. Temperatures in April and October average in the low 70s. Be prepared for cold weather between mid-October and mid-April. Winter temperatures stay mostly in the 30s to 50s, but there are periods of really cold weather and one or two good snowfalls each year. Summers are hot and humid, often in the 90s, but heat spells are always broken by cooler, drier periods.

Food & Lodging: Nashville has surprisingly few great restaurants for a city its size, but the ones it does have are outstanding. And don't overlook the indigenous Southern food or the host of welcoming ethnic restaurants reflecting the city's burgeoning immigrant population, everything from Ethiopian to Iranian to Vietnamese. The Hermitage and Union Station are grand downtown hotels. Staying at the suburban Opryland Hotel is a unique experience, but it's hard to get from it to the rest of town. Chain establishments cluster around interstate interchanges and the West End.

Nashville skyline.

NASHVILLE

■ MUSIC CITY AND MORE

"Welcome to Nashville." This recorded message by a star whose name you might recognize is the first thing you'll hear as you arrive at Nashville's airport, inviting you to enjoy the sights in "Music City, U.S.A." Chances are that someone on your flight is carrying a guitar case off the plane. As you move through the airport, you'll pass a stage that offers live music, then, at the bottom of the escalator, come face-to-face with a magnificent Gibson guitar in a display case. If you didn't know it before, you'll know by the time you claim your bags. Nashville is the headquarters of the country music business.

Yet mention country music to someone from Nashville, and you'll likely face a blank stare. Nashvillians are a bit uneasy with this one-dimensional image of their city. Not because they worry that the rest of the world regards them as a bunch of sequined hillbillies, though some proper Nashvillians and academic elites still do worry. The music business is as mainstream in Nashville now as the music is in America. If you lived in Nashville, your next door neighbor might be a musician, your kid's soccer coach might be a songwriter, or your Sunday school teacher a recording company executive. Their unease stems instead from the fact that there is so much more music than country, and there is so much more to Nashville than

music. Nashvillians are eager for you to know that, particularly if you're considering investing or visiting here.

Nashville is an old town, settled in 1780 by pioneers drawn to the Cumberland country's natural richness. Wealth drawn from the soil produced a resplendent collection of mansions during the eight decades before the Civil War. The Hermitage, President Andrew Jackson's home, is the best known, but it's only one of several open to the public; the balance, clarity, and harmony of its neoclassical architecture is repeated again and again throughout this city famous for classical buildings—most notably for the State Capitol (completed in 1859), and for the world's only full-size replica of the Parthenon (1897), standing in flower-filled Centennial Park.

The Parthenon reflects that, for a century before it became Music City, Nashville was known as the "Athens of the South" in recognition of its status as an academic center. Vanderbilt is the best known university, but it's only one of 15 or so colleges and universities including Meharry Medical College, which has educated more black doctors than any other school in the country.

An unknown artist painted this view of Nashville as it appeared from Lower City Island around 1860—between the completion of the capitol (at far right) in 1859 and the demolition of the suspension bridge in 1862. (Tennessee State Museum, Nashville)

GREAT LEAP WESTWARD: THE BEGINNING OF NASHVILLE

The settlement of Middle Tennessee was deliberate and premeditated, instigated by land speculators the colonial governor of North Carolina branded as "an infamous Company of land Pirates." Richard Henderson was their leader. Through his Transylvania Company, Henderson in 1775 negotiated with Cherokee leaders the purchase of much of present-day Tennessee and Kentucky. The fact that it was not Cherokee land didn't deter Henderson, nor did the fact that the colonial governments didn't approve of the purchase. In those days, Kentucky was part of Virginia and Tennessee was part of North Carolina. Neither colonial government wanted someone stirring things up beyond the Appalachians. More than a thousand Cherokees gathered at Sycamore Shoals on the Watauga River in present-day Upper East Tennessee where Henderson persuaded leaders Attakullakulla, Oconostota, and Savanucah to swap twenty million acres for several wagon loads of goods. Dragging Canoe, Attakullakulla's son, protested the deal, foreseeing only trouble for his people. He proclaimed: "I will not lose these lands without a fight." He didn't.

In 1778 Virginia voided Henderson's purchase. Realizing that North Carolina would follow, he concluded that he needed to get some settlers to the North Carolina portion of his purchase. Henderson figured that it would be difficult to get them off the land once they were there. He recruited two strong but very different men to lead the settlement, James Robertson, a leader in the Watauga settlements, and John Donelson, an older, better educated Virginian who had served in that colony's legislature.

The settlers were headed for a place on the Cumberland River called the French Lick—lick for the salt lick at the foot of a bluff and French for the traders who had set up shop there off and on since the late 1600s. It was surrounded by thick grasses, canebrakes, and giant trees, a true Eden with deep, rich soil, plentiful water, and abundant game.

Robertson early in 1779 led an exploratory party of eight men—seven white and one black—to the French Lick. Their destination was about 250 miles as the crow flies from their mountain valley home. The impenetrable Cumberland Plateau blocked the way, so they took a long route through the Cumberland Gap and what is now Central Kentucky. Once at the lick on the Cumberland, they cleared land and planted corn. This would tell the world they intended to stay. And it would provide food for the settlers when they arrived.

Robertson returned to the Watauga and with Donelson, recruited families to make "the great leap westward" as historian Walter Durham calls it. Robertson took most of the men and the stock overland. Donelson brought the women and children by water, floating down the Holston and Tennessee Rivers, then poling up the Ohio and Cumberland. (For routes, see History map on pages 16-17.)

It took Robertson's group two months. Some families joined them along the way, so that by the time they reached the site of today's Nashville, their party numbered nearly 400 men, women, and children. On Christmas Day, 1779, Robertson's weary but excited party trudged across the frozen Cumberland River and up to the bluff above the lick. Everyone who had started the trip made it.

The Donelson party was not so fortunate. Delayed by horribly cold weather and low water, the 30-boat flotilla didn't get underway until February 1780. Dragging Canoe had in the meantime parted company with the rest of the Cherokees and led his followers to new homes along the Tennessee River near today's Chattanooga. He intended to make good on his promise not to give up land without a fight. When the Donelson boats passed these lower Cherokee towns, they were met with a vicious attack that claimed several lives, including a newborn infant lost overboard. Navigating the tortuous, rocky Muscle Shoals wasn't easy either, but by March 20, 1780, the boats had reached the mouth of the Tennessee River. The settlers then faced the seemingly impossible task of pushing their boats upstream on the high waters of the Ohio and the Cumberland Rivers.

John Donelson wrote in his journal:

> Our situation here is truly disagreeable. The river is very high and the current rapid, our boats not constructed for the purpose of stemming a rapid stream, our provisions exhausted, the crews almost worn down with hunger and fatigue, and know not what distance we have to go, or what time it will take us to our place of destination.

Tears of joy and of grief were shed on April 24, 1780, as the half-starved Donelson party rounded the bend and labored the final mile to the bluff where Robertson's group had built a stockaded fort. The joy was for the reunited families, including Robertson's. The grief was for the 30–40 friends and loved ones who had perished on the thousand-mile voyage. The settlers named their fledgling community in honor of Francis Nash, a North Carolinian killed in the war for independence being fought back over the mountains.

Nashville spreads out over the meeting of two landforms, the Central Basin and the Highland Rim, blessing it with a richly varied natural environment that the town has had the good sense to save in an award-winning park system. Nestled in the mountain-like Harpeth Hills are two places that evoke more pride and produce more pleasure for Nashvillians than all the country music sites combined, the Warner Parks and the Radnor Lake State Natural Area. Together they protect nearly 4,000 acres of rugged forests and gentle meadows, rushing streams and placid lakes, an abundance of wildlife, and more than 300 species of wildflowers.

Nashvillians are eager to be perceived as big league for something besides country music. To prove it, in the late 1990s they lured a National Football League team from Houston and built the comfortable stadium that dominates Cumberland River's east bank. The Titans won the AFC championship their first year, earning a trip to the Super Bowl. The city landed a National Hockey League expansion franchise and built the stunning arena on Broadway for the Predators. The annual Iroquois Steeplechase is the oldest continuing run in the nation. It's always been a big league event.

A spectator at the Iroquois Steeplechase uses a pink parasol for sunscreen—and style.

Kathleen LaGue performs at Fan Fair.

In truth, though, it's country music that draws most of the ten million visitors a year to Nashville. Music City for them usually means two places, the part of downtown called "The District" and the Opryland area. The District is a five-block collection of restored buildings packed with galleries, shops, restaurants, pubs, and music venues. It's home to the Ryman Auditorium, the Wildhorse Saloon, and some genuine honky-tonks left over from the old days, such as the legendary Tootsie's Orchid Lounge. The Country Music Museum and Hall of Fame is nearby. Opryland is the mammoth suburban complex that includes the Opryland Hotel, the Grand Ole Opry House, the General Jackson showboat, the Opry Mills mall, and a nearby collection of lowbrow tourist attractions that market themselves as "Music Valley."

Nashville's big event for country music lovers is the CMA Music Festival known locally as **Fan Fair,** the one-of-a-kind party the industry throws for four days each June for more than 25,000 fans who pack a steady line-up of concerts and mingle with the stars. For details, call the Country Music Association at 615-244-2840.

More resourceful visitors will find the music off the beaten tourist path. With hundreds of recording studios and dozens of music publishing houses, Nashville produces more recorded music than any place in the United States other than Los Angeles. The thousands of singers, musicians, writers, and arrangers who make their living in Nashville are the best in the world at what they do. You can hear them perform someplace in town every day of the year, making all kinds of music in all kinds of settings, from bluegrass to blues to classical in big halls and intimate clubs, in coffee houses and in school auditoriums.

■ THE DISTRICT   *map page 159, C-2*

"The District" is the catchy handle for the downtown entertainment district between Fifth Avenue and the river that's popular with visitors and locals alike. Some purists lament the emergence here of "Nashvegas," but most people are pleased to see once derelict "Lower Broad" (Broadway below Fifth) put to productive use, even if there are a few excesses. The architecture alone makes it worth a visit, on Second Avenue in particular, to study the hooded windows, fancy cornice brackets,

One of Lower Broadway's best known institutions is Gruhn Guitars, arguably one of the finest guitar stores in the world.

(courtesy Hatch Show Prints)

and decorative pediments in one of the nation's largest collections of Victorian commercial buildings. Boisterous crowds fill Riverfront Park for summer's "Dancin' in the District," hockey and football fans pour out of the arena and stadium the rest of the year, and tourists wander The District's streets all day, every day.

Don't be put off by a few tacky souvenir shops on Lower Broad (map page 159, C-3), for there are some places you shouldn't miss. One is **Hatch Show Prints,** which still prints posters using carved, inked wood blocks, just like it did when the Hatch Brothers started it in 1879; 615-416-2001. Another is **Gruhn Guitars,** a dealer in fine and vintage instruments that are enticingly displayed in the show-room; 615-256-2033. And there is the refreshingly old-fashioned **Ernest Tubb Record Shop,** opened by the late Texas Troubadour in 1947; 615-255-7503.

◆ **RIVERFRONT PARK**   *map page 159, C-2/3*

Nashville started on the Cumberland River bank. That's a good place to start your visit. It's dressed up today by Riverfront Park, scene of Nashville River Stages, a three-day music festival held each May, and a music-oriented Independence Day celebration that draws more than 100,000 people. The park's grass terraces are quiet and peaceful most of the time, a perfect place to lay back and enjoy a sunny respite.

Riverfront Park is the start of **City Walk,** a 15-stop marked walking tour of downtown Nashville that begins at **Fort Nashborough,** the small reproduction of the fort the settlers built in 1780. Standing outside are oddly skinny likenesses of

Nashville riverfront, circa 1872. (Tennessee State Library and Archives)

Nashville's founders, James Robertson and John Donelson, shaking hands, a memorialization of their April 1780 reunion that gave birth to Nashville *(see page 154).*

If you'd like to travel to and from Opryland to the sound of honking great blue herons instead of cars, consider one of Nashville's true jewels, just a stone's throw from downtown. The east bank for most of the trip is in the **Shelby Bottoms Greenway**, an 810-acre preserve the herons share with another 180 bird species. There are nine miles of trails for hiking and biking. The greenway also includes an observation deck and a Cumberland River scenic overlook.

Shelby Bottoms Greenway

NASHVILLE

◆ **RYMAN AUDITORIUM**   *map page 159, B/C-2/3*

It's called "The Mother Church of Country Music." It was from 1943 until 1974 the home of the Grand Ole Opry, the one institution that more than any other popularized the music we now call "country." The red-brick, barn-like Gothic building didn't start as a music hall, though. It started as the Union Gospel Tabernacle, built in 1892 by a hard-driving steamboat magnate named Tom Ryman to honor his religious conversion. It soon became a major concert hall, hosting everything from opera to boxing matches to political conventions. Will Rogers, Katharine Hepburn, W. C. Fields, John Philip Sousa, Marian Anderson, Bob Hope, Arthur Rubinstein, Jascha Heifetz, Roy Rogers, Elvis Presley, Bruce Springsteen, and Enrico Caruso—they're just a few of the artists who've performed at the Ryman.

(above) Built as a tabernacle by steamboat magnate Tom Ryman and later home to the Grand Ole Opry, the restored Ryman Auditorium today frequently hosts music concerts.

(opposite) Nashville, the recent revitalization of downtown means that the very new—in this case the Bell South Building (the "Bat Building")—stands cheek-to-jowl with the old.

The owner toyed with demolishing it after the Opry left for Opryland, but instead poured $8.5 million into a restoration that includes a welcoming entrance watched over by a sculptured likeness of Captain Ryman at the wheel of a riverboat. The Ryman stands today as one of the nation's great performance venues, hosting concerts ranging from the Academy of Saint-Martin-in-the-Fields to Willie Nelson. Sprinkled throughout it are memorabilia, photographs, and displays about some of the Opry's all-time great performers, such as Hank Williams, Patsy Cline, and Loretta Lynn. It's open for self-guided tours, but the best way to experience the Ryman is sitting on its hard, curved oak pews enjoying a live performance. Between Fourth and Fifth Avenues, north of Broadway; 615-889-3060.

◆ UNION STATION   *map page 159, A/B–3/4*

Broadway changes at Fifth Avenue into what is has been called "Upper Broad," a half-mile of grand public buildings that climaxes at Union Station, the national historic landmark that's now a first-class hotel.

The Always Patsy Cline *revue is held at the Ryman Auditorium, which housed the Grand Ole Opry in its previous incarnation.*

The Louisville & Nashville Railroad flaunted its power and wealth when in 1900 it built the station in the Richardson Romanesque style popularized by Henry Hobson Richardson in the late 19th century. It must be a pretty good sample, for the National Trust for Historic Preservation's guide to American architecture cites Union Station as the example of the style. The station is fanciful and medieval looking, with a 239-foot clock tower topped by a statue of Mercury, the Roman god of commerce and travel. The interior rivals the exterior, with the cavernous barrel-vaulted ceiling of the waiting room—now the hotel lobby. The room is richly decorated with stained glass, wrought iron, and carvings that would be too costly to think of in public buildings erected today. 1001 Broadway; 800-996-3426 or 615-726-1001.

Architectural historians consider Union Station a classic example of Richardsonian Romanesque style.

■ CAPITOL HILL   *map page 159, B-2*

The hill that makes up most of downtown is kept alive during the day by workers in government, finance, insurance, and law, and during the night by patrons of TPAC, the **Tennessee Performing Arts Center.** TPAC's three theaters, Jackson, Polk, and Johnson, each named for a Tennessean American president, are home to regular performances by the Nashville Symphony, Nashville Ballet, Nashville Opera, Tennessee Repertory Theater, and Circle Players, and touring Broadway musicals. 505 Deaderick Street; 615-782- 4000.

The broad plaza spreading out from the Doric-columned 1925 War Memorial Building fills up in October with tents, giving the place the look of a medieval fair. It's actually the **Southern Festival of Books,** bringing together readers, writers, publishers, and booksellers for a long weekend packed with literary events.

◆ STATE CAPITOL   *map page 159, A-2*

Dignified, serious, and dominating all around it, the Tennessee State Capitol stands today as it did when it was completed in 1859, one of America's finest examples of Greek Revival architecture. "All the civilized world acknowledges the existence of permanent principles established by the wisdom, strength, and beauty of the proportions and symmetry of the Grecian Temples," wrote William Strickland. The Philadelphian was one of the most sought-after builders of his day, and when Tennesseans in the 1840s finally decided it was time for a permanent capitol, they lured Strickland to Nashville. He spent the rest of his life here, creating in addition to the Capitol, the unique Egyptian Revival church that still welcomes visitors at Fifth and Church. Strickland was obviously pleased with the Capitol. Following his wishes, he is interred in the building. Capitol: Charlotte Avenue between Sixth and Seventh.

In May of 1880, an equestrian statue of Andrew Jackson was unveiled in front of the Capitol Building as part of Nashville's centennial celebration. (Tennessee State Library and Archives)

NASHVILLE

The State Capitol as seen from the War Memorial Plaza.

East of the Capitol is a grassy ledge that hardly anyone visits. That's a pity, for it's a peaceful, interesting place with monuments to three Tennessee presidents. The remains of James and Sarah Polk lie in a Strickland-designed tomb. A bronze likeness of Andrew Johnson faces east, which makes sense. He was a staunch East Tennessee Unionist. Sculptor Clark Mill's dramatic creation of Andrew Jackson as a general on a rearing horse was the first equestrian statue in America. If it looks familiar, maybe you've seen the exact copy across from the White House. Or the third copy in front of St. Louis Cathedral in New Orleans, site of the 1815 victory over the British that propelled Jackson to national fame and to the presidency.

Anyone interested in women's rights should put the Tennessee Capitol on their list of pilgrimage sites, for it was here that women in the United States won the right to vote. Pro- and anti-suffrage forces converged on Nashville in August 1920 as the General Assembly meeting in special session was considering whether to join the 35 states that had ratified the 19th Amendment. It needed 36 states for passage.

The State Senate approved the amendment 25-4, and a house vote was scheduled for August 18. The crucial vote came on a motion to table the amendment. It was a tie, 48-48. Just one more vote to table would have defeated the amendment. The amendment passed, 49-46. The antis were shocked. They thought they had the votes to defeat it. But Harry Burn, a 24-year-old East Tennessean, changed his vote. He explained his reasons:

> *I* believe in full suffrage as a right; second, I believe we had a moral and legal right to ratify; third… my mother wanted me to vote for ratification.

◆ **BICENTENNIAL CAPITOL MALL**   *map page 159, A-1*

Tennessee celebrated its 200th birthday in 1996 by fashioning a welcoming, 19-acre urban park that combines lessons in Tennessee geography and history with a great place for downtown workers to take their lunchtime walks. "Stay out of that water!" You'll hear this admonition as children break for the 31 ground-level fountains representing Tennessee's major river systems. The fountains are designed for play, however, and not a dry child leaves the place in warm weather.

The symmetrical mall repeats the classical theme so prevalent throughout Nashville and even has a 2,000-seat Greek theater. The mall's west margin is the Wall of History that chronicles the state's story, and its east margin is the Wall of Counties, divided, as always, by the three Grand Divisions. Adjacent to it are plots planted in vegetation native to East, Middle, and West Tennessee. The rear of the mall contains the moving **World War II Memorial** with its eight-ton solid granite globe, the largest of its type ever made, rotating on a thin cushion of water.

Running along the west side of the mall is the Nashville Farmers' Market.

James Robertson Parkway; 615-741-5280.

Thomas Hart Benton's mural The Sources of Country Music *can be seen at the Country Music Hall of Fame and Museum. (Country Music Hall of Fame® and Museum)*

■ NASHVILLE MUSEUMS

Tennessee State Museum
map page 159, B-2

It's hard to find beneath the hanging James K. Polk Building—yes, it actually hangs from the steel superstructure—but when you get there you'll see Daniel Boone's rifle, Davy Crockett's powder horn, Sgt. York's Medal of Honor, and one of the nation's best Civil War collections. The Military Museum, across the street in the War Memorial Building, houses exhibits on America's foreign wars and includes a radio broadcasting FDR's Day of Infamy speech and an Eisenhower-style jacket worn by Ike himself. 505 Deaderick Street; 615-741-2692.

Country Music Hall of Fame and Museum *map page 159, C-3*

Don't care for country music? Go anyway. You'll be dazzled by more than 3,000 stage costumes, original song manuscripts, antique instruments, Elvis's 1960 gold Cadillac, and Thomas Hart Benton's last mural, *The Sources of Country Music*. You'll recognize the legends in the Country Music Foundation's Hall of Fame, and you'll find others influential in the business that you've probably never heard of. Demonbreun Street between Fourth and Fifth Avenues; 800-852-6437 or 615-416-2001.

Cheekwood
map page 183, A-5

Sitting atop a hill adjacent to the Warner Parks is the 1920s Georgian Revival mansion Leslie Cheeks built with the Maxwell House Coffee fortune. You can easily spend a full day here, starting with the museum that features 19th- and 20th-century American paintings, porcelains, and period furniture, and ending on the 55-acre grounds that offer gardens and a mile-long sculpture trail. Annual events are the Wildflower Fair in April and the Trees of Christmas. 1200 Forrest Park Drive; 615-356-8000.

Adventure Science Center
map page 159, C-6

Even adults can't keep their hands off the exhibits covering health and natural and physical science. The Sudekum Planetarium hosts regular shows. 800 Fort Negley Boulevard; 615-862-5160.

Frist Center for the Visual Arts
map page 159, B-3

The Frist family has transformed the 1934 classically inspired art deco post office next to Union Station into the region's premier visual arts center. 919 Broadway; 615-244-3340.

Tennessee Agricultural Museum
map page 183, B/C-6

The state's rich agricultural tradition is shown off in the horse barns built by flamboyant Roaring Twenties financier Rogers Caldwell at his Hermitage-inspired estate. You can see more than 2,600 farm implements and rural household items from pioneer times to the arrival of electricity in rural America. Ellington Agricultural Center off Edmondson Pike or Trousdale Drive; 615-837-5197.

Tennessee Central Railway Museum
map page 183, B/C-4

Rolling stock and memorabilia highlight this volunteer-run museum named for the line that once connected Middle and East Tennessee. The museum sponsors year-round rail excursions on the old TC to Watertown, a quiet, Victorian-era village that hosts events such as the Mile-Long Yard Sale in April, the Jazz Festival in July, and Christmas in the Country in December. 220 Willow Street; 615-244-9001.

Nashville Public Library
map page 159, B-2/3

Nashville's longstanding tradition of classicism is celebrated in the architecture of the new main public library, designed by architect Robert A. M. Stern. Its state-of-the-art Civil Rights Room, completed in December 2003, captures the drama and history of the 1960s. 615 Church Street between 6th and 7th avenues; 615-862-5800.

■ A NASHVILLE MUSIC SAMPLER

Live music in Nashville is, some would say, a good news/bad news story, good for audiences because the town is bursting at the seams with talent looking for an outlet, bad for artists because the glut of talent makes it difficult to earn a living.

Whether you enjoy the music at the major venues or the small clubs will depend on your taste, but you can count on top quality at both. Nashville's long list of clubs offers superb live music of all kinds. Check Nashville's daily paper, *The Tennessean,* or the weekly *Nashville Scene* for listings.

Benefit concerts offer some of Nashville's best live music. A while back, for example, five Grammy winners, Vince Gill, Nanci Griffith, Emmylou Harris, Rodney Crowell, and Guy Clark, were corralled by their dentists into performing to a packed Ryman benefitting a charity dental clinic. It was a relaxed affair, without all the special effects that often accompany concerts these days, a chance for them to show off their raw talent. Events like this are repeated over and over around

town. It's one of the joys of living in Nashville, but there is no reason for alert visitors to miss out. Just check the listings in the papers.

Recent performers have included John Hiatt (top) and Chris Whitley (left).

Larger Music Venues

Ryman Auditorium *map page 159, B-2*
116 Fifth Avenue, N.; 615-254-1445.

Wildhorse Saloon *map page 159, C-2*
120 Second Avenue, N.; 615-251-1000.

Grand Ole Opry House *map page 183, D-3*
2800 Opryland Drive off Briley Parkway,
TN-155 615-883-2211.

Gaylord Entertainment Center
map page 159, C-3
501 Broadway; 615-770-2000.

Starwood Amphitheater
3839 Murfreesboro Road; 615-641-5800.

Smaller Music Clubs

Bluebird Café *map page 183, A-6*
Leans to the acoustic side and features
top songwriters. 4104 Hillsboro Road in
Green Hills; 615-383-1461.

Bourbon Street Blues & Boogie Bar
map page 159, B/C-2
A big time New Orleans–style blues
joint. 220 Printers Alley; 615-242-5837.

Radio Café *map page 183, C-3*
An East Nashville acoustic haunt. 1313
Woodland Street; 615-262-1766.

Station Inn *map page 159, A-4*
One of the world's best-known bluegrass
spots. 402 12th Avenue, S.; 615-255-
3307.

The Sutler *map page 183, B-5*
Intimate Melrose neighborhood club
with great alt-country and neo-folkies.
2608 Franklin Pike; 615-292-5254.

BB King's Blues Club
A gritty, soulful blues club with a menu of
simple but flavorful regional classics.
152 2nd Ave. N; 615-256-2727.

Exit/In *map page 183, B-4*
Been around for years; famous for future
stars who perform before anyone's ever
heard of them. 2208 Elliston Place; 615-
321-4400.

3rd & Lindsley *map page 159, D-5*
Blues, rock just south of "The District."
818 Third Avenue, S.; 615-259- 9891.

■ WEST END *map page 183, A-4/5*

"Music City" and the "Athens of the South" live together in the leafy crescent west
of downtown. You might think that town and gown keep to their own sides of the
street, but they don't. Belmont University and the music industry cooperate to
offer a much-in-demand music business major. Vanderbilt University Press and
the Country Music Foundation collaborate to produce music-related books, shar-
ing production and distribution costs and, hopefully, profits. And, too, some of
Nashville's great musicians are affiliated with university music schools.

BLUEBIRD CAFÉ

*T*he Bluebird Café is located in a strip mall, hidden in among retail stores, past a nursery, down the road from the mall at Green Hills. It looked ordinary from the front, like maybe a small diner. Inside though, it was—as we say down south—ate completely up with atmosphere. Dark, smoky, with framed eight-by-ten glossies of all the famous people who'd played there tacked up all over the place, the Bluebird was a small room with a bar on one side and tables everywhere else. Somewhere back in the corner, a kitchen sat hidden and out of the way. Pipes in the ceiling had been painted and left exposed.

Truth is, the Bluebird Café isn't a hell of a lot to look at. But it is one of the most sought-after venues in the city. If you were an insider in the music business, showcasing at the Bluebird meant you'd arrived.

—Steven Womack, *Way Past Dead*, 1995

Singer-songwriters line up for a chance to play at the Bluebird Café.

◆ **MUSIC ROW** *map page 159, A-5*

It's not really a row. It's the several square blocks around 16th and 17th Avenues South where most of the world's $2 billion-a-year country music business is transacted, where record labels, song publishers, booking agencies, artist managers, and performing rights organizations have their offices. Fans seem to enjoy strolling past the mixture of converted houses, post-modern buildings, and, in one case, an artfully restored convent, bearing familiar names like Warner Brothers, RCA, Columbia, Sony, Capitol, and MCA, aware that inside, make-or-break decisions are being made that will forever alter the life of some aspiring singer or songwriter.

The Row's studios produce music other than country. Paul McCartney has recorded here, and so have Neil Diamond and Bob Dylan, some of the many non-country artists who have slipped into town to take advantage of some of the world's best facilities. The gateway to Music Row is the little park where 16th and 17th meet Demonbreun Street. It's named for Owen Bradley, who—along with

Chet Atkins—gets the credit for making Nashville the recording center

(top) A corporate music studio on Music Row. (left) RCA's Studio B is the oldest remaining country music studio on Music Row. Here, Chet Atkins and George Barnes record guitar tracks at RCA. (Country Music Hall of Fame® and Museum)

WHOSE COUNTRY IS THIS, ANYWAY?

A cold war is raging in Nashville. It's the never-ending struggle for the soul of country music, the battle over how far the music should stray from its traditional rural Southern and Western roots. One camp wants to make it sound, well, less "country." They want "crossover" hits that appeal to the broader pop market. This is essential, they say, for otherwise, the market share of Nashville-produced music will remain forever small.

The other side wants "traditional" hits that retain the rural flavor. Otherwise, the core fans will be alienated and will look elsewhere to satisfy their musical tastes. Whenever country goes pop, they point out, as it did in the 1970s and again in the late 1990s, the market share declines. A respected music critic put it this way in 1999: "As the crossover trend dominates, country is once again in danger of losing identity." Keep the fiddle and the steel guitar, plead the traditionalists.

This cold war between the crossover advocates and the traditionalists doesn't promise to end anytime soon. In fact, with fewer conglomerates owning all the major record labels and radio stations, and with more creative decisions being made by business people rather than music people, the cold war is intensifying. Occasionally it breaks out into a hot war. On stage at the 1974 Country Music Association awards, singer Charlie Rich took his cigarette lighter to the envelope that named pop-folkie John Denver CMA Entertainer of the Year. At the 1999 CMA awards, in front of a national network TV audience, traditionalist superstar Alan Jackson stopped mid-song and walked off the stage to protest the latest drift toward pop.

Songwriters Larry Cordle and Larry Shell put their pens to work in protest. Their song, "Murder on Music Row," borrows from the traditional Appalachian murder ballad to lament the killing of traditional country music by "the almighty dollar." Cordle, a bluegrass artist, recorded the song, then Jackson recorded a country version with fellow traditionalist George Strait. It was a big hit in 2000. Perhaps the song's success should send a message to the industry decision-makers.

it is today. Bradley was an orchestra leader who, in 1954, purchased a house on 16th Avenue with his brother, Harold, and opened a recording studio in an attached army-surplus Quonset hut. Owen became head of Decca Records' Nashville division in 1958. Atkins, already a noted guitarist, had become RCA's Nashville head the year before, the same year RCA opened its now-legendary Studio B on 17th Avenue.

◆ **BELMONT MANSION** *map page 183, B-4*

On the hill above where 16th and 17th converge into Magnolia Boulevard, a portico of massive Ionic columns looks down as if it were the big house and Music Row the plantation. The portico fronts Belmont University, the Baptist-affiliated school.

The real treasure is behind the columned building, Belmont Mansion, or "Belle Monte" as Adelicia and Joseph Acklen called it. They built the lavish Italian country house in the decade before the Civil War. Enter the quad, and you'll see right away that this is no ordinary college building. Climb the steps, ring the doorbell, and you'll be ushered in for a tour of the extravagant mansion's 11,000 square feet of living space in 36 rooms. They're filled with a fabulously rich collection of Victorian furnishings that includes marble statuary Adelicia brought back from her 1865–67 European trip when she was presented to the court of Emperor Napoleon III of France.

An anonymous artist painted this landscape of the Belmont estate, circa 1860.
(Fine Arts Center at Cheekwood, Nashville)

NASHVILLE

Belmont today.

"A real-life Scarlett O'Hara" is how Adelicia Acklen is often portrayed. The wealth she inherited from her husband, Isaac Franklin, a slave trader and planter 28 years her senior, reportedly made her the nation's wealthiest woman. You'll learn on the tour that her inheritance, increased by the skill of her second husband, Joseph, included thousands of acres of the richest cotton land in Louisiana. Joseph died there during the Civil War, and fearing that her cotton would be lost, Adelicia made her way to the Lower Mississippi. Manipulating both Confederate and Union officers, she managed to ship the crop to England where she sold it for nearly a million dollars. Adelicia was married a third time, at age 50, to Dr. W. A. Cheatham, an early advocate for the mentally ill, from whom she eventually separated for reasons she kept to herself. She was building a house in Washington, where her daughter Pauline lived, when she died—at age 70 on a shopping trip to New York.

Chamber music concerts are now played in the mansion's salon. 1900 Belmont Boulevard; 615-460-5459.

◆ **VANDERBILT UNIVERSITY**
map page 183, B-4

As you wander onto the original
Vanderbilt campus from either
West End or 21st Avenues, it's
the flower-filled grounds that
first grab your attention. Trees
planted when the university was
founded in the 1870s are now
giants—seven are state champi-
ons for their species—leading to
Vanderbilt's designation as an official arboretum. The nationally
ranked research university was

founded after the Civil War as a Methodist school, promoted by Bishop Holland
N. McTyeire. His wife was a cousin to the second wife of Cornelius Vanderbilt,
the ruthless New York shipping and railroad magnate. McTyeire persuaded the

Commodore to make dona-
tions that eventually totaled $1
million for the new school.
Opened in 1875, the university
cut its ties with the Methodists
in 1914.

Vanderbilt was enhanced as
a place to visit in the 1970s
when it absorbed its neighbor
across 21st Avenue, **George**

*(top) Kirkland Hall, Vanderbilt
University's first building, was done
in Empire Revival Victorian style,
as shown in this 1875 photograph.
The hall was changed to its current
Italianate Edwardian style (left)
in 1905. (top photo, Vanderbilt
University Photo Archives)*

NASHVILLE

Peabody College, a nationally recognized teachers college whose lineage reaches back to a school started in 1785 by pioneer Presbyterian minister Thomas B. Craighead. Stroll up the maple- and oak-fringed-lawn on the 1911–1915 campus modeled after Thomas Jefferson's University of Virginia, and you'll pass through what one architectural historian called "a veritable encyclopedia of classical architecture." Over on the main campus, don't miss the **Fine Arts Gallery** in the Old Gym on West End. It features the Samuel H. Kress collection of Renaissance paintings. West End Avenue and 21st Avenue, S.; 615-343-1704.

◆ CENTENNIAL PARK   *map page 183, B-4*

February's first hint of spring fills this spacious urban park with joggers, duck feeders, and Frisbee-throwing college students. May brings crowds to see the glorious tulip garden and to drop a few bucks at the annual Tennessee Crafts Fair. June brings them back for the more selective American Artisan Festival.

The park's centerpiece is the **Parthenon,** the world's only full-scale, exact replica of the original in Athens. It's worth a visit just to study the painstakingly accurate sculpture in the pediments and the plaster casts made from the originals at the British Museum. It's worth a visit, too, to see the art gallery's permanent exhibition of 63 American paintings donated by James M. Cowan.

The Parthenon, built for the 1897 Tennessee Centennial Exposition, exemplified the period's interest in classic architecture. Over-the-top exotic architecture was also in vogue, such as the Giza-style pyramid and Greek Revival halls—complete with exaggerated capitals and massive Ionic columns. (Tennessee State Library and Archives)

NASHVILLE

Civil engineer Eugene C. Lewis accepted responsibility for constructing the Tennessee Centennial Exposition held here a year late in 1897. Mindful of Nashville as the "Athens of the South," Lewis conceived the idea to reproduce the Parthenon for the exposition art center. He received from King George I of Greece architectural and archaeological studies, drawings, and photographs. Jacques Carrey, a French diplomat, had made extensive drawings of the Parthenon in Athens in 1674, before it was accidentally blown up. Lewis managed to get them.

Other exposition buildings were temporary, but Lewis's Parthenon was to be permanent. The plaster exterior didn't last, though, and in 1920, the city commissioned architect Russell Hart to rebuild it. It took a year longer to complete than it did to build the original, circa 500 BCE. One important element was missing from Hart's interior. The original Parthenon housed Phidias's statue of the goddess Athena Parthenos. That shortcoming was remedied in the 1980s when Nashville sculptor Alan LeQuire created his magnificent replica of the original. The sculpture, which took seven years to complete, stands today as the world's largest piece of indoor sculpture; West End Avenue at 25th Avenue; 615-862-8431.

The Parthenon got its finishing touch in the 1980s when Nashville sculptor Alan LeQuire completed a replica of the Athena Parthenos.

The Jubilee Singers of Fisk University took a European tour in 1871, during which Queen Victoria's court painter Edmond Havell completed this portrait. (Fisk University Galleries)

◆ FISK UNIVERSITY   *map page 183, B-3*

It feels like a long way from Music Row to Fisk, but it's not, just a few blocks north up 17th Avenue. And music was important at Fisk long before anyone dreamed of country music. Working through Union General Clinton B. Fisk, the American Missionary Association after the Civil War started the school for newly emancipated slaves. The old army barracks at the foot of Capitol Hill that housed the school were in bad shape by 1871, and to raise money for improvements, a student singing ensemble went on tour. They came to be called the Jubilee Singers, after Leviticus 25:10: ". . . you shall proclaim liberty throughout the land to all its inhabitants. It shall be a jubilee to you." The popularity of their Negro spirituals allowed them to raise money for a new campus. Their 1871 European tour culminated in a performance before Queen Victoria and brought back enough money for a new building. To this day, it's a great honor for a Fisk student to be a Jubilee Singer.

Glorious Victorian Gothic **Jubilee Hall** is the oldest building in the nation dedicated to educating African Americans. It's a national historic landmark. Visitors can arrange a tour through its tall, original wooden doors to see the floor-to-ceiling group portrait of the Jubilee Singers. Queen Victoria was so moved by them that she commissioned the portrait by her court painter, Edward Havell. You'll be moved, too, reading brief autobiographies of the original 11 singers who had just a few years earlier been singing around slave cabins.

The fact that it's off the beaten tourist path enhances the charm of Fisk's little **Carl Van Vechten Gallery of Art,** which, like nearby Vanderbilt's, is in an old gym. Van Vechten was a photographer with close ties to the writers and artists of the Harlem Renaissance. After the death of pioneer photographer Alfred Stieglitz, Van Vechten facilitated donation of the photographer's collection to Fisk by Stieglitz's widow, artist Georgia O'Keeffe. The collection includes Stieglitz photographs as well as paintings by O'Keeffe, Picasso, Cezanne, Renoir, and Toulouse-Lautrec. The museum also has an outstanding collection of African-American art. Corner of Jackson Street and 18th Avenue N.; 615-329-8720.

■ OPRYLAND   *map page 183, D-3*

Opryland is the empire that country music built. It started small in 1925, in a cramped studio where a part-time string band played over the radio for the first time. It is today a 480-acre complex featuring a non-stop extravaganza of world-class entertainment, accommodations, and activities, some related to country music, some not. The name "Opryland" derives from a place that is no more, the music-based theme park that operated from 1972 until 1998.

◆ OPRYLAND HOTEL   *map page 183, D-3*

It's not uncommon for traveling Nashvillians to hear, "Nashville. I've been there. To a convention at the Opryland Hotel." It is, after all, one of the world's largest, with 2,884 guest rooms and 600,000 feet of exhibit and meeting space. Nashvillians, though, bristle at such comments. They don't see the Opryland Hotel as the "real Nashville." It's a completely contrived environment, cleverly designed to keep guests on the property. Yet when Nashvillians entertain out-of-town guests, odds are they'll take them to the hotel. Not to patronize the 30 shops and 15 restaurants, or even to see the giant murals depicting Tennessee history. They go, instead, to experience the three massive indoor gardens. Unbelievable is about the only word that does them justice. You'll not find anything like them, anywhere.

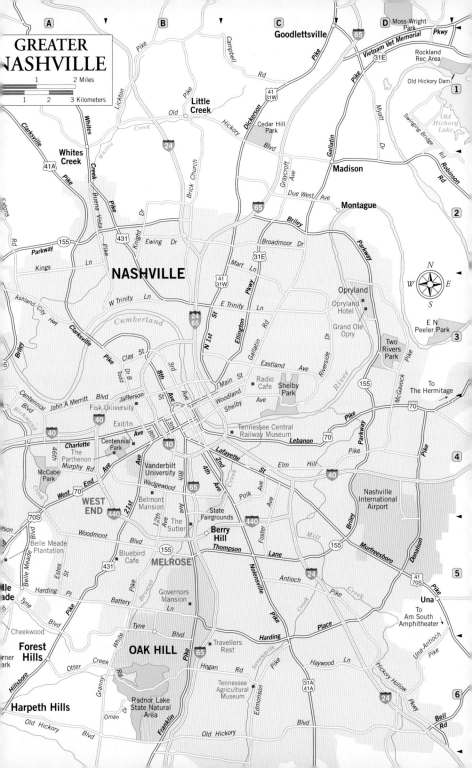

The Conservatory is a tropical paradise featuring more than 10,000 plants representing 215 species under a seven-story, one-acre glass roof. It's adjacent to the Cascades, of equal size, featuring three plunging waterfalls ranging in height from 23 to 35 feet; the Dancing Waters Fountain, which hosts a nightly laser show to live music; and an elevated walkway though the whole thing. The Delta is larger than the other two combined, and features an indoor river complete with boat rides, and plants that include palms, magnolias, mahoganies, and camellias. Linger a while in these magnificent indoor gardens, and you'll see why so many guests never see the "real Nashville."

The month before Christmas is a good time to see the Opryland Hotel. As part of the Country Christmas celebration that features a host of activities, the hotel is decked out in more than two million lights. 2800 Opryland Drive off Briley Parkway (TN-155); 615-889-1000.

The atrium of the Opryland Hotel.

◆ **GRAND OLE OPRY**   *map page 183, D-3*

It's the world's longest-running live radio show, and it's responsible for Nashville's being the music center it is today. You can hear it every Friday and Saturday night on clear-channel 650 AM, WSM. Don't expect, though, to hear many of today's top stars, for the Opry regulars are for the most part entertainers past their prime. But if you like traditional or *real* country music, as opposed to the homogenized version played on commercial radio, you'll like the Opry. Even if you don't, you'll enjoy the performance in the state-of-the-art 4,400-seat Opry House that's noted for its excellent acoustics. The Opry is produced in 15-minute segments that each feature five or six acts. All this coming and going on stage seems a bit chaotic. But that's part of the Opry's charm.

The advent of radio gave National Life and Accident Insurance—"**W**e **S**hield **M**illions" was its slogan—an opportunity to market insurance through the new medium. In 1925 WSM hired George D. Hay from Chicago's station WLS and started a "barn dance" like the one Hay ran in Chicago. Hay used the term "opry" in contrast to the grand opera the station broadcast, and the name stuck. The show became an instant hit, and grew and grew.

The Opry in the 1930s evolved into its current form and took country music to a new, national level. Roy Acuff's arrival from Knoxville signaled a change from a local show featuring part-time "hillbilly" string bands to a national program featuring professional soloists. Pee Wee King, born Julius Frank Anthony Kuczynski, joined the Opry in 1937 and introduced western music, moving the Opry and country music still further from the hillbilly image. The same year WSM increased to 50,000 watts covering most of eastern North America, and in 1939 NBC started broadcasting Opry segments. The Opry began selling advertising. It was no longer just an insurance marketing tool but was itself something to sell. WSM in 1934 started the Artists' Service Bureau to promote and book tours by Opry members. That, together with the strict requirement that members appear on the Opry a certain number of dates each year, caused country musicians to headquarter in Nashville. Before long businesses opened serving Opry members, including in 1942, Acuff-Rose, the song publisher started by Acuff and pop songwriter Fred Rose. 2802 Opryland Drive off Briley Parkway (TN-155); 615-871-6779.

NASHVILLE

NASHVILLE

STARS OF THE COUNTRY MUSIC HALL OF FAME

ROY ACUFF
1903–1992, Maynardville, TN
Acuff joined the Grand Ole Opry in 1938, became its host in 1939 and remained there for 50 years. The undisputed "King of Country Music," he was its greatest champion, shepherding country's evolution from home-folk hillbilly to a worldwide phenomenon. In 1974, when the Opry moved from the Ryman Auditorium to Opryland on the outskirts of town, President Richard Nixon came to honor the event and was given the famous on-stage lesson on how to operate a yo-yo, another Acuff specialty.

Songs: *Wabash Cannonball, Great Speckled Bird, Steel Guitar Blues, Freight Train Blues, Wreck on the Highway, Precious Jewel, Night Train to Memphis, Tennessee Waltz.*

JOHNNY CASH
1932–2003, Kingsland, AR

A country music icon and international celebrity, the influence of the "Man in Black" cannot be overrated. Only John R. Cash and Elvis Presley are members of both the Country Music and the Rock and Roll Halls of Fame. His career skyrocketed after his live concert at Folsom Prison in 1968. Then came his TV show. Bob Dylan, Mahalia Jackson, Gordon Lightfoot, even The Who were featured, plus an unknown singer-songwriter he championed named Kris Kristofferson.

Songs: *Cry Cry Cry, The Ballad of Ira Hayes, Folsom Prison Blues, I Walk the Line, Big River, Ring of Fire, Rock Island Line, Guess Things Happen That Way, Drive On, A Boy Named Sue.*

PATSY CLINE
1932–1963, Gore, VA

Though her stardom lasted only three years before it was cut short by a plane crash in 1963, Patsy Cline left an indelible mark on country music and on the American psyche as well. Known for her exceptionally clear voice and haunting personal delivery, her popularity has, if anything, increased over the years. Interestingly, she initially didn't like two of her biggest hits, *I Fall To Pieces* and *Crazy* (written by Willie Nelson). Her singing style, and subsequent success, came neither easily nor quickly. Much credit needs to be given to the producer Owen Bradly who tempered her early honky-tonk leanings with the subdued, clean arrangements that allowed the pristine beauty of her voice to emerge.

Songs: *Walkin' After Midnight, I Fall To Pieces, Crazy, She's Got You, Leavin' on Your Mind, Imagine That, A Courtyard and Then Goodbye, Faded Love, Sweet Dreams.*

THE CARTER FAMILY: ALVIN PLEASANT, SARA, AND MAYBELLE
Alvin Pleasant 1891–1960, Maces Springs, VA; Sara 1898–1978, Wise County, VA; Maybelle 1909–1978, Nickelsville, Virginia

It's hard to imagine what country music would be like today without the Carter Family. They burst into American homes during the winter of 1938 via the super-powered Mexican radio station XERA, and their influence has never waned. In 1943, the Carter Family broke up, but Maybelle and her daughters continued as Mother Maybelle and The Carter Sisters. June Carter married Johnny Cash. Today, Carter and Cash daughters are extending the Carter Family legacy.

Songs: *Will the Circle Be Unbroken, Wabash Cannonball, Wildwood Flower, Keep On The Sunny Side, I'm Thinking Tonight of My Blue Eyes, Dixie Darling, You Are My Flower, Hello Stranger, Oh Take Me Back* and some 300 others.

LESTER FLATT AND EARL SCRUGGS
Lester 1914–1979, Overton County, TN;
Earl born 1924, Cleveland County, NC
Between Flatt's picking wizardry and Scruggs's overwhelming banjo, Flatt & Scruggs became the twin towers of bluegrass, outshining even their great mentor, Bill Monroe. Recognizing that their fortunes would be better served if they lit out on their own, they left Monroe and The Blue Grass Boys in 1948 to form their own group, Lester Flatt, Earl Scruggs and The Foggy Mountain Boys—for which Monroe refused to talk to them for 20 years. Still, it was Flatt & Scruggs who brought bluegrass into the American mainstream.

Songs: *Foggy Mountain Breakdown (Bonnie And Clyde), Rollin' In My Sweet Baby's Arms, 'Tis Sweet To Be Remembered, Earl's Breakdown, Cabin on the Hill, Petticoat Junction, The Ballad of Jed Clampett (The Beverly Hillbillies), You Are My Flower,* and so many, many more.

MERLE HAGGARD
born 1937, Oildale, CA
"Hag" actually did turn 21 in prison. When he was 17, he and a buddy, both drunk and thinking it was 3 a.m., attempted to crowbar their way into a restaurant—it was still open at the time. Although he turned his life around with music, he never turned his back on his roots. A talented songwriter *(Swinging Doors, The Bottle Let Me Down),* his embrace of his troubled past *(Branded Man, Mama Tried, Hungry Eyes* and the deeply humble *Footlights)* has endeared him to working men and women everywhere. With a buttery-rich voice second only to George Jones's, he is a country music icon who steadily tours small venues.

Songs: *Mama Tried, Sing a Sad Song, Two of Us, Okie from Muskogee, Irma Jackson, Movin' On, The Fightin' Side of Me, Big Time Annie's Square, Daddy Frank (Guitar Man), I Take Pride In Who I Am, Footlights.*

George Jones
born 1931, Saratoga, TX

Perhaps as famous for his tumultuous marriage with Tammy Wynette as for his achingly beautiful tales of love and heartbreak, Jones has owned real estate at both the very top and the very bottom of the country music world. In 1968, (just divorced, largely due to his drinking), he fell in love with hairdresser-turned-country singer, Tammy Wynette *(pictured above; see page 189)*. Six years later, country music's ideal couple—the "President and First Lady of Country Music"—were splitting up, thanks again to Jones's drinking. He declared bankruptcy, kept drinking, and missed so many engagements that he became known as No-Show Jones. In 1999—driving drunk and *sans* seatbelt —he totalled his Lexus SUV while talking on a cell phone, and almost died. Nevertheless, he remains country music's greatest living male vocalist and music stylist.

Songs: *White Lightning, We Can Make It, These Days I Barely Get By, If My Heart Had Windows, Still Doin' Time, Loving You Could Never Be Better, If Drinking Don't Kill Me, He Stopped Loving Her Today, Memories of Us, Hundred Proof Memories.*

Loretta Lynn
born 1935 Butcher Hollow, Johnson County, KY

The ultimate Appalachian rags-to-riches story, Loretta Lynn married at 13, and had six children and a grandchild by 29. She went on to record 16 number-one and 60

hit singles. The movie based on her autobiography, *A Coal Miner's Daughter,* was made into a film staring Tommy Lee Jones (as her husband "Mooney" Lynn) and Cissy Spacek. Mooney died in 1993, but the Lynn's sprawling ranch outside of Nashville is still open to the public as the Loretta Lynn Campground and Museum.

Songs: *Success, Before I'm Over You, Blue Kentucky Girl, You Ain't Woman Enough, Don't Come Home A-Drinkin' (With Lovin' On Your Mind), First City, Pregnant Again.*

BILL MONROE
1911–1996, Rosine, Kentucky

Bill Monroe is the father of bluegrass—he and his Blue Grass Boys created it. How did a new musical form come about? Most say it was the influence of his uncle, Pen Vandiver, a fiddler who raised Monroe after his parents died. Monroe launched the careers of many artists including Flatt & Scruggs, the Stanley Brothers, and countless others. The departure of Flatt and Scruggs in 1948 deeply embittered him, and, in one of the most famous feuds in country music, he refused to speak with them for 20 years. One of those Monroe-influenced musicians was

Elvis Presley, who, on his one-and-only appearance at the Opry, apologized backstage to Monroe for having changed *Blue Moon of Kentucky.* Monroe replied by promptly re-recording the song to share some of the blazing fame of the young rock idol. Monroe died in 1996, his musical legacy standing second to none in America.

Songs: *Mule Skinner Blues, Uncle Pen, Footprints In the Snow, Blue Moon of Kentucky, Kentucky Waltz, Blue Grass Special, Rocky Road Blues, Heavy Traffic Ahead.*

WILLIE NELSON
born 1933, Fort Worth, Texas

Songwriter par excellence *(Crazy, Hello Walls, Funny How Time Slips Away)*, counter-culture icon, movie star, outlaw legend, with a voice that can pop a beer tab at 50 yards, Willie is perhaps the most adventurous—and loved—country singer in America. Sure, there's all those other guys (and gals), but Willie stands alone. He's paid some major dues, lost marriages, a royal skinning by the IRS, but he's had fun, delivered some great movie lines, and some fabulous music, and demonstrated to more than one generation that it's possible to live free.

Songs: *Crazy, Family Bible, Touch Me, Night Life, Funny How Time Slips Away, Whiskey River, Blue Eyes Crying in the Rain, Mamas Don't Let Your Babies Grow Up to Be Cowboys, Georgia on My Mind, All of Me, Always on My Mind.*

DOLLY PARTON
born 1946, Sevierville, Tennessee
Not your everyday multi-millionaire singer/actress /comedienne/femininst icon/philanthropist/theme-park developer. Sexy, sassy, smart—real smart—with a voice carved out of Southern crystal, Dolly has never strayed far from her roots despite superstar success. Her recent recordings for *Little Sparrow* embrace her musical beginnings, standing out beautifully against the "young country" stars' crowding the airwaves. One of 12 children from a musical, dirt-poor Applachian family, she cut her first single, *Puppy Love,* when she was 14. Dollywood, modeled after Disneyland, is world-class empire building. "I look like a woman," she's fond of saying, "but I think like a man."

Songs: *Coat of Many Colors, Puppy Love, Dumb Blonde, Touch Your Women, Joshua, My Tennessee Mountain Home, Jolene, I Will Always Love You, Here You Come Again, 9 to 5, Traveling Man, If I Lose My Mind, Mule Skinner Blues.*

HANK WILLIAMS
1923–1953, Butler County, Alabama
Arguably the greatest country songwriter who ever lived, his life was plagued by chronic back pain, alcohol and drug abuse, and dubious care—his "doctor" was an ex-felon who shot him up with painkillers the night he died, at age 30. Nevertheless, his work embodies the heart and soul of country music.

Songs: *Jambalaya, Your Cheatin' Heart, Hey Good Lookin', I'm So Lonesome I Could Cry, Honky Tonk Blues, Cold Cold Heart, You Win Again, Ramblin' Man, Why Don't You Love Me Like You Used To Do, Take These Chains From My Heart, Kaw-Liga.*

TAMMY WYNETTE
1942–1998, Itawamba County, Mississippi
The "First Lady of Country Music," Tammy Wynette will ever be remembered for her "teardrop" voice, ringing vocals, and the personal apology she received from First Lady Hillary Clinton for disparaging *Stand by your Man.*

Songs: *Stand by Your Man, Your Good Girl's Gonna Go Bad, I Don't Want to Play House, Josey,* D-I-V-O-R-C-E, *Kids Say the Darndest Things, Run Woman Run, Apartment #9.*
(all photos courtesy Michael Ochs Archives, Los Angeles)

■ HARPETH HILLS   *map page 183, A-6*

Downtown workers start their mornings gazing out of their office towers at what seem like distant mountains silhouetting the southwestern horizon. When the haze clears by coffee break, a closer look reveals that they're not mountains, but a range of steep green hills just a few miles away. These are the Harpeth Hills, poking into the Central Basin from the Western Highland Rim. Nestled in the hills are the Warner Parks and the Radnor Lake State Natural Area. Together they protect nearly 4,000 acres of rugged forests and gentle meadows, rushing streams and placid lakes, an abundance of wildlife, and more than 300 species of wildflowers. The two preserves were once part of plantations whose big houses still stand, Belle Meade and Travellers Rest, both impeccably restored and open to the public. (See pages 198–199.)

◆ WARNER PARKS

Lots of people are always doing lots of things in the Warner Parks—walking, hiking, horseback riding, bicycling, picnicking, golfing—yet the twin parks named

Willow Pond at Percy Warner Park.

for brothers Percy and Edwin never seem crowded—except for the second Saturday in May. Then 30,000 fun-lovers pack the hillside above the Iroquois Steeplechase to party to the sound of thundering thoroughbreds.

Percy Warner was chairman of Nashville's parks board in 1926 when his son-in-law, Luke Lea, was developing Belle Meade Plantation into Nashville's most prestigious neighborhood. Warner convinced Lea to donate to the city the forested hills at the end of Belle Meade Boulevard. Following Percy's death, Edwin helped expand the parks to their current size. Visitor Center: TN-100 at Old Hickory Boulevard (TN-254); 615-370-8050.

◆ RADNOR LAKE STATE NATURAL AREA   *map page 183, B-6*

If you walk softly on the gentle Lake Trail, taking care not to disturb the ducks or the turtles sunning themselves on logs, you'll feel as if you're in the wilderness rather than in the middle of a metropolitan area home to more than a million people. This preserve takes in the entire basin of the headwaters of Otter Creek from ridge to ridge. It's mostly locals who walk the trails into the rich, deep forest and

Moonrise over Radnor Lake.

along the ridge crests, though it's not unheard of to encounter a water- and tree-starved country music fan from the desert Southwest seeking refreshment at Radnor.

More than 250 bird species have been spotted at Radnor, and the 80-acre lake is popular with waterfowl, as 22 species winter here. It was the birds that led to Radnor's preservation. After the L&N Railroad built the lake in 1919 to provide water for its steam engines, the lake became a haven for migratory waterfowl and other birds. Albert F. Ganier of the Tennessee Ornithological Society, himself a railroad man, convinced the L&N to maintain the basin as a wildlife preserve. But the railroad sold the property, and in 1973, it looked as if the basin would be developed. A community-wide preservation effort resulted in Radnor's becoming the first area protected by Tennessee's 1971 Natural Areas Preservation Act. Visitor Center: 1160 Otter Creek Road off Granny White Pike; 615-373-3467.

■ PLANTATION HOUSES

Nashville grew out of the agricultural economy that flourished before industry supplanted farming as the principal employer. The plantation houses that survive from those days are among the most enjoyable places to visit.

From 1804 to 1819, Andrew Jackson lived in the cabin, which Cornelius Hankins painted in 1895, after a powerful storm had taken its toll on the property. (Tennessee Historical Society)

The colonnaded portico of the Hermitage (added in 1834, after a fire) set the standard for many Greek Revival Southern plantation homes.

◆ **THE HERMITAGE**   *map page 207, C-2*

Relief from ever-expanding sprawl is immediate as you turn onto Rachel's Lane and pass through peaceful fields still alive with the songs of meadowlarks. There's an almost palpable sense that something really important is up ahead. The home of our seventh president, Andrew Jackson, is a national historic landmark and one of the most visited homes in America.

The Hermitage is more than a house where a famous man lived, but if that were all it was, it would still be a spectacular place to visit. The Greek Revival portico, added following an 1834 fire, set the standard for Southern plantation homes that was followed until that way of life ended violently three decades later. From the time you pass through the mansion's front door, just as Jackson and his guests did, until you leave by the detached kitchen, you can't escape the feeling that at any moment, Jackson will return from a ride on his plantation to greet you. That's how intimately the Hermitage is presented.

The Hermitage shows visitors something of life on an Upper South plantation, where cotton was grown but wasn't king. And not just the life of the master. The

ANDREW AND RACHEL: A LOVE STORY

Having been president of the United States, Andrew gets top billing at the Hermitage, but he wasn't the only Jackson living here. In fact, Rachel, his wife, spent more time at the Hermitage before her untimely death than Andrew did, as the general was often off on a military campaign.

Rachel was the daughter of John Donelson, one of Nashville's founders. She was unhappily married to one Lewis Robards and was living with her mother when, in 1788, Andrew Jackson arrived on the Cumberland frontier and boarded with the widow Donelson. The jealous and abusive Robards sensed right away that there was something between Rachel and Andrew. After a confrontation with Jackson, Robards left for Kentucky. In 1790, a rumor spread that Robards intended to return and take Rachel to Kentucky, by force if necessary. Andrew graciously agreed to escort the young wife (and other travelers) to far away Natchez to escape Robards.

Back in Nashville, Andrew heard that Robards had divorced Rachel, so he hurried back to Natchez

"Beyond the Mansion" self-guided tour enters the world of the 140 African Americans who in the 1840s labored in bondage on Jackson's thousand acres. On a late February walk past daffodils in full bloom by the spring house, the hawk soaring effortlessly above and the bright red cardinals standing out against the dark cedars are likely to be your only companions as you emerge into a field dotted with interpretative signs explaining life at the field quarters. In warmer weather, archaeologists will be painstakingly sifting through the rubble around the duplex slave dwelling foundations in search of clues about slave life.

And then there is the man himself. During two terms as president, Jackson so dominated the political life of the nation that the era is still called the Age of Jackson. "Jacksonian Democracy" forever changed the political life of the country. James Madison, one of the authors of the U.S. Constitution, had warned, "democracies have ever been spectacles of turbulence and contention; have ever been found where, in 1791, according to the "official" version, the couple married. There is no record of it, however. And it turned out that Robards didn't obtain his divorce until 1793. So Andrew and Rachel weren't married, not legally at least.

They finally did marry, for real, in 1794. The passion of their early romance never dimmed, and they remained devoted to each other.

When Jackson ran for president in 1828, his opponents brought up the circumstances surrounding his marriage. Rachel, though, remained on the peaceful grounds of the Hermitage. Jackson won, and in December of that year, Rachel traveled into Nashville to shop for the clothes she would need as first lady. She came across a pamphlet rebutting charges that she was an adultress and bigamist, and was shocked to learn the extent to which the old story of her marriage had been injected into a national campaign. Rachel went into a decline from which she never recovered. She was dead by December 18. Andrew blamed his opponents for Rachel's death. He never got over it.

*(both paintings courtesy of
The Hermitage, Nashville)*

incompatible with personal security or the rights of property; and have in general been as short in their lives as they have been violent in their deaths." Jackson's election was a complete repudiation of Madison's concept of limited democracy. Jackson was the first president who was not from the elites of the Eastern Seaboard, a "self-made man"—that term came into use during Jackson's presidency—a man of the people. "The people are sovereign," said Jackson, "their will is absolute." And while we may grumble today about the influence of "special interests," Jacksonian Democracy is essentially the system we still have in America.

But there were limits even on Jacksonian Democracy. "The people" Jackson held in such reverence meant white males. It didn't include women, blacks, and certainly not Indians. Jackson's Indian removal policy is a blemish on his presidency that cannot be overlooked. 4580 Rachel's Lane, off TN-45; 615-889- 2941.

◆ BELLE MEADE PLANTATION   *map page 183, A-5*

The massive proportions of the 1853 house on "The Queen of Tennessee Plantations" is the first thing visitors notice when the costumed guide opens the front door and welcomes them into Belle Meade mansion. After their eyes adjust to the dim light, they see that the many portraits on the walls are not of people. They're of horses, lots of horses. Therein lies the story of Belle Meade. During the second half of the 19th century, this farm, run by William Giles Harding and his son-in-law, William Hicks Jackson, was one of America's best-known stud farms. Secretariat, Northern Dancer, and Riva Ridge are just some of the Kentucky Derby winners descended from Belle Meade's Bonnie Scotland. The fact that seven U.S. presidents stayed here attests to Belle Meade's importance. "Uncle Bob" Green, the groom who established a name for himself as a judge of fine horses, first as a slave, then as a free man, was important at Belle Meade. He gets about as much attention here as Harding and Jackson.

Belle Meade's furnishings are lavish. Each of the hundreds of Victorian-era pieces seems to have its own unique character. It's a challenge to absorb it all. Take time to wander about its remaining 24 tree-shaded acres and to prowl through the colossal 1892 Carriage House and Stable with its display of antique carriages. 5025 Harding Road (US-70S); 800-270-3991 or 615-356-0501.

Horsebarn at Belle Meade Plantation.

Iroquois, the first American-bred horse to win the English Derby (in 1881) retired to stud at Belle Meade, where he is buried. (courtesy of Belle Meade Plantation)

◆ TRAVELLERS REST   *map page 183, B-6*

John Overton first called his 1799 home "Golgotha," named for the "hill of skulls" in the Book of Matthew. Because the house was built on a prehistoric burial mound, workers turned up skulls and artifacts, some of which are on display today at Travellers Rest. The white clapboard house in the Federal style and its generous collection of period furnishings will seem plain and simple if you visit it after Belle Meade or Belmont. But remember, when Overton built it, this was still the frontier. Few people in those days lived in anything but log houses.

Overton was a lawyer and a judge like his friend and political ally Andrew Jackson, and in the days before law schools, aspiring lawyers "read law" under an established lawyer. The judge provided housing for his pupils, first in the 1808 addition, then after his marriage at age 50 to the widow Mary White May, in a brick outbuilding. Overton is linked to other parts of Tennessee, as Mary was from the family that founded Knoxville, and Overton, Jackson, and James Winchester were the founders of Memphis. 636 Farrell Parkway off Franklin Road (US-31); 615-832- 8197.

AUTHOR'S CHOICE:
NASHVILLE AREA LODGING AND RESTAURANTS

LODGING

Apple Brook Bed, Breakfast, & Barn
An 1896 farm house-turned-inn near Natchez Trace Parkway west of town. 9127 TN-100; 877-646-5082 or 615-646-5082.

Birdsong Lodge
Fully restored luxury inn built in 1912 as summer home of the Cheek family that made a fortune as creators of Maxwell House Coffee. Rooms plus a private cottage, all overlooking Sycamore Creek and convenient to Nashville. 1306 Highway 49 E., Ashland City; 615-792-1767.

Hancock House
Log inn between Nashville and Gallatin was originally the pre-1878 stage stop and turnpike toll house. Detached stone house and cabin in addition to the rooms. 2144 Nashville Pike (US-31E); 615-452-8431.

Hermitage Hotel
Nashville's grand downtown hotel, built in 1910 with a magnificent, richly marbled lobby, restored to its former grandeur. 231 Fifth Avenue N.; 615-244-3121.

Hillsboro House
Cozy Victorian inn convenient to Vanderbilt and Music Row. Located at 1933 20th Avenue, S.; 800-228-7851 or 615-292-5501.

Loews Vanderbilt Plaza Hotel
Family-friendly luxury next to Vanderbilt University and near Music Row. 2100 West End Avenue; 615-320-1700.

Montgomery Bell State Park
map page 207, A/B-2
Fine, new inn on shore of CCC–built lake at popular park on Western Highland Rim west of Nashville. US-70, White Bluff; 800-250-8613 or 615-797-3101.

Opryland Hotel
With 2,884 guest rooms and 15 restaurants, Opryland is a destination in itself. 2800 Opryland Drive; 615-889-1000.

Union Station Hotel
Stepping inside this national historic landmark is a must on any trip to Nashville. Converted to a first-class hotel. 1001 Broadway; 800-996-3426 or 615-726-1001.

Restaurants

Arnold's Country Kitchen
When National Public Radio broadcast "All Things Considered" from Nashville, this crowded cafeteria is where writer John Edgerton brought the hosts to share the joy of Southern cooking with the rest of the nation. 605 Eighth Avenue, S.; 615-256-4455.

Jack's Bar-B-Que
Jack Cawthon is a serious student of barbecue, and it shows at his District establishment frequented by locals and visitors alike. 416 Broadway (also at 334 W. Trinity Lane); 615-254-5715.

Jimmy Kelly's
One of the last bastions of Old Nashville, this family-owned steakhouse is a throwback to the days when such restaurants were essentially private clubs for the wealthy. The menu is conservative and the corn cakes justifiably famous. 217 Louise Avenue; 615-329-4349.

Loveless Motel and Restaurant
Nashville's most famous restaurant, in an old tourist court, noted for breakfasts of country ham, gravy, biscuits, homemade preserves, and crowds. Next to Natchez Trace Parkway terminus. 8400 TN-100; 615-646-9700.

Mad Platter
Dependably good fusion dishes in an intimate setting in historic Germantown north of downtown. 1239 Sixth Avenue N.; 615-242-2563.

Merchants
Upscale dining in elegantly restored Victorian hotel in The District. 401 Broadway; 615-254-1892.

Park Cafe
This neighborhood bistro is casual enough for jeans, but the food is tasty enough for a special occasion. The menu is a fusion of Asian, Southwestern, and Left Bank. 4403 Murphy Road; 615-383-4409.

Rotier's
The Rotier family has been serving Nashville's best burgers and Southern cooking to generations of Vanderbilt students and grads. Once you've had a cheeseburger on French bread, you'll be hooked. 2413 Elliston Place; 615-327-9892.

Sunset Grill
Music Row celebrity hangout in Hillsboro Village that manages to be elegant and casual at the same time, serving dependably good new American cuisine with emphasis on pasta and fish. 2001-A Belcourt Avenue; 615-386-3663.

Swett's
Call it what you will—soul food, country cooking, Southern cooking—this popular North Nashville cafeteria serves the best in town. 2725 Clifton Road (also in the Farmer's Market); 615-329-4418.

Zola
Creative menu with a Mediterranean flavor of Greek, Turkish, Moroccan, and Italian dishes. Consistently a local winner. 3001 West End Avenue; 615-320-7778.

MIDDLE TENNESSEE

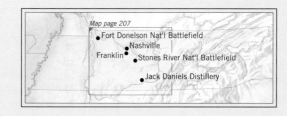

Map page 207
Fort Donelson Nat'l Battlefield
Nashville
Franklin
Stones River Nat'l Battlefield
Jack Daniels Distillery

◆ HIGHLIGHTS

◆ AREA OVERVIEW

Travel Basics: Middle Tennessee's heartland is a pleasing blend of natural and man-made environments, a handsome pastoral landscape rivaling the Pennsylvania Dutch country, Virginia's Shenandoah Valley, and the Kentucky Bluegrass. It's a land of tree-lined rivers bending through rich bottoms thick with corn, of bluegrass pastures rolling up to wooded hills, and of forests that radiate in the spring with redbud and dogwood. The countryside is dotted with columned antebellum mansions, Victorian-era cottages, and substantial early 20th-century farmhouses and is laced with quiet lanes bordered by carefully laid stone fences. Historic districts in the towns show off neat Victorian storefronts and well-tended houses from the early 1800s through the 1930s. The highlands are less fertile and more wooded than the heartland. Nature is the main attraction. Wildflowers fill the woods in spring, and fall colors are brilliant. It's an area noted for its abundance of waterfalls and clear blue lakes.

Getting Around: The tree-shaded hearts of Middle Tennessee's cities and towns are delightful places to explore on foot. Thick growths of "you could be anywhere" commercial clutter surround the town centers, but once beyond them, it's hard to find a

MIDDLE
TENNESSEE

road that doesn't offer a pretty drive. That goes for the main roads and the less traveled roads as well. It's a region well suited for wandering. Slicing diagonally across the western highlands, the Natchez Trace Parkway is one of America's most scenic roads.

Climate: Spring, arriving as early as late February and lingering until mid-May is especially beautiful, as is fall, which lasts from early October until Thanksgiving, sometimes Christmas. Between mid-October and mid-April temperatures stay mostly in the 30s to 50s, but there are periods of cold weather and a few snowfalls. Summers are hot and humid, often in the 90s. Northern counties tend to get a little more snow and ice than those to the south, and the highlands are slightly cooler than the heartland.

Food & Lodging: Fine dining is pretty much limited to a handful of places in the donut counties around Nashville. Elsewhere, search out good country cooking. Every town has a favorite. Miss Mary Bobo's Boarding House in Lynchburg is world famous. The number of small inns is on the rise, with at least one in or near most every heartland town. Lodging options are leaner in the highlands. State park cabins are nice options, and there are hotels at a few of them. Chain motels crowd around interchanges on the six interstate highway tentacles that reach out from Nashville.

Sunrise along Countyline Road in Middle Tennessee's Dickson County.

MIDDLE
TENNESSEE

■ EDEN OF THE WEST

The center of the Midstate is called the heartland to distinguish it from the more wooded, less fertile highlands surrounding it. Most of the heartland is made up of the Central Basin, a jagged-edged, oval-shaped depression averaging 120 miles in north-south length and 60 miles in east-west width. To the long hunters who explored it in colonial times, and to the settlers who followed, the heartland was a true Eden, a luxuriant, well-watered, uninhabited land filled with game.

From the time the first settlers followed James Robertson across the frozen Cumberland River on Christmas Day 1779 until the threat of Indian attacks ceased around the time Tennessee became a state in 1796, the pioneers stayed close to their forts, or "stations," near the river. When the threat of attack abated, settlers spread out as a succession of treaties with the Cherokees and Chickasaws expanded the legal limits of settlement. Like ripples from a stone thrown into a pond, pioneer settlements grew outward in ever-widening circles. Farmers cleared flat land and kept the hills in trees, creating the mosaic of field and forest you see today.

The frontier period was over by 1820, and the antebellum period had begun. When the nation broke apart in 1861, the Middle Tennessee heartland was one of the nation's richest agricultural areas. The heartland counties make up 40 percent of the Midstate, but on the eve of the Civil War, they possessed 80 percent of the wealth. An acre of land in the heartland was worth four times as much as an acre in the highlands.

Geography and politics dictated that Middle Tennessee would be a pivotal battleground in the Civil War. The Cumberland and Tennessee Rivers and the north-south railroads were obvious avenues for Union advances into the Confederacy. And President Abraham Lincoln saw no way to liberate pro-Union East Tennessee from Confederate control other than to send troops through the middle part of the state. The battlefields of Fort Donelson, Stones River, Spring Hill, and Franklin are today among the most visited places in the region.

Recovery from war's devastation was well under way by the end of the 1870s. Fine new Victorian houses and striking Gothic Revival churches soon filled the towns. The elaborate courthouses you see today went up. Factories opened, and over the years, agriculture came to be less and less important economically. Now most employment is in manufacturing.

Falls Mill near Old Salem is an idyllic picnic spot 10 miles southwest of Winchester in Franklin County.

The Middle Tennessee heartland is struggling to hold on to its unique character. Abetted by public policy that promotes growth at all costs, sprawl is gobbling up the verdant countryside. The American Farmland Trust ranks the subregion as one of the most threatened farming areas in the nation. A commonly expressed fear is that Greater Nashville will soon look like Greater Atlanta or Anywhere, U.S.A. Maybe it will. But for now, at least, much of the uniqueness of the Middle Tennessee heartland can still be enjoyed.

■ FRANKLIN   *map page 207, B-2*

"Franklin: The Handsomest Town in Tennessee." This claim by the seat of prosperous Williamson County is no exaggeration (it's made in the title of the 1999 bicentennial history of the town). Franklin's inhabitants impeccably care for houses dating from the early 1800s that line its tree-shaded streets. Its merchants entice shoppers into an assortment of shops and galleries in 19th-century commercial buildings that helped Franklin earn honors for downtown preservation from the National Trust for Historic Preservation. If you're looking for a good way to spend a crisp early November afternoon, you won't do better than strolling through Franklin's historic districts beneath golden sugar maples illuminated by autumn's slanting sun.

The Confederate monument which overlooks the town square in Franklin.

MIDDLE TENNESSEE

Elevation in feet
6,642
3,000
2,500
2,000
1,500
1,000
500
300

20 Miles
10   20   30 Kilometers

○ Towns with food and/or lodging listings

ALABAMA

N
W   E
S

The soldier atop the Confederate monument in the square looks down on the 1859 Courthouse with its four cast iron columns. Study the Courthouse up close, and you'll see a plaque honoring more than 60 Revolutionary War veterans buried in the county. Why, you ask, were there so many veterans here, when this county wasn't even settled until nearly two decades after the Revolution ended? Because North Carolina, lacking funds to pay its soldiers, paid them with land grants in what is now Middle Tennessee. Much of the Midstate was settled on these grants.

Franklin is a fine town to settle into for a few days. Stay at a locally run inn and eat at small restaurants to absorb the flavor of the place and overhear conversations about the concerns of Tennessee. **Dotson's** is a classic Middle Tennessee "meat and three" (vegetables), and it draws its share of music celebrities. It's at 99 E. Main Street. **Jack Russell's** at 2179 Hillsboro Road provides innovative American cooking with a Southern slant. At **Merridee's Breadbasket,** 110 Fourth Avenue, S., the aroma of fresh baking will whet your appetite, and you won't be let down by anything you try.

A 700-acre working cattle and horse farm out in lush countryside serves as the setting for the elegant **Peacock Hill Inn**; 6994 Giles Hill Road in College Grove; 800-327-6663.

■ BATTLE OF FRANKLIN

It was at Franklin on a late November afternoon in 1864 that the Confederate Army of Tennessee hit a roadblock in its attempt to reclaim the state.

Gen. John Bell Hood threw his tattered Southerners against the fortified Federals commanded by Hood's West Point classmate Maj. Gen. John M. Schofield. It was a disaster for the Confederates: they lost 1,750 men compared to 189 Federals. Development has smothered most of the battlefield, but some important places remain and are open to the public. The place to start the tour is the Carter House.

◆ CARTER HOUSE   *map page 207, B-2*

Fountain Branch Carter and his family hid in terror in the cellar of this substantial 1830 farm house while outside the boys from the North, from the South, and from in between—Kentucky and Missouri—went at each other in some of the Civil War's fiercest fighting. When it was over, word arrived that Carter's son Tod, a young officer in Hood's Confederate army who hadn't been home in three years, lay wounded a few yards from the house. He died at home within two days.

The personalized tour of this national historic landmark includes outbuildings that were here during the fighting. The small office has no less than 207 bullet holes through its wooden walls. It's chilling to think of what those bullets did to human flesh. The museum behind the step-gabled brick house has a decidedly Southern cast, which accounts for why you don't see much about General Hood. He is blamed for the disaster. 1140 Columbia Avenue (US-31); 615-791-1861.

◆ CARNTON PLANTATION AND CONFEDERATE CEMETERY
  map page 207, B-2
John and Carrie McGavock were living in this handsome 1826 plantation house when violence came to their door on November 30, 1864. The ten surrounding acres are tranquil today, but they were the scene of unspeakable horror that night, as wagon after wagon of mangled men were dropped off at the makeshift hospital.

Confederate cemetery at Carnton Plantation in Franklin.

A CONFEDERATE SOLDIER REMEMBERS

*A*bout two hours after sun up the next morning we received the order to "Fall in, fall in, quick, make haste, hurrah, promptly, men; each rank count two; by the right flank, quick time, march; kept promptly closed up." Everything indicated an immediate attack. When we got to the turnpike near Spring Hill, lo! and behold; wonder of wonders! the whole Yankee army had passed during the night. The bird had flown. We made a quick and rapid march down the turnpike, finding Yankee guns and knapsacks, and now and then a broken down straggler, also two pieces of howitzer cannon, and at least twenty broken wagons along the road. Everything betokened a rout and a stampede of the Yankee army. Double quick! Forrest is in the rear. Now for fun. All that we want to do now is to catch the blue-coasted rascals, ha!ha! We all want to see the surrender, ha! ha! Double quick! A rip, rip, rip; wheuf; pant, pant, pant. First one man drops out, and then another. The Yankees are routed and running and Forrest has crossed Harpeth River in the rear of Franklin. Hurrah, men! keep close up; we are going to capture Schofield. Forrest in in the rear; never mind the straggler and cannon. Kerflop we come against the breastworks at Franklin.

FRANKLIN

"The death-angel gathers its last harvest."

*K*ind reader, right here my pen, and courage, and ability fail me. I shrink from butchery. Would to God I could tear the page from these memoirs and from my own memory. It is the blackest page in the history of the war of the Lost Cause. It was the bloodiest battle of modern times in any war. It was the finishing stroke to the independence of the Southern Confederacy. I was there. I saw it. My flesh trembles, and creeps, and crawls when I think of it today. My heart almost ceases to beat at the horrid recollection. Would to God that I had never witnessed such a scene.

⊱ ⊰

*I*t was four o'clock on that dark and dismal December day when the line of battle was formed, and those devoted heroes were ordered forward, to

> *Strike for their altars and their fires,*
> *For the green graves of their sires,*
> *For God and their native land.*

As they marched on down through an open field toward the rampart of blood and death, the Federal batteries began to open and mow down and gathering to the garner of death, as brave, and good, and pure spirits as the world ever saw. The twilight of evening had begun to gather in a precursor of the coming blackness of midnight darkness that was to envelop a scene so sickening and horrible that it is impossible for me to describe it.

—Sam R. Watkins, *Co. Aytich, A Side Show of the Big Show,*
describing events at the Battles of Franklin and
Nashville, 1864 (published in 1882).

Lt. Robert B. Hurt, Jr. was a member of the Confederate 55th Tennessee Infantry and died during the fierce fighting at Franklin. (Library of Congress)

Dead and dying filled the house. The bodies of four of the six Confederate generals killed at Franklin were laid out on the columned porch that stretches across the back. After the war, the McGavocks donated two acres for the reinternment of 1,500 dead Southerners who had been hastily buried in shallow mass graves. 1345 Carnton Lane, off Lewisburg Avenue (US-431); 615-794-0903.

◆ FORT GRANGER   *see Franklin, map page 207, B-2*

Federal commander John M. Schofield watched the battle at Franklin from this 1862 earthen fort atop a Harpeth River bluff. He was joined by a battery of Ohio light artillery that poured killing fire down on the advancing Confederates. A sometimes muddy trail leads from Pinkerton Park to Fort Granger, which has scattered among its mounds and ditches interpretive tablets explaining the configuration of Civil War fortifications. Pinkerton Park off Murfreesboro Road (TN-96) east of downtown Franklin.

◆ WINSTEAD HILL   *see Franklin, map page 207, B-2*

Standing at the small memorial park south of town, you get the same view the Confederates had before they launched their suicidal frontal assault. It was here that Patrick Cleburne, the Irish-born division commander who counseled against the attack, remarked to a subordinate: "Well, Govan, if we are to die, let us die like men." The six Confederate generals killed at Franklin, including Cleburne, are a grisly Civil War record. Half a mile south on the main road is Harrison House, the stately 1848 mansion where Hood and his generals passionately disagreed over the wisdom of the Franklin attack. Columbia Pike (US-31) south of Franklin.

■ MAURY COUNTY

"The Dimple of the Universe" is how one historian labeled this part of Tennessee. The combination of deep rich soil, diversified agriculture, and slave labor created immense wealth in the three decades before the Civil War. The planter class felt obliged to show it off with the architecture of "Southern nationalism," the classically inspired mansion. It's a wonder so many of them remain, but they do, and they're the main attraction in Maury County. Visitors during the annual tours in May, September, and December, when mansions in private ownership are spruced up and opened to the public, are fortunate. Tour details: 888-852-1860 or 931-381-7176.

◆ **SPRING HILL**   *map page 207, B-3*

Things seem about as you'd expect in a quaint village that's been here since 1808. There is a lovely little Carpenter Gothic church, pillared mansions, and a collection of tidy smaller homes. On the southern edge of town, though, you start to sense something is not quite right. Commercial development seems oversized for such a small place. You'll likely hear an accent that sounds more like Michigan than Middle Tennessee. As you pass an expressway called "Saturn Parkway," look to your right and you'll see the source of your unease. Partially hidden by some man-made hills is one of the world's largest industrial plants where more than 8,000 workers (mostly Midwestern transplants) assemble Saturn automobiles. For tours, call 800-326-3321 or 931-486-5778.

◆ **SPRING HILL CIVIL WAR SITES**

Confederate Gen. John Bell Hood thought he had the perfect plan on November 29, 1864. His Army of Tennessee had outflanked John M. Schofield's Federals at Columbia and were poised to block the road to Franklin and Nashville. The Union army would be trapped. But the Confederates camped for the night a few hundred yards short of the road. While they slept, the men in blue walked quietly past. The failure of the Southerners to block the road in what has come to be known as "The Affair at Spring Hill" remains a mystery to this day.

Another Spring Hill Civil War mystery is the killing of Confederate Maj. Gen. Earl Van Dorn by Dr. Charles Peters in May 1863. Van Dorn, described by fellow officers as having a weakness for women, had been keeping company with Jessie McKissack Peters, the doctor's wife. Peters shot the general when the two of them were alone in Van Dorn's headquarters at Ferguson Hall. Maybe it was murder. Maybe it was a fight. Maybe it was a political act. Some suspected Dr. Peters of being a Union spy. The third person in the triangle, Jessie, was heard to remark: "Now ain't that the devil, a sweetheart killed, and a husband run away, all in the same day."

Spring Hill's marked Civil War tour rolls through the grassy countryside past Oaklawn, the 1835 mansion where Hood slept while Schofield got away; Ferguson Hall, the 1854 mansion where Dr. Peters killed Gen. Van Dorn; and the preserved battlefield where fighting broke out when the Confederates reached Spring Hill. Tour details: 888-852-1860.

◆ **RIPPAVILLA**   *map page 207, B-3*

The father of Nathaniel Cheairs offered him a substantial bribe not to marry Susan McKissack. All six previous Nathaniel Cheairses had married Sarahs. Nat and Susan married anyway, and in 1855 they completed one of the region's most handsome homes. It was over breakfast at Rippavilla on the morning of November 30, 1864, that the reckless John Bell Hood quarreled with the other generals over who was responsible for letting the Yankees slip away in "The Affair at Spring Hill." For five of them, it was their last meal.

Rippavilla has been completely refurbished to meet fine 1860 standards. It doubles as a regional visitor center. It houses a superb, albeit small, Civil War museum with a display on Union army camp life, artifacts found on this property, and a sword of Confederate general Nathan Bedford Forrest, who commanded the cavalry at Spring Hill; 5700 Main Street (US-31) in Springhill; 931-486-9037.

The dining room at Rippavilla.

■ THE ANTEBELLUM TRAIL

Columned mansions are the ultimate symbol of the Old South. We're at once attracted and dismayed by them, drawn to their classical beauty and visions of romantic life in them, repulsed by the system of human bondage that built them. Figuring that more of us are drawn then repulsed, tourism boosters conceived the Antebellum Trail to show off the 60-mile chain of mansions from Nashville down through Brentwood, Franklin, Spring Hill, Columbia, and Mount Pleasant. Some are historic sites open to the public. Dozens more are private residences that have been carefully and lovingly restored. Each locale has at least one annual tour that welcomes visitors into some of the private homes; call 800-381-1865.

HISTORIC HOMES

1798 CRAGFONT

map page 207, C/D-1
also see page 245

Architecture: Georgian (limestone)
A grand pioneer home built by Brig. Gen. James Winchester, veteran of George Washington's army. The exquisite interior is full of Federal-period furnishings.

East of Gallatin, off TN-25 at 200 Cragfont Road; 615-452-7070.

Cragfont.

1815-1860 OAKLANDS

map page 207, C/D, 2/3
also see page 230
Architecture: Federal and Italianate
Scene of a daring raid in July, 1862 by Confederate General Nathan Bedford Forrest, it also served as the personal residence of Jefferson Davis during his December 1862 inspection of the South's Army of Tennessee.

900 N. Maney Avenue Murfreesboro; 615-893-0022.

Oaklands.

MIDDLE
TENNESSEE

1816 JAMES K. POLK ANCESTRAL HOME

map page 207, B-3
also see page 221

Architecture: Federal
Family home of James K. Polk, the 11th U.S. president, who died within three months of leaving office.
301 W. Seventh Street, Columbia; 931-388-2354.

The Hermitage.

1819, 1830 THE HERMITAGE

map page 207, C-2
also see pages 195-197

Architecture: Greek Revival
Home of Andrew Jackson, seventh president of the United States, this much-visited mansion set the standard for Southern plantations that followed. Rebuilt in 1830s after a fire.

4580 Rachel's Lane, Hermitage, off TN-45; 615-889-2941.

1826, 1847 CARNTON PLANTATION

map page 207, B/C-2
also see page 209

Architecture: Federal and Greek Revival
Commandeered by the Confederates as a hospital during the Battle of Franklin, it became a scene of unspeakable horror; four of the six Confederate generals killed at Franklin were laid out on the columned back porch. The 1,500 Confederates who died here are interred in the private cemetery.

1345 Carnton Lane off Lewisburg Avenue (US-431) in Franklin; 615-794-0903.

Carnton Plantation.

1828 WYNNEWOOD

map page 207, D-1
also see page 245

Architecture: Log Structure
The largest log structure in Tennessee. Opened as a stagecoach stop, the building has a generous kitchen with a huge assortment of 19th-century cooking implements.
Old TN-25 in Castalian Springs, east of Gallatin; 615-452-5463.

Wynnewood.

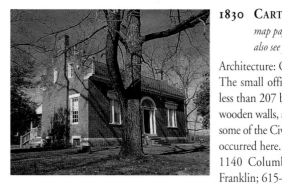

Carter House.

1830 CARTER HOUSE

map page 207, B-2
also see page 208

Architecture: Georgian and Federal
The small office outbuilding has no less than 207 bullet holes through its wooden walls, a chilling reminder that some of the Civil War's fiercest fighting occurred here.
1140 Columbia Avenue (US-31), Franklin; 615-791-1861.

1830 CHERRY MANSION

map page 255, E-4
also see page 259

Architecture: Federal and Colonial Revival
Union General Ulysses. S. Grant spent a quiet night here on April 5,1862, prior to the ferocious Battle of Shiloh.

101 Main Street, Savannah (in West Tennessee; not open to the public).

MIDDLE TENNESSEE

1840s SAM DAVIS HOME

map page 207, C-2
also see page 232

Architecture: Greek Revival
Home of Sam Davis, "Boy Hero of the Confederacy" who, captured as a spy at 21, refused to reveal his sources and was hanged.

1399 Sam Davis Road, Smyrna; 888-750-9524 or 615-459-2341.

1845 RATTLE & SNAP

map page 207, B-3
also see page 223-224

Architecture: Greek Revival
Considered perhaps the grandest antebellum plantation house in America, legend has it that William Polk of North Carolina won the acreage in a betting game called "Rattle & Snap."

TN-243 between Columbia and
    Mount Pleasant; 800-258-3875
    or 931-379-5861.

Rattle & Snap.

Belle Meade.

1853 BELLE MEADE

map page 183, A-5
also see page 199

Architecture: Greek Revival
Union and Confederate forces skirmished here. Later, it became one of the world's most significant Thoroughbred horse farms.

5025 Harding Road (US-70S),
    Nashville; 800-270-3991 or
    615-356-0501.

1853 BELMONT

map page 183, B-4
also see page 176

Architecture: Italianate

An 11,000-square-foot, 36-room extravaganza, Belmont housed Union officers during the Battle of Franklin and Nashville. The art collection of Adelicia Acklen, "a real-life Scarlet O'Hara," reflects a fabulous era.

1900 Belmont Boulevard,
Nashville; 615-460-5459.

Belmont.

1855 RIPPAVILLA

map page 207, B-3
also see page 214

Architecture: Greek Revival

Over breakfast here the morning of the Battle of Franklin, John Bell Hood quarreled with the other Confederate generals. For five of them it would be their last meal.

5700 Main Street (US-31) in Spring Hill; 931-486-9037.

Rippavilla.

MIDDLE
TENNESSEE

◆ **COLUMBIA**   *map page 207, B-3*

On the eve of the Civil War, Columbia was the third largest city in Tennessee, and the seat of the state's wealthiest county. The square around the 1904 Beaux-Arts Courthouse still flourishes with trade transacted in historic buildings, some dating back to the 1820s. The historic districts west of the square are packed with more than 150 historic houses that show off nearly every style of domestic architecture from the 1810s to the 1930s.

Locust Hill, an 1840 plantation home, offers a rare opportunity to stay in one of the antebellum houses visitors travel to Maury County to see. Try rooms decorated with antiques and homemade quilts or stay in a converted smokehouse; 1185 Mooresville Pike; 931-388-8531.

The aroma of barbecue cooking over hickory fills downtown Columbia. Follow your nose to **Nolen's Barbeque** and you won't be disappointed (100 W. Fifth Street). Down home cooking can be found in Columbia's vibrant, historic town square at **Henri's On the Square**.

King Mule and His Queen enjoy Mule Day, in Columbia in 1949. The town has been known for its fine mules since it supplied them for the British Army during World War I. (Tennessee State Library and Archives)

Washington B. Cooper's portrait of James K. Polk, circa 1846. (Tennessee State Museum, Nashville)

James K. Polk Home

map page 207, B-3

Our 11th president is not widely known, but historians rate the disciple of Andrew Jackson as one of the most successful. If you like having California in the United States, you can thank James K. Polk. If you don't, you can blame him. More territory was added to the United States during his 1845–49 presidency than at any other time.

James's parents built this unpretentious Federal-style house in 1816 while he was away at the University of North Carolina. It's outfitted with many of the furnishings used by the President and Sarah Childress Polk at the White House. The only Speaker of the United States House of Representatives to be elected president, Polk entered his presidency with clearly stated goals. One was to make the United States a coast-to-coast nation. He achieved his goals and kept his pledge to serve only one term.

"No president who performs his duty faithfully and conscientiously can have any leisure," Polk wrote shortly before leaving the White House. The two portraits of Polk hanging side-by-side vividly display the effect of his philosophy. They're both by the same painter, one early and the other late in Polk's four-year term. One is of a young-looking man, the other of an old-looking man. Polk died within three months of leaving office. 301 W. Seventh Street; 931-388-2354.

Columbia Mule Day

You've probably not given much thought to how mules are bought and sold. If you'd like to know—and have fun in the process —come to the Columbia Mule Day the first weekend in April. From the 1840s until World War II, this was the nation's major mule market. It's more of a party now, but there is still no shortage of mules. There's a mule-driving show and a parade featuring miles of mules.

The details of the Athenaeum Rectory refer to Moorish architecture rather than the more typical Italianate or Greek Revival styles.

The Athenaeum Rectory

This 1835 "Moorish-Gothic" residence is unlike anything else you'll see around here or anywhere else. It served as the Rectory, or headmaster's house, for the Athenaeum, a school founded by Vermont native and Princeton graduate Franklin Gillette Smith, that provided a quality classical education to girls from 1852 to 1903. Smith's descendants lived in the Rectory until they donated it to the public in 1973, which accounts for the presence of so many original furnishings, including the chandelier and the European-made glass doors. 808 Athenaeum Street; 931-381-4822.

◆ WEST OF COLUMBIA

The largest concentration of antebellum mansions for which Maury County is famous lies west of Columbia, out toward Mount Pleasant and Hampshire. You'll know them by markers placed by the APTA, the Association for the Preservation of Tennessee Antiquities. Old Zion and Cross Bridges Roads and the town of Mount Pleasant have their share of impressive houses, but the grandest are on the old highway between Columbia and Mount Pleasant, TN-243.

The columned mansions were built by second-generation Tennesseans whose fathers settled this rich land after an 1805 Indian treaty made it legal. They were progressive farmers, practicing crop rotation and diversification, raising hemp, corn, oats, wheat, tobacco, rye, and livestock. William Polk won some of his land playing a game called Rattle & Snap and referred to his acreage as his "Rattle & Snap land." When son George Washington Polk built a palatial mansion in the 1840s on his share of that acreage, he gave it that name.

Rattle & Snap   *map page 207, B-3*

Regarded by many as the grandest of all antebellum plantation houses—not just in Tennessee, but anywhere—Rattle & Snap dominates a rise in front of a forested hill at the end of a long, flower-lined lane leading through brilliant green pasture. The iron capitals topping the imposing Corinthian columns were manufactured in Cincinnati; the marble mantle came from Italy and the iron grillwork from Pittsburgh. A German landscape architect designed the gardens and greenhouses.

Like any grand house that's been around this long, Rattle & Snap has its share of intriguing stories, including being saved from the torch during the Civil War when Union officers belonging to the Masonic order saw a portrait of the mansion's owner, George Washington Polk, in which he, too, was wearing a Masonic ring. None of the stories, though, is quite as fascinating as the renovation you see today. Amon Carter Evans, retired publisher of *The Tennessean,* the Nashville newspaper, acquired the property in 1979 and reportedly poured $8 million into it. Henry A. Judd, retired chief restorationist for the National Park Service who restored Independence Hall in Philadelphia, headed a team of historians, architects, archaeologists, artisans and designers. No effort was spared. TN-243 between Mount Pleasant and Columbia; 800-258-3875 or 931-379-5861.

St. John's Church   *map page 207, B-3*

St. John's Episcopal Church presents an intriguing silhouette standing among the tall trees on its broad, stone-fenced grounds at the intersection of Zion Road and TN-243. Its squared tower and tall arched windows

Rattle & Snap.

MIDDLE TENNESSEE

St. John's Episcopal Church, just west of Columbia.

recall an English country church: it is, in fact, a copy of a church in Devon, England. Leonidas Polk, another of William's sons, entered the Episcopal priesthood after finishing West Point and eventually became bishop of Louisiana and founder of the University of the South at Sewanee *(see page 145)*. Leonidas convinced his brothers to build this charming brick plantation chapel in 1842.

Ambling among the monuments and tombstones, you'll notice several bishops' graves. Though St. John's ceased to have an active congregation in 1915, Tennessee's Episcopal bishops are still buried here by tradition.

Confederate President Jefferson Davis talked Leonidas Polk into accepting a commission in the Confederate army, and though he had little military experience, Polk became a lieutenant general commanding a corps in the Army of Tennessee. A shell from a Union cannon struck him dead during the Atlanta campaign in the spring of 1864.

Later that year, Gen. John Bell Hood led the tattered army back into Tennessee, and the men marched right past St. John's Church. A young general, Patrick Cleburne, was taken by the serenity of the place. "If I am killed in the impending battle I request that my body be laid to rest in this, the most beautiful and peaceful spot I ever beheld." A few days later, after the Battle of Franklin, the Irishman's lifeless body was lowered here into the cold Tennessee ground.

Zion Church

The other antebellum church out this way is a short distance up Zion Road from the TN-243 intersection. The unusual step-gabled building was completed in 1849. The strict Presbyterians who built it migrated from South Carolina in 1805 to escape the riotous living of more recent Scots-Irish immigrants. The Zionists were horrified by their dancing, drinking, horse racing, and gambling. The Zion group purchased the land from the heirs of Gen. Nathanael Greene who North Carolina had rewarded for his Revolutionary War service with a grant of land in what would become Tennessee. One of the many distinctive features of this still-active church is the location of the doors. They're on either side of the pulpit so late arrivals must face the stares of the congregation.

■ NATCHEZ TRACE PARKWAY *map page 207, A-4 to C-2*

You can think of the Natchez Trace Parkway as a pretty place for a leisurely Sunday drive. It is that, of course, but it's much more. The parkway is a 445-mile linear national park weaving in and out of environments ranging from steep forested ridges to swampy bottoms. The deer you're sure to see grazing at sunset are among the 57 species of mammals along the parkway, and the hawk you'll see soaring

Redbud in bloom over Swan Creek along the Natchez Trace Parkway.

*(following pages) Sunrise view of Harpeth Hills outside Nashville
(see page 192) in Middle Tennessee*

effortlessly above belongs to one of 215 species of birds. It takes only a few steps from a parking area to be surrounded by wildflowers, particularly in April, when the stream banks are purple with phlox. Bicyclists like the parkway, though only a few each year make the whole trip from Nashville to Natchez. The parkway has hiking and equestrian trails as well.

The buffalo path—turned Chickasaw Trail, turned Boatmen's Trail—became an official national road when the Mississippi Territory was annexed to the United States. On orders from President Thomas Jefferson, in 1801–03 the army upgraded the road. Lodging was in crude inns called "stands." One night in October 1809, famed explorer Meriwether Lewis was a guest at Grinder's Stand. His mentor Jefferson had named him governor of the Louisiana Territory, and Lewis was making his way to Washington from the territorial capital of St. Louis. Lewis was shot and died at Grinder's under circumstances that people have been arguing about ever since. Most scholars believe the cause was suicide.

The **Meriwether Lewis National Monument,** established in the 1920s, is part of the parkway now, and makes a nice park, complete with hiking trails through the oak-hickory forest in the rugged headwaters of Little Swan Creek. NTP Milepost 385.9 at TN-20 *(map page 207, A-3).*

■ CEDAR COUNTRY

Ubiquitous cedar thickets dot the landscape southeast of Nashville. They're remnants of vast stands of tall, red cedars that once covered much of Middle Tennessee's Inner Central Basin. The trees so impressed the early settlers that they named the nearest town Lebanon after the Cedars of Lebanon in the Bible. Reckless commercial exploitation in the early 20th century doomed all the big trees, and these thickets of smaller ones are what's left.

If you were picking your way through a thicket and came upon a rocky opening that looked as if someone had taken a wrecking ball to a concrete parking lot, and you weren't impressed, you wouldn't be the first person. Until fairly recently, these barrens or "glades" were regarded as good-for-nothing wasteland. Elsie Quarterman knew better. The Vanderbilt University botanist wrote her 1948 dissertation on "Plant Communities of Cedar Glades of Middle Tennessee," and for the next 40 years, she spread the word about the uniqueness of the cedar glades. They are home to plants and communities of plants not found anywhere else on earth. Now they're protected on state and federal lands, as well as on lands acquired by the Nature Conservancy.

Cedars of Lebanon State Park

map page 207, C/D-2

The glades here are actually mini-deserts where summer temperatures can be 10 to 30 degrees hotter than in the surrounding forest. You can sample these flower-filled openings on easy trails that meander in and out of eerie limestone formations, cedar and hardwood forests, and, of course, the glades, at Cedars of Lebanon State Park. This park got its start the way most Tennessee state parks did, as a 1930s New Deal land conservation and public works project. Some 792,000 cedars were planted on badly eroded land, and today, the park and adjacent state forest hold the world's largest eastern red cedar forest.

The U.S. Department of the Interior has named Cedars of Lebanon a National Natural Landmark. South of Lebanon on US-231 off I-40; 615-443-2769.

Long Hunter State Park

map page 207, C-2

Not far from Cedars of Lebanon, on the shore of J. Percy Priest Lake closer to Nashville, more glades are protected at Long Hunter State Park. As at Cedars of Lebanon, the trails are level and easy. You don't have to be a big-time hiker to enjoy them. The trails at both parks are nice any time of the year, but April and May are the best times to see the profusion of flowers. Long Hunter is south of Mount Juliet off I-40 on TN-171; 615-885-2422.

■ MURFREESBORO   *map page 207, C-2*

Murfreesboro, Tennessee's capital before it moved to Nashville, was the site of one of the biggest battles of the Civil War, and was at different times the principal western base for both the Union and Confederate armies. It's still an important city, home to Middle Tennessee State, Tennessee's third largest university, and up the road at Smyrna, the **Nissan plant** where each year 400,000 cars and trucks roll off the line. For tours, call 615-459-1444.

Murfreesboro has an elegant, well-preserved heart rich in historical and architectural treasures. A stroll from the square out maple-lined East Main Street is a visit through a living architectural museum. The Corinthian-columned, 1859 **courthouse** is one of five in Tennessee that pre-date the Civil War. It was the target of one of the most successful raids by one of the war's most successful raiders, Gen. Nathan Bedford Forrest (see page 33). In July 1862, his horsemen in gray swooped into the Federally occupied town and liberated the Southern prisoners held in the building. The courthouse was the scene, too, of the Old South's last fling in the Midsouth, the grand Confederate officers' ball on Christmas Eve 1862. History does not tell us how many of the party-goers fell in the horrendous battle the following week.

MIDDLE TENNESSEE

Ask anyone where to get the best home-cooked meal in these parts, they'll send you to **City Café** at 113 E. Main Street. Two other places that are distinctly local are the **Front Porch Café** at 114 E. College Street, which serves sandwiches, quiche, turnovers, and salads in the parlors of a stately century-old funeral home. (If you drive to nearby Christiana, try **Miller's Grocery** at 7011 Main Street. Once a country store, it is now a popular restaurant with made-from-scratch "country gourmet" food.)

An elaborate 1903 Queen Anne mansion with character and grandeur is now the **Byrn-Roberts Inn.** With eleven fireplaces and a wrap-around porch, it's located at 346 E. Main Street; 888-877-4919.

◆ OAKLANDS   *map page 207, C-2/3*

The broad, colonnaded porch sweeping around this sumptuous brick mansion comes into view as you make your way up Maney Avenue. The enormous 12-foot windows should prepare you for what you'll find inside. But they don't. You'll be astounded by the front parlor, with its 16-foot ceilings and fabulous period furnishings. Of course, that's how the Maney family wanted guests to react when they built the place, or at least the last major addition. Oaklands is actually three houses, dating from 1815 to 1860, which expanded as two generations grew in size and wealth.

By the time Nathan Bedford Forrest's Confederate cavalry staged its daring Murfreesboro raid in July 1862, Federals under Col. William W. Duffield had already occupied Oaklands. They left the wounded Duffield here, where he was nursed by the Maney family and by his wife who had come down from Detroit. After the war, the Duffields sent the Maneys a beautiful silver service and other gifts. The most famous visitor to Oaklands during the war years was Confederate President Jefferson Davis. He stayed at Oaklands in December 1862 during his inspection of the South's principal western army. 900 N. Maney Avenue, Murfreesboro; 615-893-0022.

An impromptu music jam held in Murfreesboro during Uncle Dave Macon Days, an event in honor of the legendary banjo player.

◆ STONES RIVER NATIONAL BATTLEFIELD   *map page 207, C-2*

Don't let names like the "Slaughter Pens" and "Hell's Half Acre" scare you away. The jigsaw of field and forest on the edge of this fast-growing city is a pretty place. The savage battle on December 31, 1862–January 2, 1863 was anything but pretty, however. It was one of the bloodiest of the Civil War, a staggering 13,249 Federal casualties and 11,739 for the Confederates. It was a draw from a military standpoint. But because the Confederates retreated, it was considered a victory in the North, which needed one to lift sagging morale. The battle was the opening round of nearly two years of fighting along the railroad linking Nashville to Atlanta via Chattanooga, where some historians believe the war's outcome was decided. The nation's very first Civil War monument is here, erected by the men of Hazen's Federal brigade while they were based in Murfreesboro following the battle. 3501 Old Nashville Highway; 615-893-9501.

The Federals built **Fortress Rosecrans,** the Civil War's largest earthen fort, after the battle to protect the enormous depot where they massed men and material for their next push south. Paved paths wind through the remnants of dirt ramparts that once stretched for nearly three miles. The fort provides access to Murfreesboro's heavily used four-mile Greenway along the banks of Stones River and Lytle Creek. Fortress Rosecrans is at 3501 Old Nashville Highway (TN-96). Another access is at Cannonsburgh Village, the collection of reconstructed log buildings bearing the town's original name at 312 Front Street.

◆ SAM DAVIS HOME   *map page 207, C-2*

The 168-acre Davis farm is a welcome relief from the sprawl consuming Smyrna, the railroad town 12 miles from Murfreesboro. Sitting on a rise at the end of a cedar-lined drive behind a 350-year-old oak, the house went through the transition in the 1840s so common in Middle Tennessee—a two-story, central-passage log house made over in the Greek Revival style, with a columned portico, clapboard siding, and an "L" addition. The tour provides a choice interpretation of life there before the Civil War. The Davis farm is one of the few antebellum plantations that still has slave quarters on it.

But what about Sam Davis, the "Boy Hero of the Confederacy," who grew up here? Davis was one of the "Coleman Scouts," a shadowy outfit of intelligence-gathering Confederate cavalrymen operating behind Union lines. Following his capture near Pulaski in November 1863—with documents he was taking to the

Confederates at Chattanooga—Gen. Grenville Dodge gave Davis a choice: reveal the identity of the person who gave him the documents or be hanged as a spy. "I would rather die a thousand deaths than betray a friend or be false to duty," the 21-year-old Davis declared as he was led to the gallows. Dodge was so moved by his bravery that years later, when funds were being raised for the Sam Davis statue on the State Capitol grounds, Dodge—the man who became famous after the war for building the Union Pacific Railroad—sent a contribution. 1399 Sam Davis Road; 615-459-2341.

■ DUCK AND ELK RIVERS RAMBLE   *map page 207, D-3 and page 16*

Middle Tennessee is at its best where two topographical regions meet. The varied landscape is both pleasing to the eye and rich in ecological diversity. That's what you'll find where the parallel Duck and Elk Rivers and their feeder streams have carved Central Basin valleys out of the Highland Rim, producing a mix of hills and valleys that is some of Tennessee's handsomest country. A leisurely zigzag here leads to quaint Victorian railroad towns, waterfalls crashing into laurel-lined gorges, the birthplace of the Tennessee Walking Horse, and the quiet hollow where some of the world's best whiskey is made. Realizing that they have a good thing to show off, boosters have put together **Tennessee Backroads Heritage** to promote tourism and give guidance to visitors. Call them at 800-799-6131.

◆ HOOVER'S GAP   *map page 207, D-3*

Start your ramble at I-24 exit 67 where the interstate and US-41 squeeze through the steep ridges separating the watersheds of the Cumberland and Tennessee Rivers. The Confederate flag fluttering atop the little hill signals **Beech Grove Cemetery.** The dead buried here lost their lives in a small but important June 1863 battle that started what has come to be called the Tullahoma Campaign. In just eleven days, and with hardly any casualties, the Federal army maneuvered the Confederate army out of Middle Tennessee all the way to Chattanooga. Though overshadowed at the time and ever since by concurrent events at Gettysburg and Vicksburg, the campaign was a turning point in the Civil War.

The retreating Southerners hastily buried their dead in shallow graves in the fields where they fell. When veterans from this area returned after the war, they moved the remains to the pioneer cemetery. This is believed to be the nation's first Confederate cemetery. The marble markers in neat rows each have chiseled the

*Ralph W. Earl painted this Middle Tennessee scene of the Cumberland River in 1823.
(Museum of Early Southern Decorative Arts, Winston-Salem, North Carolina)*

MIDDLE
TENNESSEE

same sad inscription: "Unknown Confederate Soldier." You'll notice a sign marking the Tullahoma Campaign Trail. Pamphlets for a tour of the campaign can be
obtained from Tennessee Backroads Heritage.

◆ **WALKING HORSE COUNTRY**   *map page 207, D-3*

If you're fortunate enough to be here in early spring, you'll enjoy the clusters
of daffodils along the road to **Bell Buckle,** a likeable Victorian railroad town that
has revived itself by converting its commercial row into businesses geared toward
visitors—crafts and antique shops, a book store, and a country café that hosts a
live radio show on Saturday afternoons. The leafy campus on the edge of town is
Webb School. Sawney Webb, its founder, relocated the school here in 1886 to get
away from the saloons near its previous location. The school is the site of a juried
arts-and-crafts show each October, one of several annual events that bring out-
siders to Bell Buckle.

Wartrace, another railroad town just down the road, brags about being the "Cradle of the Tennessee Walking Horse," the distinct breed noted for its gentle temperament and smooth ride. It evolved as a utility horse that did not wear out riders in these steep hills. In the early 1930s, horse trainer Floyd Carothers and his wife, Olive, bought the 1917 hotel that faces the railroad. In meetings at the hotel, Carothers, Albert Dement, and Harry Davis conceived the idea for a walking horse show. The first one was in 1939, and Strolling Jim, trained by Carothers behind the hotel, was named the first grand champion. (Strolling Jim is buried on the hotel grounds.)

The ten-day **Tennessee Walking Horse National Celebration** at nearby Shelbyville has been going strong ever since. It regularly draws 250,000 visitors. If you'd like to get into walking horses even more, visit one of the farms on the list you can get at the Chamber of Commerce; 931-684-3482.

Gov. Prentice Cooper rides Tennessee's first walking horse champion, Strolling Jim, in 1938. (courtesy of Mrs. Prentice Cooper)

To stay on a 230-acre working farm in the lush, rolling countryside, consider the spacious **Parish Patch Farm & Inn** at 1100 Cortner Road near Normandy. Its **Cortner Mill** restaurant is located a mile away on the same property and occupies an old mill on the Duck River; 931-857-3017.

◆ OAK BARRENS   *map page 207, D-3*

The edge of the Highland Rim *(see map page 16)* is covered with a shallow-soiled, swampy forest the pioneers called the Oak Barrens. Where streams fall off the Rim into the Central Basin there are some splendid natural areas worth a stop. Just outside Manchester is **Old Stone Fort State Archaeological Park.** Arrive in mid-April, and you'll swear there's just been a snowstorm. That's how thick the dogwood is. The park's centerpiece is an earthen and rock wall, built over 500 years from A.D. 80 to 550 that encloses a plateau between two forks of the Duck River. Anthropologists tell us that it was really not a fort.

The falls of Duck River in the Old Stone Fort State Archaeological Park.

It was a ceremonial site used by people of the Woodland period, which lasted from about 2,300 to 1,100 years ago. In the park's magnificent natural setting hiking trails run along small gorges through which streams crash in a series of waterfalls. There is a nice little museum showcasing both prehistoric and historic Native American cultures. US-41 North; 931-723-5073.

Rutledge Falls is off the old road between Manchester and Tullahoma, next to a grassy oasis in the Barrens and marked by a lovely little Gothic Revival church. It's a loud, broad stair-step cascade that takes the creek into a small gorge fringed in mountain laurel. Closer to Tullahoma is the **Short Springs State Natural Area,** oddly marked by a huge unnatural water tower. Sparkling creeks tumble off the Highland Rim in several falls, and trails weave in and out of one of the most dazzling displays of wildflowers found anywhere.

Tullahoma, on the high point between the Duck and Elk Rivers' watersheds, got its start in the 1850s as a construction camp on the Nashville & Chattanooga Railroad. The collection of richly decorated Victorian houses facing the railroad gives evidence of the town's post–Civil War prosperity. Charming **Holly Berry Inn** at 302 N. Atlantic Street sits along the row of well-tended Victorian houses facing the tracks; 931-455-4445. **Ledford Mill**—an 1884 gristmill converted into a restful inn—is set in the hollow where Shipman's Creek tumbles off the Highland Rim; on Ledford Mill Road; 931-455-2546.

Middle Tennesse wildlife: A harmless rough green snake (top) winds around an azalea branch; and (right) a rare luna moth, with a wingspan of about three inches, rests on a pin oak leaf.

The city is best known as the home of the U. S. Air Force's **Arnold Engineering Development Center,** the world's most advanced and largest flight simulation facility. President Harry S. Truman in 1951 dedicated the center, named for Gen. Henry H. "Hap" Arnold, commander of America's air forces in World War II. For tours, call 931-454-5655.

Local places to enjoy a meal include **Daddy Billy's,** a rustic pub serving sandwiches, soups, salads, and a good assortment of beers to the sound of fast freights rumbling past. And at the **Downtown Café** you can pick up the latest gossip and home cooking "Where People Meet to Eat." Located at 119 N. Jackson Street.

◆ LYNCHBURG   *map page 207, C/D-4*

The highway lined with tall pines leads to one of Tennessee's most celebrated landmarks, the **Jack Daniel's Distillery.** It's right where it was in 1866 when Jack Daniel registered it as the nation's first government-registered distillery. You've no doubt seen the ads that portray the distillery and its environs as a folksy place

(above) The original office of Jack Daniel himself, in Lynchburg.

(opposite) The cupola of the Lynchburg Courthouse, built circa 1885.

where ole boys make whiskey the way they always have. Well, it's true. The whiskey is made just like it's always been, right here in this little hollow. You'll learn on the hour-long tour that Jack Daniel's is *not* bourbon. It's Tennessee Whiskey, the product of a unique charcoal mellowing process. Tours from 9–4:30. Follow the signs; 931-759-6180.

The square surrounding the 1885 Courthouse in tiny, well-kept Lynchburg houses tourist businesses now, selling both the tasteful and the tacky. The interior of the Hardware & General Store is the real thing, a well-preserved store from the turn of the last century.

Jack Daniel used to dine at **Miss Mary Bobo's Boarding House** and his distillery now owns this venerable institution. Fried chicken, fresh vegetables, cornbread, biscuits, and other Southern-style food served family style are the best you'll find anywhere. Located on Main Street. Call first, 931-759-7394, as reservations are a must.

To enjoy the peace and quiet of this small town in a cozy 1877 house within walking distance of Jack Daniel's Distillery, stay at the **Lynchburg Bed & Breakfast** on Mechanic Street; 931-759-7158.

◆ FAYETTEVILLE   *map page 207, C-4*

The road from Lynchburg follows the fertile valley of Mulberry Creek past several stately mansions before reaching the Elk River town of Fayetteville. You'll enter on broad, tree-shaded Mulberry Street, lined with one glorious house after another, and soon come to the courthouse square. It's a long way from Fayetteville to the nearest mall. It shows. The square hums with business. This is a place where kids still ride their bikes to town for an ice cream cone.

Local people eat out at **Cahoots** at 114 W. Market Street, located in what was in 1867 the city jail; and they put up their friends at **Bagley House,** an elegant Victorian inn with antique-furnished rooms set on 13 acres. It was once home to Warren Bagley, who invented the panoramic camera. 1801 Winchester Highway, (US-64); 931-433-3799.

MIDDLE TENNESSEE

■ SUMNER COUNTY   *map page 207, C-1*

Like Maury County south of Nashville, Sumner County to the north is noted for its historic houses. Not the columned mansions of the antebellum period, but homes built by first generation Tennesseans during the frontier period. A day or less is all you need to enjoy the simple elegance of the grandest houses built on America's immediate post-Revolutionary frontier.

◆ MANSKER STATION FRONTIER LIFE CENTER   *map page 207, C-1*

One of the forts the Cumberland settlers built for protection has been reconstructed in **Goodlettsville's Moss-Wright Park,** a large expanse of green along a shimmering creek that's the boundary between the region's first two counties. Mansker Station Frontier Life Center, as the name suggests, is more than a hand-hewn reconstructed stockaded fort, accurate in every detail. It's a living history museum. At periodic camps and at the 18th Century Colonial Fair each May, men in tri-cornered hats and knee britches are splitting rails, doing blacksmith work and carpentry while women in full-length dresses weave and cook and wash over open fires. It's crowded, noisy, muddy, and smelly, just like it must have been in the 1700s when it was crammed with men, women, children, pigs, cows, chickens, and who knows what else.

Legend has it that Kasper Mansker was born to German parents on the ship that brought them to the New World. He was one of the "long hunters" who ventured into the wilderness from the fringe of colonial America before 1779. ("Long hunters" would stay away for long periods, often months—hence their name.) They took back stories of the uninhabited Eden west of the Appalachians that tantalized future settlers. The station presided over by Kasper and Elizabeth White Mansker was one of the most important on the frontier. It held a crude inn, or tavern, copied in the reconstruction, where the weary slept two or three to a bed or on bear or deer skins on the rough floor. The station hosted travelers as well as newly arrived settlers seeking shelter before they built their own houses. Andrew Jackson stayed for awhile at Mansker's. Caldwell Drive off Long Hollow Pike (TN-174); 615-859-3678.

Bowen-Campbell House, completed in 1787, was built almost entirely of local materials.

◆ BOWEN-CAMPBELL HOUSE   *map page 207, C-1*

This house shares the park with the fort. It was completed by Virginia natives William and Mary Russell Bowen in 1787. It may not seem like much by today's standards, a plain two-story, one-room-deep brick house, but on the frontier, it was a mansion. The glass was hauled on horseback from Lexington, Kentucky, the hardware from Pennsylvania. Other than that, everything used in the construction came from the place. The costumed guide offers insight into the way people lived in those days. It wasn't easy, even for the well-to-do. Caldwell Drive off Long Hollow Pike (TN-174); 615-859-3678.

◆ ROCK CASTLE   *map page 207, C-1*

The orderly layers of hand-cut limestone blocks—no two are the same—are as straight now as they were when they were laid by some of the same craftsmen who built the Bowens' house. That's because the builders dug through five feet of soil to rest them on bedrock. Rock Castle was a house of monumental proportions for its day. The beautiful black walnut trim of the interior, in the study in particular, is so refined that it's difficult to conceive how it was produced in this remote wilderness.

The man who worked here was Daniel Smith. A Virginian, he was a renowned surveyor responsible for setting the Virginia–North Carolina boundary west of the Appalachians, what today is the Kentucky-Tennessee line. He took for his compensation land in the Cumberland country and moved his family here in 1784. Few people contributed as much to Tennessee's early development as Daniel Smith. He was one of the trustees who laid out the new town of Nashville; a charter trustee of Davidson Academy, the region's first school; secretary of the Southwest Territory, appointed by President George Washington; chairman of the committee that drafted Tennessee's first constitution; a United States senator; and a general in the militia. No wonder Thomas Jefferson said of him, "For intelligence, well-cultivated talents, for integrity, and usefulness, in soundness of judgment . . . he was equaled by few men." All these duties took Smith away from

Hank and three of his friends hang out in Orlinda, Robertson County.

Rock Castle, so it was his wife, Sara, who oversaw the house's construction that was finished around 1795. Off Indian Lake Road South off US-31A in Hendersonville; 615-824-0502.

◆ CRAGFONT   *map page 207, C/D-1*

Cragfont is the grandest of the pioneer homes. Perched atop a bluff and visible for miles when the leaves are down, Gen. James Winchester's monumental stone house feels like a mansion, even by today's standards. The veteran officer of George Washington's army had the resources to bring stone masons, carpenters, and joiners all the way from his native Maryland to work on the house. Construction started in 1798. The exquisite interior is full of Federal-period furnishings, including many pieces from the Winchester family. Off TN-25 east of Gallatin; 615-452-7070.

◆ BLEDSOE'S FORT HISTORICAL PARK   *map page 207, C/D-1*

Just up the road from Cragfont is Bledsoe's Fort on the site of Isaac Bledsoe's station. Isaac had visited the spot on a hunting expedition in 1772 and chose it for his home when he came for good. He and his brother Anthony were both prominent men on the Cumberland frontier. Both lost their lives in Indian attacks. Now that you've seen how the frontier elite lived, you can see here how most people lived. Nathaniel Parker's 1784 log cabin is a typical family home. The stone cottage, though just as small, is not typical. It looks like something from Ireland. That's because it was built by Irishman Hugh Rogan, probably around 1798. The path that wanders through the woods, carpeted in early spring with periwinkle and spring beauty, includes a stretch of the Cumberland Road, or Avery Trace, the first road directly linking the Cumberland settlements to distant East Tennessee. TN-25 east of Gallatin.

◆ WYNNEWOOD   *map page 207, D-1*

This is the last stop on your Cumberland frontier tour. It sits on a slope below some tall cedars that are probably as old as the house itself. The national historic landmark, the largest log structure in Tennessee, dates from just after the frontier period, to 1828, when it was opened as a stagecoach inn. Its generous kitchen has a huge assortment of 19th-century cooking implements. It's a challenge to figure out their uses. Old TN-25 in Castalian Springs, east of Gallatin; 615-452-5463.

■ CLARKSVILLE   *map page 207, B-1*

Clarksville is the city tobacco built. It's in the Black Patch, the area straddling the Tennessee-Kentucky line that produces most of the world's dark-fired tobacco, the kind that goes into chewing tobacco and snuff. The tobacco wealth's legacy is the collection of architectural gems in Clarksville's historic heart. Fortunately, the brightest gem was hardly touched by the rare winter tornado that hit town in 1999.

The old **Federal Building and Customs House** is one of the most flamboyant buildings in Tennessee. Completed in 1898, it served as a post office and as the customs house for the tobacco export business. The slate-roofed building is jazzed up with steep gabled dormers, decorative terra cotta around all the openings, arched windows, and copper eagles perched on each corner of the roof. The building is now incorporated into the **Customs House Museum and Cultural Center,** which combines permanent historic and art exhibits with interactive science and history exhibits to delight children. 200 S. Second Street; 931-648-5780.

The Customs House Museum and Cultural Center in Clarksville.

Wilma Rudolph runs for the gold in the 100-meter race during the Rome 1960 Olympics. (photo by Jerry Cooke for Sports Illustrated)

About a quarter-mile away at the southern end of the Cumberland River-Walk you'll find a statue of one of Clarksville's most famous citizens, Wilma Rudolph. Stricken with polio as a child and in braces until she was ten, Rudolph didn't just overcome her disability and learn to walk. She became one of the most celebrated runners in history. She was a member of the Tennessee State University "Tigerbelles" who together won a total of 23 Olympic medals. Rudolph herself won three gold medals at

the 1960 Rome Olympics. College Street and Riverside Drive; 931-645-7476.

In Clarksville's downtown historic district, **Blackhorse Pub & Brewery** is known for its fancy antique bar. Hand-crafted beer complements a menu of salads, sandwiches, pasta, and gourmet pizza (134 Franklin). **Red's Bakery** at 101 Riverside Drive serves hot cobblers, pies, cakes, and pastries. **Rose Garden Tea Room** offers outstanding breakfast and tea room fare in a warm but over-decorated 1886 Victorian mansion at 512 Madison Street.

Phila Hach prepares Thanksgiving dinner for her guests. (courtesy of Hachland Hill Inn)

MIDDLE TENNESSEE

In the woods outside Clarksville you'll find the **Hachland Hill Inn,** run by a noted chef and author, Phila Hach. Located at 5396 Rawlings Road; 931-647-4084. The inn includes three cedar log cottages. Southern favorites come from the kitchen, and some international dishes do as well.

◆ DRIVING THROUGH CLUTTER TO THE COUNTRYSIDE

To get out of Clarksville you'll have to navigate miles of auto-dominated commercial clutter, fueled by the payroll from nearby **Fort Campbell,** home of the Army's 101st Airborne Division. For tours, call 270-798-3215.

Once through it, you'll find a delightful countryside. Notice that about every third building is a tall barn, often painted dark red or black, with some sawmill slabs piled next to it. This is where tobacco is smoke-cured. The lush farmland between Clarksville and Springfield is particularly beautiful, especially the acreage that was part of the plantation started by Joseph Washington. He migrated here in 1796, the year his cousin George signed the bill making Tennessee a state. You'll find those lands south of Adams and Cedar Hill.

■ DOVER   *map page 207, A-1*

Sitting atop a Cumberland River cliff—which accounts for its name—Dover was once a thriving river port where products were shipped from the massive Cumberland Iron Works. It's a sleepy little place today, known mostly as a gateway to the Land Between the Lakes and for Fort Donelson National Battlefield.

◆ FORT DONELSON NATIONAL BATTLEFIELD   *map page 207, A-1*

Like so many battlefields, Fort Donelson is a lovely place, a patchwork of field and forest overlooking a wildlife area rich in waterfowl and other birds. The events here in February 1862, early in the Civil War, proved crucial to its ultimate outcome. Federal land and water forces under the previously unknown Gen. Ulysses S. Grant—who at Dover earned the nickname "Unconditional Surrender"— opened the Cumberland as a path into the heart of the Confederacy. Grant eventually commanded all U. S. forces and was elected president after the war. You can take a driving tour to most of the battle sites, including the Dover Hotel where

Confederate winter quarters at Fort Donelson.

Grant accepted the surrender from his old friend, Simon Bolivar Buckner. And you can take a hike through the meadows and into the deep oak-hickory forest that's rich with spring wildflowers. US-79 west of Dover; 931-232-5706.

■ UPPER CUMBERLAND   *page 207, D&E-1&2*

When Tennesseans speak of the Upper Cumberland, they usually refer to the counties in the Cumberland River watershed upstream from Carthage. It includes much of the Cumberland Plateau but also takes in the Eastern Highland Rim that spreads out beneath the Plateau's jagged western escarpment.

The main attractions are twin lakes created by dams on Cumberland tributaries, **Center Hill Lake** *(map page 207, D-2)* on the Caney Fork and **Dale Hollow** on the Obey *(map page 207, E & F-1)*. Their clear, blue waters lap against a combined thousand miles of shoreline in rugged, hardwood-covered hills.

Two of the most dramatic waterfalls in the state are just above Center Hill's slack water. At **Burgess Falls State Natural Area** *(map page 207, E-2)*, near Cookeville, the 130-foot stair step fall for which it's named is arguably the most beautiful in a region blessed with a multitude of beautiful falls. And it's only one of several in the mile-long stretch of the Falling Water River. At **Rock Island State Park** near McMinnville, the Caney Fork plunges through a 200-foot-deep gorge in a series of cascades.

❖

In the 1890s, textile magnate Clay Faulkner enticed his wife to move out from the town of McMinnville by building one of the region's grandest Queen Anne–style mansions. **Falcon Manor** is now an inn with lavish Victorian furnishings; located at 2645 Faulkner Springs Road, McMinnville; 931-668-4444.

The unusual stair-step fall at Burgess Falls State Natural Area.

WEST TENNESSEE

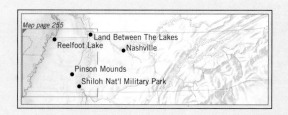

Map page 255

Land Between The Lakes
Reelfoot Lake
Nashville
Pinson Mounds
Shiloh Nat'l Military Park

◆ **AREA OVERVIEW**

Travel Basics: West Tennessee is the end of the state between the western Tennessee River Valley and the Mississippi River. Most of the region lies within the Gulf Coastal Plain, giving its landscape and its culture the flavor of the Deep South. No tall ridges, deep valleys, or swift streams. You'll find instead faintly sloping fields lined in neat rows of cotton, soybeans, and corn, and lazy rivers weaving through swampy bottoms. There are quaint southern towns, but almost no contrived tourist attractions, and not much sprawl. So while the region may not be what people expect to see in Tennessee, a good case can be made that West Tennessee is the most bona fide slice of the Volunteer State.

Getting Around: The major highways crisscross the region along routes of the railroads that shaped its development. The pace tends to be slow on the abundant back roads. Sooner or later you'll end up behind a piece of farm machinery taking its own sweet time. No roads run along the two big rivers, the Tennessee and the Mississippi, so getting to points of interest along their banks takes some doing.

WEST TENNESSEE

Climate: Tennesseans keep an eye on the West Tennessee weather. Most weather systems move into this long skinny state from the west. Between March and May severe thunderstorms occasionally occur. With its lower elevation, the Weststate is slightly warmer than the rest of Tennessee, with average summer maximums in the low 90s. Cold weather is a possibility from October through April but temperatures average in the low to mid 50s.

Food & Lodging: West Tennesseans love barbecue and catfish. You can't travel far without passing a barbecue joint, either a roadside shanty or a full-service restaurant. Catfish, rolled in cornmeal and deep fried, is a staple on the ubiquitous Southern-style buffets. Lodging options are thin except along I-40 and the main roads. Tourism boosters provide information on the refreshingly old-fashioned yet modern fishing camps and resorts on Kentucky Lake, 731-642-9955; and Reelfoot Lake, 731-253-2007.

*Photographer Joseph Allen (right) with a friend after
a successful fishing excursion on Reelfoot Lake.*

■ A DIFFERENT TENNESSEE

"Rural West" is how Middle and East Tennesseans often refer to the western end of the state outside greater Memphis. If you hear them say it's all flat and boring, that's a giveaway that they haven't studied it too closely. Most likely only from their windshields whizzing to and from Memphis on I-40. West Tennessee's treasures may not be as obvious or as arresting as those elsewhere in Tennessee, but they're there. Take, for example, the Wolf River along the Mississippi border. It's slow and meandering, drifting quietly in and out of cypress swamps and sliding effortlessly between beds of water lilies. So quiet, so still. Not even remotely like the rushing streams in the eastern two-thirds of the state. But no less intriguing. The region's culture is still firmly planted in the soil. Most every county has an annual festival celebrating a favorite crop—cotton, tomato, strawberry, peach, forest products—or a "World's Biggest" something—fish fry, barbecue, coon hunt. Every event crowns a "Miss" whatever. Beauty pageants are big deals in West Tennessee. Miss Tennessee is crowned each year in Jackson.

■ KENTUCKY LAKE PRESERVES *map page 255, E-1&2*

When the TVA strayed into Kentucky in the 1940s to plug the Tennessee River with concrete, it created what was then the world's largest reservoir. The lake and public lands along its 2,300-mile shoreline offer unlimited fishing, sailing, hiking, hunting, bird watching, cycling—just about every form of outdoor recreation except downhill skiing. **Land Between the Lakes** is the huge national recreation area named for the peninsula between Kentucky Lake and Lake Barkley. The open, grassy prairies that once dotted Tennessee have been replicated and are home to bison and elk.

It's not all fun and games at LBL. Homeplace 1850 is a collection of sixteen restored log structures where workers in period dress go about the daily grind of farming, cooking, weaving, sewing, and other tasks necessary to survive on a family farm in the mid-19th century. Park information: 931-232-6457.

◆ STATE PARKS *map page 255, E-1*

Paris Landing State Park is beautifully sited overlooking the widest part of Kentucky Lake, where the Big Sandy embayment meets the main stem on the Tennessee. The point between the two stems is one of three units of the Tennessee

The Wolf River winds through cypress swamps along the Mississippi border.

National Wildlife Refuge, which each winter hosts 150,000 ducks and 75,000 geese. **Paris Landing Inn,** a modern hotel-restaurant in the state park enjoys a world-class setting overlooking Kentucky Lake. US-79; 800-250-8614.

Two state parks on either side of the lake, **Nathan Bedford Forrest** on the west and **Johnsonville** on the east, result from one the Civil War's oddest battles, the November 4, 1864 duel between Forrest's Confederate cavalry and the Union navy, the only cavalry versus navy engagement of the war. From atop Pilot Knob on the Tennessee River's west bank, Forrest's gunners destroyed the huge Johnsonville supply depot. 731-584-6356.

Further upstream, two rustic preserves are noted for their spring wildflowers and bluff-top views of wintering ducks and geese. **Lady Finger Bluff** is a TVA area and **Mousetail Landing** is a state park.

■ SHILOH NATIONAL MILITARY PARK   *map page 255, D/E-4*

It's a lovely place to be in April, the rolling plain west of the Tennessee River. Its canopy of oaks, light green with spring's delicate new growth, is broken by grassy openings fringed in the white of dogwoods. Fallen peach blossoms give the appearance of pink snow on the warming ground.

This setting for the Shiloh National Military Park renders the carnage of April 1862 even more incomprehensible. You'll learn at the visitor center that the iron markers describing the events are coded by shape and color to make it easier to tell what happened. It's still not easy. As you drive, walk, or bike the gentle roads, you'll see that

most of the fighting was not in fields, but in the tangle of woods, creeks, and bogs. As you penetrate the woods searching for one of the 475 iron markers or 152 monuments, try to imagine a hundred thousand men fighting here for two long days. Information: 731-689-5696.

Civil War re-enactors at Shiloh National Military Park.

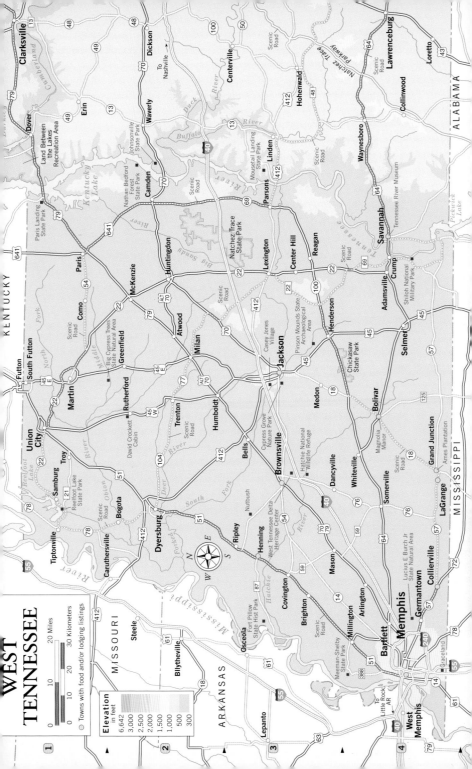

SHILOH: CREEKS TURNED RED

It's a lovely name, Shiloh, said to be Hebrew for "place of peace." It was anything but that in April 1862. More Americans died in two days of fighting than in all the wars in the history of the country to date. The carnage of this early battle shocked the nation— or two nations, depending on your perspective— and brought home the grim reality about the War Between the States; it wasn't going to be over quickly, and it would touch the life of every American. No exceptions.

The little Methodist meeting house gave its name to history because it stood between two great armies, the Federals on the Tennessee River commanded by Maj. Gen. Ulysses S. Grant and the Confederates at the rail junction of Corinth under Gen. Albert Sydney Johnston. The Federals wanted Corinth, but Grant had orders to wait for reinforcements before he moved. The Confederates decided to get the jump, and on April 2 started what was to be a fast, one-day advance to attack the unsuspecting Yankees. The muddy march from Corinth moved painstakingly slow. It took the Southerners three days to get in position to hit Grant's Federals. All the while, Federal reinforcements under Don Carlos Buell were getting closer and closer.

The Confederate attack at dawn on April 6 completely surprised the Union troops, overrunning their camps and pushing them nearly to the river. Johnston confidently proclaimed: "Tonight we will water our horses in the Tennessee River." A bullet that entered Johnston's leg behind the knee was masked by his boot, and it wasn't until he became weak from the loss of blood that he realized he'd been hit. A simple tourniquet might have saved his life, but Johnston had sent his surgeon to tend to wounded Federal prisoners. Within thirty minutes, the Confederacy's senior field leader was dead.

The thick woods were that night filled with unspeakable horrors, as thousands of dead and dying men lay helplessly about in a driving rain. A Mississippi private described what he saw:

> Vivid flashes of lightning rent the heavens and . . . sickening sights fell before my eyes… I saw a large piece of ground literally covered with dead heaped and piled upon each other. I shut my eyes upon the sickening sight…

It looked at the end of the day as if a complete Confederate victory was within reach. Gen. P. G. T. Beauregard, who took over from Johnston, wired Richmond that the Confederates had "gained a complete victory." Grant, though, didn't see it that way. Buell's troops arrived overnight, and the next morning, April 7, the Federals counterattacked. As they pushed harder and harder, chaos in the Confederate ranks went from bad to worse until Beauregard concluded it was time to return to Corinth. The North had won a stunning victory. But at a horrific cost. Death played no favorites at Shiloh, as mothers and wives on both sides would never again lay eyes on the more than 3,500 men and boys killed outright and many of the 17,000 wounded who never made it home.

*Union Infantry defend an artillery battery during
the Battle of Shiloh. (Library of Congress)*

STANLEY AT SHILOH

Born in Wales and nurtured in a workhouse, Henry Morton Stanley survived near disasters at sea and a stint in the Confederate army before being hired by the New York Herald Tribune in 1871 to search for a English explorer in Africa. Meeting this man at Ujiji, Stanley uttered the famous words, "Dr. Livingstone, I presume." Below, Stanley describes events in April of 1862, when he participated in the battle of Shiloh.

*A*s I moved horror-stricken, through the fearful shambles, where the dead lay as thick as the sleepers in a London park on a Bank Holiday, I was unable to resist the belief that my education had been in abstract things, which had no relation to our animal existence. For, if human life is so disparaged, what has it to do with such high subjects as God, Heaven, and Immortality? And to think how devotional men and women pretended to be, on a Sunday! Oh, cunning, cruel man! He knew that the sum of all real knowledge and effort was to know how to kill and mangle his brothers, as we were doing to-day! Reflecting on my own emotions, I wondered if other youths would feel that they had been deluded like myself with man's fine polemics and names of things, which vanished with the reality.

I overtook my regiment about one o'clock, and found that it was engaged in one of those occasional spurts of fury. The enemy resolutely maintained their ground, and our side was preparing for another assault. The firing was alternately brisk and slack. We lay down, and availed ourselves of trees, logs, and hollows, and annoyed their upstanding ranks; battery pounded battery, and meanwhile, we hugged our resting places closely. Of a sudden, we rose and raced towards the position, and took it by sheer weight and impetuosity, as we had done before. About three o'clock, the battle grew very hot. The enemy appeared to be more concentrated, and immovably sullen. Both sides fired better as they grew more accustomed to the din; but, with assistance from the reserves, we were continually pressing them towards the river Tennessee, without ever retreating an inch.

—Sir Henry Morton Stanley, *Autobiography,*
describing events in 1862, published in 1937

■ SAVANNAH   *map page 255, E-4*

Near Shiloh lies the quaint river town of Savannah. Glance to the left from the bridge leading into town for a glimpse of the columned Cherry Mansion standing watch over the Tennessee River. Grant stayed here with its Union-sympathizing owners—Savannah was overwhelmingly pro-Union—and spent a quiet night on April 5 before the roar of guns drew him to the field.

Savannah's **Tennessee River Museum** has exhibits on paleontology, archaeology, steamboats, and the Civil War; 731-925-2364. Down the road 12 miles at Pickwick Landing State Park, you can golf, fish, or just relax.

Early photos of Savannah and prints of Tennessee River steamboats decorate **Woody's**, a brick and paneled down-home eatery at 705 Main Street. The good food here is fancier than you'd expect. **Hagy's Catfish Hotel** just off TN-22 is not a place where fish sleep, but a celebrated family-style restaurant on the banks of the Tennessee River with special catfish dishes.

■ COTTON KINGDOM

West Tennessee's Deep South character is strongest where cotton was once king, in the Delta country that forms a broad crescent around Memphis. The remnants of bygone days, when the toil of many created wealth for the privileged few, are the historic districts filled with remarkable town houses in all the styles that were important in the 19th century. The towns are linked by roads that are often nothing more than ribbons of asphalt through the rolling fields. Now and then they'll dip through tunnels of overhanging oaks to cross hardwood-filled bottoms. Come here in the fall, and you'll be put off by the roadside litter. Take a closer look. It's actually cotton that's blown off wagons hauling it to the gin.

Picking cotton in West Tennessee, circa 1890.
(Tennessee State Library and Archives)

◆ COLLIERVILLE   *map page 255, B-4*

Characterless suburbia may be closing in on leafy Collierville, but its perfectly charming heart retains the ambiance of a prosperous post–Civil War railroad town. Three rows of redbrick buildings filled with antique and gift shops surround the shady plaza, which is dotted with comfortable benches that demand that you sit a spell. The square's fourth side is taken up by the 1902 depot and cars and locomotives of the **Memphis Transportation Museum.**

Refreshment is available in an old-time drugstore building and an old-time church. The one-time drugstore, now called the **Silver Caboose** (132 E. Mulberry Street), serves sandwiches, salads, and daily specials that include pot pies, as well as sumptuous desserts and ice cream specialities from the fountain. Excellent tea room fare is to be had at the **White Church,** a combination antique shop-and-restaurant housed in an 1873 Gothic Revival building at Poplar and Main.

◆ **LaGrange**   *map page 255, C-4*

Route 57 heads straight east from Collierville paralleling the swampy, mysterious-looking Wolf River—one stretch is even called Ghost River—to one of the region's oldest and best-preserved towns. LaGrange is so quiet it's spooky. After a spring shower, all you'll hear is the drip-drip-drip of rain falling from the massive oaks on spacious lawns. They're from the days when LaGrange was an important cotton processing and trade center with a population many times today's. War, storms, epidemics, fire, and financial downturns have reduced LaGrange's importance, but not its charm.

Walking the peaceful streets you'll come upon the home of the woman given the lofty title, "Queen of the Confederacy." She was Lucy Holcombe when she grew up in the private home now marked with the historic marker. As Mrs.

A cabin and flower gardens in LaGrange.

Francis W. Pickens, First Lady of South Carolina, her captivating personality and good looks got her likeness on Confederate money. Before the Civil War, Mr. Pickens was ambassador to Russia, where the couple's first child was born Olga Neva Francesca Eugenia Dorothea Pickens. The Czar and Czarina were her godparents and faithfully kept up with "Douschka" (Little Darling), the name by which she was always known.

◆ GRAND JUNCTION AND BIRD DOGS   *map page 255, C-4*

Bird hunters know this somnolent town at the crossing of two railroads. The **National Field Trial Championship** for pointing dogs is held here each February. The hearts of dog lovers are warmed by a visit to the **National Bird Dog Museum** with its resplendent portraits of pointing dogs, spaniels, and retrievers; 731-764-2058. The field trials are held outside town at **Ames Plantation,** nearly 20,000 acres of field and forest acquired around 1900 by Hobart Ames, the New England industrialist and avid bird hunter. It's owned now by a foundation bearing his name and is managed as an agricultural experiment station by the University of Tennessee. You can observe research on the propagation of bobwhite quails, artificial insemination in swine, and fescue fungus, but most folks visit Ames Plantation to see the baronial 1847 mansion and the reconstructed 19th-century farmstead around it.

◆ BOLIVAR   *map page 255, C-4*

When this county seat was laid out in 1824, it was named for Simon Bolivar, the South American liberator. His bust on the grounds of the ornate 1868 Italianate-style courthouse is a gift from the people of Venezuela. The courthouse was supposedly built with funds secured after the Civil War by Ulysses S. Grant, whose troops burned the earlier one. Bolivar's maple- and oak-draped streets show off well-tended houses in a variety of 19th- and early-20th-century styles, including a massive 1856 Tuscan Villa. In the middle of town is **McNulty's Wood,** a rare patch of virgin forest that's a national natural landmark.

To experience elegant Southern lodging in an 1849 town house in the historic district, try **Magnolia Manor** at 418 N. Main Street; 731-658-6700. The stairway still has a mark made by General Sherman with his sword after General Grant chastised him for intemperate remarks to their hostess.

*The monument to Simon Bolivar in front of the town's courthouse
was a gift from the people of Venezuela.*

SIMON
BOLIVAR

FROM THE GOVERNMENT
AND THE PEOPLE OF
THE REPUBLIC OF VENEZUELA
AND THE PARTNERS
FOR THE AMERICAS
VENEZUELA-TENNESSEE
TO THE CITY OF BOLIVAR
ON THE CELEBRATION
OF THE BICENTENNIAL
OF THE BIRTH OF
THE LIBERATOR
1783 · 1983

◆ JACKSON   *map page 255, D-3*

This sprawl-enveloped city, the region's de facto capital, grew up as a railroad hub, with more lines radiating out of it than any place in Tennessee except Memphis.

NC&StL Depot

If you're old enough to recall boarding a passenger train to the call of "all aboard," the feel of the classic redbrick 1907 NC&St L Depot will be familiar. It's been converted into an excellent little railroad museum. 585 S. Royal Street; 731-425-8223.

Casey Jones Village

Casey Jones Village just off I-40 is a dab of Pigeon Forge–style hokum on the West Tennessee plain, complete with "shoppes" and miniature golf. At its center is the relo-cated house where the famed engineer was living when he made his last run. In the early morning hours of April 30, 1900, his train plowed into the rear of a disabled freight train, killing Casey, and providing the story for the song that gave "the brave engineer" a place in railroad lore; 800-748-9588.

Cypress Grove Nature Park

Before man "improved" West Tennessee by sawing the trees, draining the swamps, and straightening the rivers, much of it was in bottomland hardwood forests, wetlands dominated by majestic bald cypress trees. A handsome patch of it remains at Cypress

In the parlor of the Casey Jones Home, a portrait of the famous engineer rests on the piano.

WEST
TENNESSEE

Naturalist Joyce Hansen and "The Inspector," a great horned owl, go eyeball to eyeball in the Cypress Grove Nature Park.

Grove Nature Park on US-70 W. A seemingly endless boardwalk meanders beneath trees rising tall toward the sun, to a willow-draped pond, and to the Raptor Center. Birds of prey have their own giant cages that let you see them in their natural habitat. Looking through the plexiglas, you'll come face-to-face with a huge bald eagle showing off its giant talons and hooked beak. Don't worry, these eagles, hawks, and owls weren't kidnapped in the wild to be locked up here. They're all injured and need this protection. 731-425-8364.

Pinson Mounds State Archaeological Area   *map page 255, D-3*
South of Jackson off US-45 one of the nation's premier archaeological sites is protected at Pinson Mounds. The main attraction is a series of mounds dating from the Middle Woodland Period, 200 B.C.E. to A.D. 500. The informative museum, underground in a faux mound, offers a walk though Tennessee's prehistoric past and includes the 13,000-year-old remains of a Mastodon. Emerging from the museum's rear door, you gaze upon the second tallest mound in the United States, at 72 feet, and imagine how many baskets of dirt had to be hauled to build it. The park's trails include a boardwalk through a cypress bottom on the Forked Deer River like the one upstream at Cypress Grove. For information call 731-988-5614.

WEST TENNESSEE

◆ BROWNSVILLE AREA   *map page 255, C-3*

In the middle of the clutter around the TN-76/I-40 interchange, you'll find the welcoming **West Tennessee Delta Heritage Center.** It houses an instructive cotton museum where a "please touch" sign invites visitors to sense how the fiber progresses from the field to a useful product; 731-779-9000.

As if to emphasize the continuing importance of cotton around here, the road into town passes an implement dealer where shiny new mechanized cotton pickers are lined up as if they're anxious to get to work.

Brownsville's manicured **historic district** includes houses dating from the early 1820s when West Tennessee was settled. You might be surprised by what you'll find as you wander the shady sidewalks on the self-guided tour. Temple Adas Israel, the Reform Jewish temple built in 1882, is the oldest in the state. A member of the congregation in this unquestionably Deep South town, Morton Felsenthal, spent a lifetime studying Abraham Lincoln and collecting Lincoln books and memorabilia. They're displayed at the **College Hill Center,** an 1850s building that started as a girls school; 731-772-4883.

A cotton-picking machine works its way accross a field in West Tennessee circa 1910.
(Tennessee State Library and Archives)

West Tennessee and Memphis in particular are considered to be the hog heavens of barbecue.

Trying local barbecue is part of the Tennessee experience. **Backyard Bar-B-Q** offers plates and sandwiches of pulled pork, chicken, and beef brisket, as well as giant barbecue-stuffed potatoes. You'll find it at 703 E. Main Street.

❖

The Hatchie River is the only one in West Tennessee that hasn't been channelized, and much of the designated scenic river is within the **Hatchie National Wildlife Refuge** on the outskirts of Brownsville, 11,556 acres of mostly bottomland hardwood forest. TN-76 just south of I-40 *(map page 255, C-3)*; 731-772-0501.

❖

In **Mason,** 23 miles south of Brownsville, stop by **Bozo's Hot Pit Bar-B-Q.** It's been around since 1923, when it was started by Jefferson "Bozo" Williams. Its wood-paneled dining room has been one of West Tennessee's most famous barbecue joints, and it became even more so when Larry "Bozo the Clown" Harmon sued for trademark infringement. The local Bozo won. On US-70/79.

❖

Highway 19 between Brownsville and Ripley rolls through one of Tennessee's most famous places—made so by its famous native, Tina Turner, in her song "Nutbush City Limits." You won't find a city, just a wide place in the road, where the country store across from the cotton gin serves homemade plate lunches.

◆ HENNING   *map page 255, B-3*

This classic little railroad town faces what was the Illinois Central's Chicago–New Orleans main line, the steel highway that during the Great Migration of the 1920–30s carried countless black Southerners to northern cities and to the hope of a better life. Henning is best known as the place where a young Alex Haley heard stories from his elders about their African ancestors that led him to write *Roots,* his 1976 book that won a Pulitzer Prize and spawned a TV adaption that won 145 awards including nine Emmys. The substantial home of Haley's grandparents, where the writer lived as a boy, is now the **Alex Haley House and Museum.** The world-renowned author is buried here. 200 S. Church Street; 731-738-2240.

◆ FORT PILLOW STATE HISTORIC PARK   *map page 255, B-3*

Highway 87 aims west from Henning up and down hills that belie the notion that West Tennessee is all flat. The road is on its dead-end path to the Mississippi River and to **Fort Pillow State Historic Park,** scene of one of the Civil War's most controversial engagements. The Confederates built the fort on one of the Chickasaw Bluffs, but after mid-1862, it was occupied by the Federals. Nathan Bedford Forrest's Southern horsemen attacked it on April 12, 1864, inflicting heavy casualties, particularly on the black soldiers. Partisans have argued ever since over whether it was a massacre. Not much has happened here since the Civil War, and nature has reclaimed most of it in forest and wetland. It's a beautiful place. A bluff-top overlook lets you see how the mighty Mississippi has been unruly, changing its course and leaving pieces of Tennessee stranded on the opposite bank. Park information: 731-738-5581.

■ REELFOOT LAKE   *map page 255, B/C-1*

Isolated by a big bend in the Mississippi River in the sparsely populated northwest corner of Tennessee, this pristine lake is one of the state's natural wonders. It's literally alive with wildlife—54 species of fish, 53 mammals, 238 kinds of birds, and countless amphibians and reptiles. Each winter 60,000 geese and 250,000 ducks come for a visit, but the hundred or so bald eagles grab most of the attention that time of the year.

Reelfoot's tranquility offers no hint of its violent past. A series of earthquakes rocked mid-America in 1811–12, earthquakes scientists believe were the most severe ever in North America (not including Alaska). They created a depression in the cypress bottoms that filled with water from the nearby Mississippi River, which flowed backwards. The resulting 14-mile-long, four-mile-wide lake is shallow, with an average depth of 5.2 feet. Much of it is marsh bordered by dense stands of bald cypress growing out of the water. Reelfoot is managed by state and federal agencies, whose visitor centers are good places to begin your visit. Reelfoot Lake State Park is on TN-21/22 near Tiptonville; 731-253-9652. National Wildlife Refuge on TN-157 west of Union City; 731-538-2481.

Reelfoot is not a place you can experience driving by it. You'll need a closer look. You can get it from a pontoon boat on one of the naturalist-led cruises the state park offers from May through September. The graceful form of a snowy white egret flying against the deep green backdrop is a sight you'll not forget. Nor

Canoeing on isolated Reelfoot Lake.

WEST TENNESSEE

EAGLES COME TO TENNESSEE

Benjamin Franklin wanted the turkey. James Audubon agreed with him. Congress, however, saw it differently, and in 1782 adopted the bald eagle as our national symbol. Americans have revered these majestic birds ever since. When bald eagles mature at about age five, their heads and tails change from dark brown to white, giving them their unmistakable appearance. They're big creatures, with wingspans up to eight feet.

Bald eagles mate for life and nest now mostly around the Great Lakes, in Alaska, and in Canada. They feed on fish, and need ice-free water in winter. So they head south to Tennessee. Reelfoot Lake has one of the largest wintering bald eagle populations in America. They start arriving in late October and stay as late as early April, with peak populations in January and February.

Ravaged by habitat destruction and pesticides, our proud national symbol quit nesting in Tennessee in the 1960s. But they're back. Through a process called "hacking" started in 1983, eaglets of about eight weeks of age are placed in artificial nests, then released at about 12-14 weeks. Eagles tend to return to the same area to nest, so they started coming back to Tennessee, and now live at several lakes. Eight pairs live year round at Reelfoot Lake. Incidentally, help from private organizations has been essential in the bald eagle recovery. Dollywood, the Pigeon Forge theme park, has been a leader. The airlines helped, too, providing transportation for eaglets from Alaska and elsewhere for release in Tennessee.

Bald eagles are a sight to behold. As many as 130,000 visitors each January and February join the Reelfoot Lake State Park staff for the eagle tours. Reservations are essential; 731-253-7756.

are you likely to forget the huge cottonmouth wiggling past, head held high out of the water, in a channel barely wide enough for both the boat and the snake. Canoe trips are offered in the spring, and in December–March, there are tours to see the bald eagles. If you really want to experience Reelfoot up close, try spring's Heron Rookery Swamp Tromp. You'll wade through cypress knees to a large heron rookery. As for the cottonmouths, you'll just have to accept the naturalist's assurances that they won't bother you.

(previous pages) Bald cypress trees grow in the marshy areas of Reelfoot Lake.

To spend a night in nature, try reserving a lakeside room at the **Blue Basin Cove Bed & Breakfast** off TN-78; 731-253-9064. The food's good at **Boyette's** on TN-21/22. A local institution since 1921, it serves the best in catfish, crappie and country ham, along with white beans and slaw. For frog legs, catfish, crappie (in season), and country ham served family-style, try **Lakeview,** also on TN-21/22.

"Old Uncle Henry," a Reelfoot Lake commercial fisherman prepares one of his chicken wire fish traps in 1923. (Tennessee State Library and Archives)

M E M P H I S

Map page 285

◆ **HIGHLIGHTS** *page*

◆ **AREA OVERVIEW**

Travel Basics: Lacking Tennessee's signature features such as mountains, lakes, Civil War battlefields, and presidents' homes, Memphis makes up for it by throwing a party. Not just a party, but a year-round lineup of festivals and celebrations. Most center around music, as Memphis legitimately claims to have helped birth much of America's popular music. Other events focus on food. Memphis is the world's pork barbecue capital, and each May, home to the World Championship Barbecue Cooking Contest, the self-proclaimed Superbowl of Swine. And if there is an important exhibit making the rounds of the major art centers like New York and San Francisco, chances are that it will stop in Memphis, too. This is not to say that everything of interest is staged. You can visit the studio where Elvis cut his first record, tour Graceland, his home, and sample the music on Beale Street. Memphis has a memorable zoo, outstanding museums, and splendid parks.

Getting Around: Other Tennessee cities have fake trolleys. Memphis has real ones. They'll get you where you want to go Downtown. You'll need a car elsewhere in this

MEMPHIS

sprawling city that's a checkerboard of agreeable tree-shaded neighborhoods and un-appealing commercial clutter. Directional signs are well placed on the broad, level streets arranged in a grid, except for a few diagonal mavericks like Poplar and Lamar.

Climate: Spring and fall are long, moderate seasons, though the weather can get cold anytime from October through April. Winters are relatively mild with an average January low of 31 degrees and average high of 48. Summer's heat and humidity can be oppressive. July's average high hovers around 92 degrees and at night drops only into the low to mid 70s.

Food & Lodging: The creative chefs of Memphis serve some of the best food in Tennessee, with an emphasis on dishes fusing differing styles from around the world. The Bluff City dishes out the nation's best pork barbecue and some of its best ribs. There aren't too many interesting places to stay, however. The big exception is the Peabody Hotel, one of the grandest in the nation. If you can stand the tariff and the crowds, go for it. Several comfortable chain hotels crowd around the Peabody.

The Memphis skyline rises behind a model of the Mississippi Delta on Mud Island.

MEMPHIS

The earliest known painting of Memphis was completed by John H. B. Latrobe (son of architect Benjamin H. Latrobe) in 1832, after his Mississippi wedding. (New-York Historical Society)

■ REBOUND CITY

In his short story "The Captain's Son," Pulitzer Prize–winning author Peter Taylor describes a Memphis man who married into a Nashville family.

> *He* was what we in Nashville used to think of as the perfect Memphis type. Yet he was not really born in Memphis. He was raised and educated out there but he was born on a cotton plantation fifty miles below Memphis—in Mississippi, which, as anybody in Nashville will tell you, is actually worse.

These few lines speak volumes about the relationship between Memphis and the rest of Tennessee. Memphis may be Tennessee's largest city, but to most Tennesseans, it's "out there." It's wedged in the far corner of the giant parallelogram that is Tennessee and seems "utterly foreign," to borrow the phrase of one journalist. Memphis doesn't look, feel or act like anyplace else in Tennessee. Ask a Tennessean what they think of it, and you'll likely hear: "Memphis? The biggest town in Mississippi."

Given all that, you'd think Tennesseans would stay away. But they don't. Tennesseans may not stand out like the Japanese, the Germans, and the British who make the pilgrimage to the King's hometown. But Tennesseans come to Memphis. They come to have a good time. Memphis goes out of its way to make itself fun for visitors.

Much of the fun results from the ongoing effort to remake Downtown. Flight to the suburbs in the 1960s was not unique here, but it hit the Bluff City harder than most. This was due in part to the layout. Downtown is on the edge of town, a narrow strip along the Mississippi River. The racial tension that's never far below the surface didn't help, either. Downtown Memphis hit rock bottom following the slaying here in 1968 of Martin Luther King, Jr. The city's commercial center of gravity shifted miles away to a business district that grew up around Poplar and I-240 called "East Memphis," or as you'll hear, "out east." Most residents found no reason to go Downtown anymore. Boarded up storefronts soon outnumbered going businesses.

Evidence of the ongoing effort to make Memphis appealing to visitors is a line of horse-drawn carriages, available for tours as well as transport.

The rebound started in 1975 when Jack Belz bought the derelict Peabody Hotel and spent six years and $25 million to restore it. From then on, it seems as if some new development has been started every year. Part of **Mud Island** was transformed into an intriguing Mississippi River theme park, and on the rest of it, the "New Urbanism" Harbor Town was built, one of several new Downtown residential developments. Historic Beale Street was made over as an entertainment district. Oddly enough, the 1977 death of the most famous Memphian triggered the most powerful stimulus. Colonel Tom Parker, Elvis's controversial manager, is rumored to have said upon the King's death: "It don't mean a damned thing. It's just like when he was away in the army." Crass though it may be, there is truth here, at least as far as the impact on the local economy. Presley's mansion, Graceland, opened to the public in 1982, the year after the Peabody reopened, and started pumping well over $100 million a year into the economy. Overnight, Memphis was transformed from a rusty river town into a tourist mecca.

The completion of the Pyramid arena in 1991 has helped spark a revival in **The Pinch district** on Downtown's northern edge, and at the opposite end, the renovation of South Main Street as an arts and design center continues. Across from the Peabody, a fabulous redbrick baseball park went up that's similar to Baltimore's successful one at Camden Yards. Peabody Place, another Belz project, is an eight-block, multi-use development blending the old and the new, the uniquely Memphis with generic odds and ends, such as an IMAX theater.

This rebound, this rebuilding is nothing new. Memphis was America's fastest-growing city in the 1850s, swelling with Irish and German immigrants who came

to work on the railroads and in the river trade. The city didn't do badly during the Civil War, when it was a center for both legal and illegal commerce. But after the war, things took a turn for the worse. The plantation economy of the surrounding countryside lay in ruin. Memphis filled with former slaves looking for opportunity, and in 1866, racial violence erupted, mostly between black Federal soldiers and the Irish. Then in 1867, a yellow fever epidemic broke out, only to be repeated in 1873, 1878, and 1879. Thousands died, and many, particularly the Irish and the Germans, left town for good. Death and flight reduced the city's population by more than half. The city declared bankruptcy and surrendered its charter. Newspapers in the rest of the state suggested that Memphis be burned and abandoned.

Memphis rebounded, though, largely through river and rail commerce and agribusiness. Cotton and hardwood led the way. The city became the world's largest cotton spot market through the Memphis Cotton Exchange. Edward H. "Boss" Crump brought political stability. (Too much of it, some would argue.) Today, it's not so much agribusiness as transportation and distribution that keeps Memphis going. One business alone, the FedEx Corporation, employs more than 30,000 workers. So many identical FedEx planes line up at the airport, they look like the inventory in a toy factory.

Downtown Memphis still has a way to go. At night, it's frightfully empty away from the steady hum of activity in the Peabody–Beale Street area. Then, too, much of the redevelopment feels contrived, something for tourists. Memphians who've been around long enough miss the old Downtown. But they're pleased something new is happening, and they're eager to show it off.

(left) A bird's-eye view of the busy Memphis waterfront, circa 1870. (Library of Congress)
(top) The Memphis Cotton Exchange enabled the city to become the world's largest cotton spot market. This photo was taken in 1953. (Tennessee State Library and Archives)

■ MEMPHIS AND MUSIC

They grab your attention the minute you set foot in the visitor center on Riverside Drive, the statues of B. B. King and Elvis Presley. Their dominance attests to the importance of music to Memphis. It's music that draws most visitors. And the two bronzes define the genres most identified with Memphis. Memphis calls itself the "home of the blues" and the "birthplace of rock 'n' roll."

◆ HOME OF THE BLUES

Memphis claim to be "home of the blues" stems largely from W. C. Handy, whose likeness stands in the park on Beale Street named for him. The bandleader made Memphis his home in the early 1900s to take advantage of the vibrant black music scene centered around Beale Street. A candidate for mayor, Edward Holt Crump—"Boss" Crump after he consolidated his power—asked Handy to compose a campaign song. Handy named it "Memphis Blues," and in 1912 it became the first published blues composition. It and his 1914 "St. Louis Blues" remain classics to this day. Handy was far from a traditional blues artist—he was not introduced to the music until late in his career—but he gets credit for popularizing the term "blues" and for first commercially exploiting the music, which earned him the title "Father of the Blues."

W. C. Handy (second from right, seated), the "Father of the Blues," jams with fellow musicians in this early Memphis photo. (Memphis Shelby County Library)

Little Bill Gaither, Memphis Slim, and Big Bill Broonzy pose for this publicity shot in Chicago, circa 1940. (Frank Driggs Collection)

♦ BIRTHPLACE OF ROCK 'N' ROLL

When A&E cable network ran the biography of Sam Phillips, it was subtitled "The Man Who Invented Rock 'n' Roll." Phillips started the Memphis Recording Service in 1950 to capture the blues and rhythm-and-blues artists who were leaving Memphis to record in Chicago and elsewhere. B. B. King, Howlin' Wolf, Junior Parker, and Rufus Thomas were among them. Phillips knew, though, that the market for the music was limited. He was looking for something that would appeal to the broader white audience, particularly the emerging teenage culture. Kids had a little jingle in their pockets and were ready to spend it on the new, cheap 45 RPM discs, but they were bored with bland pop music. Phillips is quoted as saying that he wished he could find a white boy who could sing like a black boy.

JOHNNY CASH ON MEMPHIS, MUSIC CAPITAL

*W*hat writers have always said about Memphis is true: musically speaking, it was the capital city of the whole Mississippi Delta, not just a river town in western Tennessee. There was no question it was where I needed to be. Ever since that Sears Roebuck radio came into our house, Memphis had been the center of the world in my head, the one place where people didn't have to spend their lives sweating bare survival out of a few acres of dirt, where you could sing on the radio. I took myself there as soon as I could after parting company with the air force.

*W*hen I made my first move on Sun, I told Sam Phillips on the telephone that I was a gospel singer. That didn't work. The market for gospel records, he told me, wasn't big enough for him to make a living producing them. My next try didn't work either—that time I told him I was a country singer. In the end I just went down to the Memphis Recording Service one morning before anyone arrived for work and sat on the step and waited.

Sam was the first to appear. I stood up and introduced myself and said, "Mr. Phillips, sir, if you listen to me, you'll be glad you did."

That must have been the right thing to say. "Well, I like to hear a boy with confidence in him," he replied. "Come on in."

—Johnny Cash with Patrick Carr, *Cash, The Autobiography,* 1997

MEMPHIS

Elvis at Sun Records on December 4th 1956. He is in the control room with Sam Phillips, Robert Johnson on the left who was with the Memphis Press. Scimitar and Leo Soroka on the right from UPI

He found one. In the summer of 1953—nobody knows exactly when—a shy but flashy 18-year-old recent high school graduate wandered into Phillips's Sun Studio on Union Avenue, ostensibly to make a record for his mother. "What kind of singer are you?" asked Marion Keisker, the only employee besides Sam. "I sing all kinds," the boy responded. "Who do you sound like?" she asked. "I don't sound like nobody." Nothing came of that first cut, but over time, Phillips concluded that the boy was a worthwhile project. On July 5, 1954, Elvis Presley recorded his first commercial release, the R&B song "That's All Right, Mama" on one side, and on the other, a sped-up version of Bill Monroe's signature bluegrass classic "Blue Moon of Kentucky." Popular music, indeed America, would never be the same.

MEMPHIS

◆ MUSIC SITES

The Memphis of the 1950–70s that ranked fourth in the nation as a recording center is long gone. As one artist put it, "Musically, Memphis today is more of a state of mind than a place." You won't find a city bursting with talent trying to break into the business, as in Nashville for example. But you will find a music scene that's not shackled by the need to conform to some corporate type's notion of what will sell. It's a trade off many Memphis music boosters are happy to make. The annual events are great times to sample the music.

May includes the **Beale Street Music Festival;** 901-525-4611.

Labor Day's **Memphis Music and Heritage Festival** is sponsored by the Center for Southern Folklore; 901-525-3655.

November is the time for **Bluestock on Beale Street;** 901-526-4280.

For club and concert listings, check the weekly *Memphis Flyer* or Friday's edition of the daily *Commercial Appeal.*

A street music processional on Beale Street.

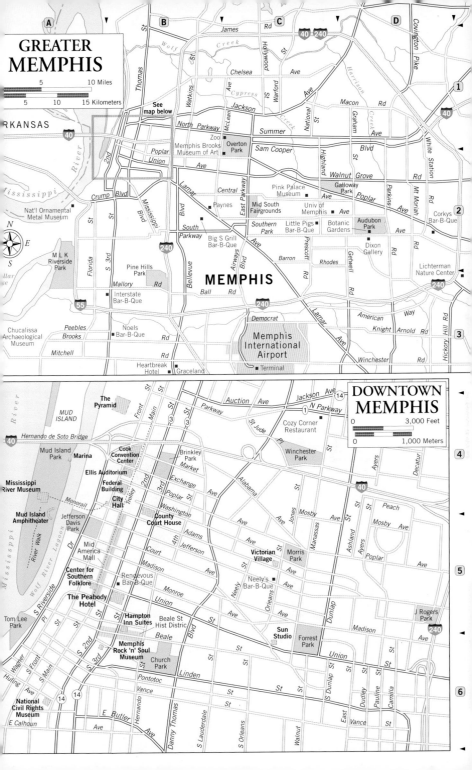

GREATER MEMPHIS

5   10 Miles

5   10   15 Kilometers

A   B   C   D

James   Rd

Wolf   Creek

Thomas   St

Chelsea   Ave

Cypress   Creek

Watkins   St

Warford

Hollywood

40   240

Harrison

Covington Pike

1

40

Jackson   Ave

McLean   St

National   St

Macon   Rd

Graham   St

White Station   Rd

See map below

North Parkway

Summer   Ave

ARKANSAS

40

2nd

Poplar   Union

Zoo

Memphis Brooks Museum of Art

Overton Park

Sam Cooper

Blvd

Highland   St

Walnut   Grove   Rd

Perkins

Mt Moriah   Rd

Mississippi River

Nat'l Ornamental Metal Museum

Crump   Blvd

Mississippi Blvd

Lamar   Blvd

Central   Ave

East Parkway

Pink Palace Museum

Galloway Park

Poplar

Univ of Memphis   Ave

Corks B-B-Que

2

N   E   S   W

Paynes

South   Parkway

Mid South Fairgrounds

Southern   Park

Little Pigs Bar-B-Que

Botanic Gardens

Audubon Park

Ave

Prescott   Rd

Dixon Gallery

Lichterman Nature Center

240

MLK Riverside Park

Florida   St

S 3rd   St

Pine Hills Park

Bellevue   Blvd

Big S Grill Bar-B-Que

Airways   Blvd

Barron   Ave

Rhodes

Getwell

MEMPHIS

55

Mallory   Rd

Interstate Bar-B-Que

Ball   Rd

240

Lamar   Ave

American   Way

Knight   Arnold   Rd

Hickory Hill   Rd

3

Chucalissa Archaeological Museum

Peebles   Brooks

Noels Bar-B-Que

Rd

Mitchell   Rd

Democrat

Memphis International Airport

Winchester   Rd

Heartbreak Hotel

Graceland

Terminal

DOWNTOWN MEMPHIS

0   3,000 Feet

0   1,000 Meters

River

MUD ISLAND

The Pyramid

Front   St

Main   St

Auction   Ave

Parkway

Jackson   Ave

N Parkway

14

Hernando de Soto Bridge

40

Mud Island Park

Marina

Cook Convention Center

Brinkley Park

Market

St Jude

Cozy Corner Restaurant

Winchester Park

Ayers

Decatur

4

Mississippi River Museum

Ellis Auditorium

Federal Building

City Hall

Monorail

Trolley

2nd   St

3rd   St

Exchange   Ave

Poplar   Ave

Alabama

40

Peach

Mud Island Amphitheater

Jefferson Davis Park

Washington

County Court House

Adams

4th

Jefferson

Jones

Mosby   Ave

Ashland

Mosby   Ave

Poplar   Ave

5

River Walk

Wolf River Lagoon

Mid America Mall

Court

Madison

Ave

Victorian Village

Morris Park

Manassas

Neely's Bar-B-Que

Ave

Dunlap

J Rogers Park

Center for Southern Folklore

Rendevous Bar-B-Que

Monroe

Neely

Orleans

Madison

S Riverside

The Peabody Hotel

Union

Ave

Sun Studio

Forrest Park

Union

240

Tom Lee Park

S 2nd   Pl

S Front   St

S 2nd   St

S 3rd   St

Hampton Inn Suites

Beale St Hist District

Beale   Blvd

Memphis Rock 'n' Soul Museum

Church Park

S Dunlap   St

Dudley   St

Pauline   St

Camilla   St

East   St

6

Wagner

Huling   Ave

14

Pontotoc

Vance

Linden

Hernando

Danny Thomas

S Lauderdale

S Orleans

Vance

National Civil Rights Museum

E Butler   Ave

E Calhoun

Walnut   St

Memphis Rock 'n' Soul Museum

map page 285, lower, B-6

This is the place to start a Memphis musical tour, at the Smithsonian Institution's Rock 'n' Soul Social Crossroads exhibition in the Gibson Guitar building a block off Beale Street. You'll see that the intersection of black and white cultures that's so often filled with tension in Memphis is the same force that produced the music that makes Memphis a holy city for music lovers. The exhibition traces the evolution of the music from the fields, churches, and kitchens of the rural South into the most popular music in history. You'll learn about Memphis jug bands, country string bands, Delta blues shouters, rockabilly, and soul. This latter genre doesn't get as much attention in Memphis as the blues and rock 'n' roll, but it was important here during the late 1960s and early 1970s. The Stax and Hi labels produced artists such as Otis Redding, Sam & Dave, Wilson Pickett, Isaac Hayes, Al Green, and the Staple Singers. Booker T. & the MGs, the racially mixed band that accompanied most of the Stax artists, included guitarist and writer Steve Cropper and organist Booker T. Jones, and had some hits on its own.

Among the many treasures on display are the soundboard used for Elvis's first recording, one of B. B. King's "Lucille" guitars, and the equipment that recorded Otis Redding's "Sittin' on the Dock of the Bay." Plan on staying here awhile, for it takes some time to listen to the abundance of toe-tapping music on the CD headset you'll be fitted with for the tour. 191 Beale Street; 901-205-2533.

One of the great stars on the Stax Records label, Otis Redding was known for his riveting and heart-wrenching performances. (Michael Ochs Archive, Los Angeles)

Miss Zena and the White Guy perform at a club along Beale Street.

Beale Street

map page 285, lower, A-5 to D-6

Music fills the air and visitors fill the street day and night along the three blocks of Beale Street that are lined with clubs, theaters, and parks. Beale Street's heritage reaches back to the first half of the 20th century when it was the most important center of black commerce and culture between St. Louis and New Orleans. Some natives turn their noses up at Beale's makeover, grousing that it's little more than a theme park. It does have its share of schlock, but it's also a place where you can hear genuinely good, authentic music ranging from internationally known acts to amateurs who set up in the public space.

Sun Studio

map page 285, lower, C-6

If rock 'n' roll can be said to have been born in one place, this is it, this tiny, undistinguished brick building in a lifeless section east of Downtown. This is where Sam Phillips started his studio in 1950. About a year after Elvis first walked in unannounced, Phillips warmed to the idea of working with him and recruited guitarist Scotty Moore and bass player Bill Black to rehearse with Elvis. Their first recording sessions here in June 1954 didn't produce much Phillips liked. Neither did the one on July 5. Not at first. Some droopy ballads, nothing to write home about.

Then during a break, Elvis picked up a

guitar and started horsing around with the R&B song "That's All Right, Mama." As Scotty put it, he started "jumping around the studio, just acting the fool. And Bill started beating on his bass and I joined in. Just making a bunch of racket, we thought." Phillips heard it from the control room. "That's it," he thought. That's what he'd been looking for. A white boy who could sing like a black boy. He dashed out of the control room and told the trio to repeat it so he could tape it. The recording was an instant hit locally. Elvis was on his way to stardom.

Phillips sold the Sun Records' contract with Elvis Presley to RCA the next year for $35,000—he says he never regretted that decision—and used the money to develop other artists. The Sun roster was packed with astounding talent. Carl Perkins recorded "Blue Suede Shoes" at Sun in 1956, and Johnny Cash recorded "I Walk the Line" here the same year. Jerry Lee Lewis's "Whole Lotta Shakin' Going On" was recorded at Sun the next year. Roy Orbison and Charlie Rich began their careers at Sun as well. The Sun Studio is by day a place that welcomes visitors and by night an active recording studio. 706 Union Avenue; 901-521-0664.

Center for Southern Folklore

map page 285, lower, B-5

The live performances here lean to the basic, what music enthusiasts call "roots." You can enjoy Southern-style food while you're listening, or browse the collection of folk art and unique gifts. 119 S. Main Street; 901-525-3655.

Sun Records in Memphis.

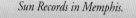

The stone wall in front of Graceland is covered with love notes and admiring messages from the King's legions of fans.

◆ GRACELAND   *map page 285, top, B-3*

"For reasons I cannot explain, there's some part of me that wants to see Graceland," sings Paul Simon in the title cut of his Grammy-winning album of that name. "I'm going to Graceland, Memphis Tennessee." He's not alone. It's said that more people visit Elvis's home than any house in America, aside from the White House. More than George Washington's Mount Vernon or Thomas Jefferson's Monticello. Elvis fan or not, you must see it when you're in Memphis.

There are two ways to view Graceland. There are two ways to view Elvis. As one writer put it, Graceland is "the collision between a rich man and poor taste." This view is represented in the gaudy Jungle Room, outfitted with furniture that Elvis's father, Vernon, is reported to have described as the most hideous he'd ever seen. This view brings to mind the Elvis people poke fun at, the jumpsuited Vegas Elvis who died here in 1977 at age 42, the man who is copied by countless impersonators and on velvet portraits.

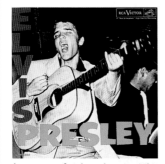

EARLY ELVIS

If Tupelo, Mississippi, was a backwater of the rural American South when Elvis Presley was born there in 1935, it was a town filled with music. Humming and singing marked the business of people's lives. Harmonies from gospel choirs drifted out church windows; rhythm spun from the open doors of juke joints at the edge of towns; dog-tired blues thrummed from the guitars of men singing on the doorsteps of rickety houses. This was a slow-moving place where opportunities were few and spare time familiar. On hot Southern nights, people sat on their front steps breathing in evening's heady fragrance, its dust, the smell of the river, of fields and of sweat—a sensual, earthy mix that Elvis absorbed into his bones. If his music was exhilarating, youthful, wild, and sexual, its power came from the grip and grind of its delta roots.

From the beginning, Elvis gravitated toward music: his mother said when he was three years old, at church, he'd creep up the aisle and try to sing with the choir. When he was ten, Elvis auditioned at a talent show at the Mississippi-Alabama State Fair. A few years later he was trying to meet Tupelo singer Mississippi Slim by standing outside the local radio station.

By 1948, when Elvis moved with his family to Memphis, he knew by heart hundreds of songs: gospel, rhythm and blues; and pop love songs by crooners Bing Crosby and Dean Martin, even Mario Lanza. In Memphis, teenage Elvis walked down a Beale Street alive with music. He hung out at music spots, played a simple guitar, and sang ballads (supposedly he didn't "sing a fast song" until his first recording session). In 1953, when Elvis was working at Parker Machinists Shop, he came over to Sun Studios to make his mother a record for her birthday present. The studio's owner, Sam Phillips, heard Elvis sing and was nonplussed. Elvis even tried out for a gospel quartet that rejected him.

But Elvis persevered. He took his looks seriously, appearing at one jam session wearing white shoes, pink pants, and a black shirt—his hair slicked back in a ducktail. Perhaps it was the outward sign of an inward determination to step out onto the stage and be a self who'd been pacing in the wings.

Late one night in the summer of 1954, playing at Sun Studios with guitarist Scotty Moore and bass player Bill Black, Elvis began joking around and loosened up. Out came out a new sound, an unstoppable force—the new Elvis, who would make Sun Records famous.

—Kit Duane

The other view of Graceland is represented in the Hall of Gold, an 80-foot-long room lined with gold and platinum records and awards from around the world. This view brings to mind a young man, a boy really, the creative genius who with his own rich imagination created his own form of music, his own style of presenting it, and his own unique persona. This is the Elvis who had 14 number-one records on the Top 100 chart, 11 on the country chart, and seven on the R&B chart and who had 21 number-one records in Britain. This is the Elvis who had 107 Top 40 hits, more than twice as many as the Beatles, and had an amazing 110 albums and singles that went gold or platinum. There has never been anyone like him. There never will be.

Visitors buy tickets across the road from the mansion at a strip mall that sells all manner of Elvis stuff. Spring for the platinum tour that includes the mansion and the satellite attractions, like his airplanes. For the total Graceland experience, come on the anniversary of the King's death on August 16 each year, to the Candlelight Vigil. Better yet, come for the whole week's activities, "Death Week" the natives call it. 3734 Elvis Presley Boulevard; 800-238-2000 or 901-332-3322.

A young Elvis impersonator on Beale Street.

◆ DOWNTOWN MEMPHIS, BEYOND MUSIC

Mud Island River Park *map page 285, A-4&5*

Mud Island is a glorified sandbar in the Mississippi River with an innovative park showcasing the river. The **Mississippi River Museum** traces the river's history and culture from prehistoric times to the present. You'll pass through a re-creation of an 1870s steam-powered packet, a reconstructed Civil War ironclad gun boat, and the pilot house of a towboat like the ones out on the river today. You'll follow the music from the fields and churches to the recording studios, learn about the legendary W. C.

Handy as you loiter about a re-created juke joint, and hear a medley of familiar music recorded along the Mississippi in the 1950–60s, from Fats Domino, Elvis Presley, Jerry Lee Lewis, Johnny Cash, B. B. King, and a host of others. Museum: 901-576-7241.

River Walk is a unique, half-mile scale model of the Lower Mississippi—one average step equals one mile of the real river—where the water level reflects the level of the river.

Just downstream from Mud Island is a dock where you can book a tour on the ***Memphis Queen Line;*** 901-527-5694.

(above) Explore a model Mississippi at River Walk on Mud Island.

(opposite) A replica of the Lower Mississippi River on Mud Island.

Peabody Hotel

map page 285 lower, A/B-5

The Peabody is a destination in its own right, the hub of activity in Downtown Memphis. The two-story Italian Renaissance-style lobby features wrought-iron chandeliers, skylights of etched glass, hand-painted beamed ceilings, and a magnificent fountain carved out of a single block of marble. Each day at 11 a.m, the lobby is jammed for the Duck March. The famed Peabody ducks waddle in, single file, to spend the day in the fountain. Crowds return at 5 p.m. to see them depart for their rooftop penthouse pond. 149 Union Avenue; 800-PEABODY or 901-529-4000.

National Civil Rights Museum

map page 285, lower, A-6

Martin Luther King, Jr., was in Memphis in April 1968 to support striking sanitation workers, and was staying at the Lorraine Motel as he usually did when he was in town. On April 4, as King stood on the motel's second floor balcony, James Earl Ray, a prison escapee from Missouri, aimed his rifle from the rear window of a building on South Main Street and fired the shot that killed King. King's room, 306, is just the way it was that day, and has been incorporated into the museum built around the motel. The exhibits follow African Americans' struggle for justice from 1619, when the first slaves were brought over, to King's assassination. At the chillingly realistic exhibits on the Montgomery bus boycott, the desegregation of Little Rock's Central High School, the Greensboro sit-ins, and the Birmingham demonstrations, you get a sense of the heroism of those who led the way, not just the leaders whose names are familiar, but the ordinary folks who had the courage to challenge the established order. 450 Mulberry Street off S. Main Street; 901-521-9699.

■ MIDTOWN MEMPHIS

Overton Park

map page 285 upper, B/C-1/2

Highlighted by oak-shaded neighborhoods of tree-lined parkways, stately homes, and the Gothic campus of Rhodes College, Midtown is separated from Downtown by the huge medical complex that includes the University of Tennessee's health science schools and world-renowned St. Jude Children's Hospital. Midtown's centerpiece is Overton Park, a 342-acre green retreat set aside in 1901 and named for John Overton, who, along with Andrew Jackson and James Winchester, developed Memphis in 1819. More than half the park is a unique urban old-growth forest of uncommonly large trees. It's hard to believe that the state of Tennessee wanted to rip it up for an interstate. Only a landmark decision in 1971 handed down by the U.S. Supreme Court kept bulldozers out.

SLOW COOKED PIG MEAT: IT'S A MEMPHIS THING

There's a popular saying that the South is a place, while "north" is merely a direction. Another transformed word down here is "barbecue"— always a noun; almost never a verb, as they use it up north. While various meats can be used to create barbecue, the orthodox version in Tennessee calls for pork ribs or shoulder slowly cooked with more smoke than fire over hardwood or charcoal.

Like the state's music, barbecue is different in different parts of Tennessee. A Carolina-style of barbecue is served in East Tennessee—smoked pork gently marinated in vinegar and black pepper. Farther west, barbecue is served with a crusted, tomato-based sauce infused with a little Caribbean flavor, mainly molasses and chili peppers.

In Memphis today there are over a hundred barbecue joints, and Memphis-style barbecue restaurants are popular in Washington (the state and the District), Los Angeles, San Diego, Salt Lake City and Denver. Even more significant, Memphis-style 'cue can be found in proud New Orleans and even around archrival Nashville.

This slow-cooked fast food represents more than a happy mingling of mountain and lowland cuisine. Martin Luther King's "table of brotherhood" would likely be laden with this food, since a really good barbecue restaurant will bring a healthy mix of white and black Memphis fans together almost as effectively as a football game. The *Encyclopedia of Southern Culture* notes, "more than any other cuisine, barbecue draws the whole of Southern society." The experienced barbecue traveler, the encyclopedia explains, is always on the lookout for parking lots where pickups are parked next to expensive imports—the object being to find the one place in town where people from all income-tax brackets eat together. In Memphis, such places include:

Big S Grill
1179 Dunnivant Street;
901-775-9127
Call first to see if Mr. Hardaway is cooking.

Cozy Corner
745 North Parkway; 901-527-9158.

Charles Vergos, Rendezvous
52 S. Second Street; 901-523-2746.
Use the entrance in the alley opposite Union Avenue entrance to the Peabody Hotel.

Interstate Bar-B-Q
2265 S. Third, a block north of I-55;
901-775-2304.

—Gary Bridgman

Overton Park's northwest corner is taken up by the **Memphis Zoo,** a source of justifiable pride in Tennessee's largest city. It's home to a respected breeding program that saves animals from extinction. 800-290-6041 or 901-333-6500.

If you're on a music pilgrimage, don't miss the park's **band shell.** Elvis Presley's July 5, 1954 recording of "That's All Right, Mama" was an instant hit locally, and the nineteen-year-old was invited to open a Slim Whitman concert here on July 30. Elvis's naive brilliance comes through in his recount of his first concert appearance. "I came offstage, and my manager told me that they was hollering because I was wiggling my legs. I went back out for an en-core, and I did a little more, and the more I did, the wilder they went." You know the rest of the story.

Entering Overton Park through the main entrance off Poplar Avenue, you'll be greeted by Edward Holt Crump. Not in person, but in the form of a big bronze likeness. Crump was one of America's last urban political bosses. He ruled local politics off and on from 1909 until his death in 1954, and dominated state politics, too, during much of that time. He was an enigmatic character. Most of the bosses were. He was corrupt and repressive, yet the governments he controlled were efficient and frugal.

Hieroglyphics decorate the entrance gate to the Memphis Zoo.

Memphis Brooks Museum of Art

map page 285, top, B/C-1

You sense quality the minute you lay eyes on the marble exterior of the 1916 building. Your anticipation is affirmed when you enter the rotunda and start your tour of one of America's top 25 art collections. Studying the stained glass and icons from the 1200s in the Medieval Treasury, filled with the soothing sounds of monastic chants, you'll feel as if you're in a European shrine instead of a stone's throw from where Elvis performed his first concert. Other areas sure to please you are the Renaissance galleries and the American gallery, featuring a Robert W. Earl portrait of Andrew Jackson, one of the founders of Memphis. Upstairs is an astounding collection of African masks. 1934 Poplar Avenue in Overton Park; 901-544-6200.

Pink Palace Museum

map page 285, top, C-2

This eclectic museum has something for everyone. Adults and children alike are intrigued by the collection of skeletons, including the one of a human and the one of a giant python. There are exhibits on the history and culture of Memphis and on the natural environments of the Midsouth, as well as a planetarium, an IMAX theater, a miniature circus, and 500 stuffed birds. It wouldn't be truly Memphis without something about trendsetting music, and sure enough, there is a mannequin dressed in one of Elvis's Army uniforms and another holding one of W. C. Handy's trumpets. Not all the Memphis trendsetters are musicians. You'll see an original Holiday Inn room from the early 1950s when the chain was started in Memphis by Kemmons Wilson. And speaking of trendsetters, that's why the Pink Palace is here. Clarence Saunders founded the nation's first self-serve supermarket chain here, Piggly Wiggly, and set out to build a 36,500-square-foot mansion faced with pink marble. He went broke. The city took it over in 1930, completed it, and turned it into a must-see attraction. 3050 Central Avenue; 901-320-6362.

■ THE REST OF MEMPHIS

National Ornamental Metal Museum

map page 285, top, A-2

The setting alone makes a visit to this out-of-the-way place mandatory. It's atop the oak-filled bluff where you look out at the towboats pushing barges through a giant S-shaped bend in the Mississippi. Pass through the ornate gate, and you'll be on grounds dotted with sculpture on your way to the gallery that hosts revolving exhibits ranging from gold jewelry to weapons to weather vanes. At the blacksmith shop, you can watch metalsmiths at work or take a class yourself. 374 Metal Museum Drive, off Crump Boulevard (I-55); 901-774-6380.

Victorian Village

map page 285, lower, C-5

On Adams Street, within sight of Downtown, in an otherwise bleak section, stands a block of astounding houses from the mid-to-late 1800s, from when cotton was king in Memphis. Calling this a "village" is a tad optimistic, but it's worth seeing. The grandest of the elaborate, lavishly furnished houses open to the public are the **Mallory-Neely House** (901-523-1484) and the **Woodruff-Fontaine House** (901-526-1469). The street is particularly worth visiting in December when it's all dressed up for holiday activities.

Dixon Gallery and Gardens

map page 285, top, D-2

Thanks to the generosity of the late Margaret and Hugo Dixon, their 17-acre estate carved out of the West Tennessee woods is now an inviting gallery and gardens. The house showcases their collection of French Impressionist paintings, including works by Monet, Cezanne, and Renoir, as well as decorative art that includes an extensive collection of porcelain. The grounds are landscaped in the English style, with formal and informal elements. The woods filled with dogwood, azalea, mountain laurel, and rhododendron are a spectacle of color in the spring. 4339 Park Avenue; 901-761-5250.

Memphis Botanic Garden

map page 285, top, D-2

This delightful oasis in Audubon Park includes a lovely Japanese garden surrounding a lake full of colorful fish and a wildflower-filled patch of mature forest that's a riot of color in spring and fall. The park is the site of one of the city's top events, October's Arts in the Park, a four-day celebration featuring every imaginable kind of visual art from throughout the nation, and more than 80 stage acts of every variety. 750 Cherry Road between Park and Southern; 901-685-1566.

Chucalissa

map page 285, top, A-3

Back in 1939, when CCC boys were digging a hole for a state park swimming pool, they discovered evidence of a prehistoric village. It turned out to be a major one that archaeologists determined had been occupied from A.D. 1000–1400. A recreation of a grass-roofed mud hut village has been built around a tall mound. It and the museum are operated by the University of Memphis. The museum provides insight into that time when the only tools the people had were made of wood, stone, and bone. Ever wonder how primitive cultures managed to stay healthy? Well, they didn't. The exhibit on health describes how the natives were afflicted with dysentery, diarrhea, toothache, and worms. Makes you appreciate modern medicine. 1987 Indian Village Drive, off Riverport Road; 901-785-3160.

■ NATURAL MEMPHIS

There is something awesome about the Mississippi River. It glides by so quietly and so effortlessly. Yet it is so powerful. Just knowing where Old Man River's water comes from begets a sense of awe. You're looking at water that started as rivulets of melting snow at Yellowstone in Wyoming, as tiny rhododendron-shrouded streams in North Carolina's Blue Ridge, and as trickles from clear blue lakes in Minnesota's north woods.

Oddly enough, though the big river forms the entire length of Tennessee's western boundary, opportunities to stand on its bank are rare. One such place is **Meeman-Shelby State Park** just north of Memphis *(map page 255, A-5)*. The park's 13,467 acres take in the river bank, the swampy cypress and tupelo-filled flood plain, and some of the Chickasaw Bluffs, which were formed over the millennia by deposits of wind-borne silt and dust. Nearly 20 miles of easy trails wander through the hardwoods, where you're likely to spot deer, wild turkey, and beaver, as well as more than 200 species of birds. A paved road stretches across the flat-as-a-pancake flood plain to a scenic landing on the river. Off N. Watkins Road (TN-388); 901-876-5215.

In East Memphis, just outside the I-240 beltway, the 65-acre **Lichterman Nature Center** has protected field and forest since the 1920s, long before Memphis grew out this far. 5992 Quince Road *(map page 285, top, D-2/3)*; 901-767-7322. A bit further out, along the Wolf River, gentle trails loop through the thousand-acre **Lucius E. Burch, Jr. Forest State Natural Area,** named for the noted Memphis attorney and conservationist. You'll experience four habitats here: river, wetland, bottomland hardwood forest, and forest edge. Access is off Walnut Grove Road east of I-240 and off Germantown Road (TN-177) *(map page 255, A/B-4)*; 888-867-2757.

If you're not inclined to stray from what probably drew you to Memphis—Elvis, Beale Street, and barbecue—but you'd like a little peace and quiet in the outdoors, try the incomparable urban old growth forest in Midtown's **Overton Park** *(see page 294)*. Or take the short **Chickasaw Bluff Trail** at Chucalissa, the 15th-century native village *(see map page 285, top, A-3; and text page 298)*.

AUTHOR'S CHOICE:
MEMPHIS LODGING AND RESTAURANTS

LODGINGS

Hampton Inn Suites–Peabody Place
Stunning decor, conveniently located in the Peabody Place development adjacent to Beale Street and the Peabody Hotel. 175 Peabody Place; 901-260-4000.

Heartbreak Hotel
Elvis theme hotel, complete with in-room Elvis movies and Graceland-based decor. For the ultimate Elvis experience. Packages include Graceland tour. 3677 Elvis Presley Boulevard; 877-777-0606.

The Peabody Hotel
Elegant, comfortable, and always crowded, it's one of America's great hotels. Hub of activity Downtown, convenient to Beale Street and other attractions. 149 Union Avenue; 800-PEABODY or 901-529-4000.

Talbot Heirs Guesthouse
Luxurious bed-and-breakfast with large suites across the street from the Peabody. 99 S. Second Street; 901-527-9772.

RESTAURANTS

Arcade
Decor is original 1950s, and yes, Elvis ate here. Today's menu has Memphis-theme dishes like Shepherd's Delight (Cybill is from here), Great Balls of Fire (The Killer recorded it here), and The Rainmaker. 540 S. Main Street; 901-526-5757.

Automatic Slim's Tonga Club
Trendy and wildly popular with locals. Southwestern and Caribbean dishes are served. 83 S. Second Street; 901-525-7948.

Brother Juniper's College Inn
Quintessential Memphis: out of the way, offbeat. Run by an Eastern Orthodox priest and decorated with icons, this University of Memphis–area breakfast spot is consistently voted the best in town. 3519 S. Walker Avenue, off Highland; 901-324-0144.

Chez Philippe
Top of the heap, serving a distinctively Memphis blend of Southern, French, and Asian. Innovative dishes—shrimp-stuffed hush puppies and salmon with barbecue sauce. Peabody Hotel; 901-529-4188.

Cupboard
Classic Southern cooking, with daily entrees including chicken and dumplings, smothered pork chops, and country-fried steak, plus fresh vegetables and homemade bread and deserts. 1400 Union Avenue; 901-276-8015.

King's Palace Café
Great gumbo, Memphis-style ribs, and plate lunches served in an authentic and intriguing Beale Street establishment left over from the old days. 162 Beale Street; 901-521-1851.

MEMPHIS

Koto

Restaurateurs Jimmy Ishii (Japanese) and Erling Jensen (Denmark) have teamed up in Midtown as they have at River Terrace to produce fusion cuisine that's so unusual it's hard to describe. One example: cheesecake tempura. 22 S. Cooper Street; 901-722-2244.

McEwen's on Monroe

"New Southern" is how the owner of this elegant downtown eatery describes it. Innovative dishes and old favorites, including, for instance, fried chicken and banana pudding, like you've never before tasted. Seasonal menu. 122 Monroe Avenue; 901-527-7085.

On Teur

Small, funky Midtown place with a devoted following that comes for great sandwiches and creative fish dishes. 2015 Madison Avenue; 901-725-6059.

Paulette's

A traditional Memphis favorite serving crepes, crab cakes, steak, chicken, and pork in pleasant, comfortable setting. Kahlua-mocha parfait pie is a dessert you won't forget, and there are other great ones as well. 2110 Madison Avenue; 901-726-5128.

River Terrace

Sunset over the river and dramatic views of the lighted DeSoto Bridge are breathtaking, and so are the fish, duck, and pork at this elegant former private club. 280 N. Mud Island Road; 901-528-0001.

BARBECUE

Ask a Memphian about barbecue, and you'll learn right away that they take the subject seriously. Devotion to a particular style or place approaches religious fervor and crosses the racial line that often divides the city. These are the places natives most often name:

Corky's
5259 Poplar Avenue; 901-685-9744.

Cozy Corner
745 N. Parkway; 901-527-9158.

Interstate
2265 S. Third Street; 901-775-2304.

Little Pigs
671 S. Highland Street; 901-323-9433.

Neely's
670 Jefferson Avenue, 901-521-9798; and 5700 Mt. Moriah Road; 901-795-4177.

Noel's
3024 S. Third Street; 901-332-9490.

Payne's
1762 Lamar Avenue and 1393. Elvis Presley Boulevard; 901-272-1523

WALKS AND WILDFLOWERS
I N   T E N N E S S E E   P A R K S

■ WILDFLOWER WALKS

Tennessee plays host each year to a lavish parade of colorful wildflowers. It starts in March—sometimes as early as February—when the spring beauties and the blood-root brighten the bleak forest floor, and it runs through October when the first killing frost takes the life out of the aster and the goldenrod. It shouldn't come as a surprise that Tennessee is home to an incredible diversity of plants blooming in the wild. With nine distinct topographic regions, elevations ranging from less than 200 to nearly 7,000 feet, varied soil types, average annual precipitation that ranges from 40 to near 100 inches, and a spread of average maximum summer tempera-tures from the mid-90s to the low 70s, Tennessee has the most varied ecology of

(above) Grasshoppers nibble on ironweed, a wildflower often seen along Tennessee hiking trails.

(opposite) Morning light illuminates a trail along Turnbull Creek in Dickson County.

any non-coastal state in the nation. It's no wonder that one naturalist tagged Tennessee the "Noah's Ark" of American vegetation.

Up high, in the dense, damp mountain forests along Tennessee's eastern border, you'll find flowers that normally are found in the harsh climate of northern New England's mountains and in the Canadian Arctic. At other places in Tennessee you'll come across wildflowers more common on the Midwestern prairies. In the moist cypress bottoms in the western end of the state, you can see some of the same flowers you would see far to the south along the Gulf Coast. In the cedar glades around Nashville, there are species that don't exist anywhere else in the world. Some of the most delightful flowers to gaze upon are the most prolific throughout Tennessee: bluebells, phlox, wood-sorrel, crested dwarf iris, may apple, and nearly all of the more than two dozen kinds of trillium.

■ TRAILS LESS TRAVELED

Tennessee is a hikers' paradise, made so by the variety of the topography, the many public lands, and the labors of generations of hiking enthusiasts. Whether it's climbing to the fir-covered summit of one of the East's tallest peaks, scrambling to a hidden waterfall through a boulder-strewn gorge, strolling through a wildflower-carpeted hardwood forest, or skimming along a boardwalk above a cypress swamp, you'll find it in Tennessee. The most popular trails are in

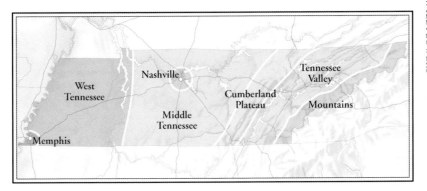

what might be called "the usual suspects," the big preserves like the Great Smoky Mountains National Park, Cherokee National Forest, Big South Fork, South Cumberland, and Land Between the Lakes, and popular smaller areas like Fall Creek Falls, Frozen Head, Old Stone Fort, and Radnor Lake. But there are many equally wonderful but less-known trails. Here are a few.

■ INFORMATION

Tennessee State Parks

> *www.state.tn.us/environment/parks/parks.htm*
> *888-867-2757*

Each park's website can be accessed by inserting the **directory name**—which we've given below each park's location—at the end of the above Tennessee State Park Department website. For example, if you'd like information on Big Ridge *(in our listings, page 306)*, replace */parks.htm* with *bigridge;* the whole web page address would then become *www.state.tn.us/environment/parks/bigridge.*

For more hiking information, see the hiking guides listed in "RECOMMENDED READING" on page 310, or contact the Tennessee Trails Association, Box 41446, Nashville, 37204-1446.

(opposite) Ooohs and Ahhs from hikers enjoying a sunrise from Mt. LeConte in the Great Smoky Mountains circa 1955. (Tennessee State Library and Archives)

WALKS AND WILDFLOWERS

♦ MOUNTAINS

Great Smoky Mountains National Park

map page 53, center;
also page 58, center right
   also see descriptions on pages 52-54
(Gatlinburg entrance: Gatlinburg, south of
Knoxville on TN 441)
www.nps.gov/grsm; 800-365-2267

Few places on earth can match the wildflower displays of the Great Smoky Mountains National Park. The 1,500 species it shows off to millions of annual visitors places it first among North American parks in the number of different kinds of blooming plants. The park also boasts the greatest diversity of arthropods (millipedes, etc.) in North America. The year 2000 marked the 50th anniversary of the Smokies Spring Wildflower Pilgrimage held each April. It's by far the most noted spring wildflower outing in Tennessee, with attendance at the three-day event exceeding a thousand people per day.
Wildflower Pilgrimage, Wed-Sun, the last week
in April. www.springwildflowerpilgrimage.
org; 865-974-2256 or 865-436-7318

Roan Mountain State Park

map page 59, right center
also see page 65
   800-250-8620 or 423-772-0190

The park features many wonderful plant areas, but is more famous as the gateway to the Catawba rhododendron that blooms on the slopes of Roan Mountain. The Rhododendron Festival in mid-June is a lot of fun—an arts and crafts fair with great food and bluegrass combined with hikes up the mountain to see the rhododendrons.

♦ TENNESSEE VALLEY

Big Ridge/Norris Dam

map page 70, top right
also see pages 97-102
Big Ridge: 865-992-5523
Norris Dam: 865-426-7461

Both of these parks on Norris Lake were established by the TVA. Norris Dam is noted for its displays of trout lilies (last week in March) while Big Ridge offers dutchman's breeches and the beautiful wake robin trillium (first weeks in April). In late May, both parks offer lush displays of Tennessee's state tree, the tulip poplar.

River Bluff Trail follows the Clinch River below Norris Dam. Off I-75 take US-441 or TN-61. Three-mile loop *(also see page 99).*

Warriors' Path State Park

map page 71, top right
(along the Holston River in the Tennessee
Valley near Kingsport off I-81)
   423-239-8531

Named for the park's proximity to the ancient war and trading path used by the Cherokee, this is another TVA parksite where you can find service berry and the remarkable and rare little brown jugs. In late April, the wild geranium puts on lavish displays.

◆ CUMBERLAND PLATEAU

Fall Creek Falls State Park
map page 130, center
also see pages 142-143
(among the gorges and waterfalls on the
Cumberland Plateau, off TN-111 south
of Cookeville)
423-881-5708

For over 60 years, this park—the most visited state park in Tennessee—has devoted the first weekend in May to the pink lady's slipper. With its spectacular waterfalls, cascades, and woodlands, the park is noted for its 19 species of rare plants and animals. It is also cherished for its mid-May displays of mountain laurel and, in early June, the enormous white blooms of the unique big-leaved magnolia that dominates the woods.

Frozen Head State Park
map page 131, center left
also see page 141
(in the Cumberland Mountains near the
Obed River National Wild and Scenic
River off TN-62 west of Oak Ridge
423-346-3318

Another stellar wildflower area where herbacious flowers reign supreme. From mid- to late April, be prepared for thick banks of white flowering trillium gracing every trail. Foam flower, larkspur, bellwort, yellow and speckled mandarin, along with blankets of other trillium species are found here in large numbers, even the delicate yellow trout lily. One of the few areas in Tennessee that the clear cutters overlooked, several coves harbor intact hardwood ecosystems that are home to important populations of the cerulean warbler.

Sewanee Perimeter Trail
map page 130, lower left
also see page 146

Located on the Cumberland Plateau within town of Sewanee. Twenty miles of student-maintained trail circle the 10,000-acre University of the South. Best parts: the 1.4-mile stretch through wildflower and waterfall-filled Shakerag Hollow from Green's View to University Gate and the one mile along the bluff from University View to Morgan's Steep.

South Cumberland Recreation Area
map page 130, lower left
also see page 143
(includes several separate preserves on the
Cumberland Plateau, with the headquar-
ters off I-24 near Monteagle northwest of
Chattanooga)
931-924-2980

This relatively new park along the Cumberland Plateau features rosebay rhododendron in the gorges, mountain laurel and big-leaf magnolia on the upper slopes, along with pink lady slippers and enormous carpets of trailing arbutus beneath the canopy.

♦ MIDDLE TENNESSEE

Bearwaller Gap Trail

map page 207, D/E-1

Dramatic trail around a Cumberland River bend at Cordell Hull Lake that climbs the tall bluffs and passes many wet-weather waterfalls. Almost six miles. Trailhead at Defeated Creek Recreation Area.

Cardwell Mountain Trail

map page 207, E-3

Trail near McMinnville; from Cumberland Caverns circles to the massive bluffs and boulders atop an outlier of the Cumberland Plateau; Five and a half miles.

Cedars of Lebanon State Park

map page 207, C-2
also see page 229
(in the Middle Tennessee cedar country near Lebanon off I-40 east of Nashville)
615-443-2769

This popular park is home to Tennessee's unique cedar glades. The soil here is thin and surface temperatures vary greatly, making for a harsh, desert-like habitat. Nevertheless, 19 rare and endemic species of plants grow profusely here, remnants of ancient prairie. Two flowers to search out are leavenworthia (early- to mid-March) and the Nashville breadroot, an endemic lupine (early April).

REDBUD TREE IN BLOOM

*I*ndeed there was a redbud tree in full bloom and two days later there were three more, so vivid against the bare gray branches of the other trees, themselves festooned with cardinals that seemed like scarlet fruits. After the redbuds came the swollen leaf buds of the hickory trees, and, startling as rouge on the cheek of a gray mule, was the soft, subtle red of the swamp maples. Both banks of the branch were sharply outlined by the first flat leaves, two by two, of the touch-me-not.

Then the dogwoods blossomed and pseudopodia of green crept over the hills, spreading almost while I watched. The frogs set up a frantic screaming in all the swampy places and suddenly there were wild blackberry bushes knee high. Then the green went uncontrolled, as the pace of spring accelerated, and climbed the huge trees to the sky. And the blackberry bushes were up to my waist. The wild plum and the sarvis trees burst into white clouds of bloom.

And the sound of the whippoorwill began on the dot of the dusk.

—Rachel Maddux (1913-1983), *A Walk in the Spring Rain and The Orchard Children,* published in 1992

Montgomery Bell State Park
map page 207, B-2
(in the oak-hickory forest on the Western Highland Rim off I-40 west of Nashville)
800-250-8613 or 615-797-9052
Two state-designated natural areas track several endangered species: Eggert's sunflower, bearded rattlesnake root, and goldenseal (heavily picked for its health benefits). The rare Tennessee snake tail dragonfly is also found here. The southern section is dominated by three subtypes of the oak-hickory forest—best examples in the state.
Montgomery Bell Trail: An 11-mile trail in Montgomery Bell State Park that can be hiked in loops of 6.2 and 7.2 miles. Two CCC-built lakes, magnificent old hardwood forest, abundant spring wildflowers, and brilliant fall colors. Trailhead in parking area.

Standing Stone State Park
map page 207, E-1
In a rugged part of Eastern Highland Rim north of Cookeville off TN-52
931-823-6347
This 11,000-acre park on the Cumberland Plateau is another great site for Spring wildflowers. The bright red fire pink is a delight as well as brilliant displays of shooting star. On the ridge of Copper Mountain, a large sinkhole features a forest cove that is especially diverse. Flora include trillium, crested iris, doll's eye, and wild geranium.

◆ **NASHVILLE AREA**

Radnor Lake
maps pages 183, B-6
(in Harpeth Hills, between Franklin (US-31) and Granny White Pikes.)
615-373-3467
The parklands surrounding this beautiful natural lake abound with wildflowers. Because so much of the surrounding land has never been disturbed, larkspur can bloom so thickly it's hard not to think they've been planted. (This is a "hot spot" for bird watching during spring migrations.)

◆ **WEST TENNESSEE**

Chickasaw Bluffs Trail
map page 255, A-4
(along Mississippi River north of Memphis)
Trail runs along Mississippi River bluff and past cypress-filled bottoms at Meeman-Shelby Forest State Park outside Memphis. Trailhead in parking area of MS River Group Camp. Eight miles.

Reelfoot Lake
map page 255, C-1
also see page s 258-273
(at Tiptonville in far northwest Tennessee)
800-250-8617 or 731-253-7756
This large natural lake, with its classic cypress swamp, was created by the New Madrid earthquake of 1811. It features many aquatic wildflowers, such as the very showy nelumbo (lotus family), and hosts the largest population of breeding waterfowl in Tennessee.

RECOMMENDED READING

■ CIVIL WAR

Cooling, Benjamin Franklin. *Forts Henry and Donelson: The Key to the Confederate Heartland.* Knoxville: University of Tennessee Press, 1987.

Cozzens, Peter. *No Better Place to Die: The Battle of Stones River.* Urbana & Chicago: University of Illinois Press, 1990.

Daniel, Larry J. *Shiloh: The Battle that Changed the Civil War.* New York: Simon & Schuster, 1997.

Hurst, Jack. *Nathan Bedford Forrest: A Biography.* New York: Vintage Books, 1993.

McDonough, James Lee and Thomas L. Connelly. *Five Tragic Hours: The Battle of Franklin.* Knoxville: University of Tennessee Press, 1983.

Seymour, Digby Gordon. *Divided Loyalties: Fort Sanders and the Civil War in East Tennessee.* Second ed. Knoxville: University of Tennessee Press, 1982.

Woodworth, Steven E. *Six Armies in Tennessee: The Chickamauga and Chattanooga Campaigns.* Lincoln: University of Nebraska Press, 1998.

■ FICTION

Agee, James. *A Death in the Family.* New York: Vintage Books, 1998. (Originally published in 1938.)

Calhoun, Frances Boyd. *Miss Minerva and William Green Hill.* Knoxville: University of Tennessee Press, 1976. (Originally published in 1909.)

Foote, Shelby. *Shiloh: A Novel.* New York: Vintage Books, 1991. (Originally published in 1952.)

Ford, Jesse Hill. *The Liberation of Lord Byron Jones.* Boston: Little, Brown, & Co., 1965.

Maddux, Rachel. *Walk in the Spring Rain.* Knoxville: University of Tennessee Press, 1992. (Originally published in 1966.)

Taylor, Peter. *A Summons to Memphis.* New York: Alfred A. Knopf, 1986.

_____. *In the Miro District and Other Short Stories.* New York: Alfred A. Knopf, 1977.

_____. *In the Tennessee Country.* New York: Alfred A. Knopf, 1994.

■ MUSIC

Arnaud, Michel. *Nashville: The Pilgrims of Guitar Town*. New York: Stewart, Tabori & Chang, 2000.

Escott, Colin. *Good Rockin' Tonight: Sun Records and the Birth of Rock 'n' Roll*. New York: St. Martin's Press, 1991.

_____ with George Merritt and William MacEwen. *Hank Williams: The Biography*. Boston: Little, Brown, & Co., 1994.

Guralnick, Peter. *Last Train to Memphis: The Rise of Elvis Presley*. Boston: Little, Brown, & Co., 1994.

Kingsbury, Paul et. al., ed. *The Encyclopedia of Country Music: The Ultimate Guide to the Music, Compiled by the Staff of the Country Music Hall of Fame and Museum*. New York: Oxford University Press, 1998.

Lynn, Loretta, with George Vecsey. *Coal Miner's Daughter*. New York: Warner Books, 1980. (Originally published in 1976.)

Nager, Larry. *Memphis Beat: The Lives and Times of America's Musical Crossroads*. New York: St. Martin's Press, 1998.

Parton, Dolly. *Dolly: My Life and Other Unfinished Business*. New York: Harper Collins Publishers, 1994.

Tichi, Cecelia. *High Lonesome: The American Culture of Country Music*. Chapel Hill: University of North Carolina Press, 1994.

■ RECREATIONAL GUIDES

Brandt, Robert. *Middle Tennessee on Foot: Hikes in the Woods & Walks on Country Roads*. Winston-Salem: John F. Blair, Publisher, 1998.

_____. *Touring the Middle Tennessee Backroads*. Winston- Salem: John F. Blair, Publisher, 1995.

DeFoe, Don, et. al., ed.. *Hiking Trails of the Smokies*. Gatlinburg: Great Smoky Mountains Natural History Association, 1994.

Manning, Russ. *The Historic Cumberland Plateau: An Explorer's Guide*. Second ed. Knoxville: University of Tennessee Press, 1999.

Richards, Ann and Glen Wanner. *Bicycling Middle Tennessee: A Guide to Scenic Bicycle Rides in Nashville's Countryside*. Third ed. Nashville: Pennywell Press, 1996.

Sakowski, Carolyn. *Touring the East Tennessee Backroads*. Winston-Salem: John F. Blair, Publisher, 1993.

Skelton, William H., ed. *Wilderness Trails of the Cherokee National Forest*. Knoxville: University of Tennessee Press, 1992.

Summerlin, Vernon. *The Compleat Tennessee Angler: Everything You Need to Know About Fishing in the Volunteer State*. Nashville: Rutledge Hill Press, 1999.

I N D E X

ACKNOWLEDGMENTS

All photographs in this book are by Joseph Allen unless noted below.

HISTORY & CULTURE:
Page 14, Library of Congress Geography and Map Division ▪ Page 15, Metropolitan Museum of Art, NYC ▪ Page 18, Smithsonian Institution ▪ Page 19, Tennessee State Museum, Nashville ▪ Page 20, T.W. Wood Gallery and Arts Center, Montpelier, VT ▪ Page 21, Tennessee State Museum, Nashville ▪ Page 23, Tennessee State Museum, Nashville ▪ Page 24, Birmingham Museum of Art, Alabama, gift of John Meyer ▪ Page 25, Chicago Historical Society ▪ Page 28 (left), National Archives ▪ Pages 28-33 (all), Library of Congress Prints and Photographs Division ▪ Page 34, Tennessee Historical Society, Nashville ▪ Page 35, Library of Congress Prints and Photographs Division ▪ Page 37, Tennessee Valley Authority ▪ Page 38, Tennessee State Library and Archives (photo by Ed Clark) ▪ Page 39, Bettmann/Corbis ▪ Page 40, Nashville Public Library, The Nashville Room ▪ Page 41, FedEx Corporation, Memphis

THE MOUNTAINS:
Page 54, Tennessee State Library and Archives ▪ Page 56, Tennessee Valley Authority ▪ Page 65, Tennessee State Museum, Nashville

TENNESSEE VALLEY:
Page 72, Tennessee State Museum, Nashville ▪ Page 73, Library of Congress Prints and Photographs Division ▪ Page 75, Tennessee State Library and Archives ▪ Page 78, First Tennessee Heritage Collection ▪ Page 80, Tennessee State Museum, Nashville ▪ Page 82, University of Tennessee Library ▪ Page 90, Tennessee State Library and Archives ▪ Page 91, University of Tennessee Archives, Special Collections, Library of the University of Tennessee, Knoxville ▪ Pages 92-93, Hunter Museum of American Art, Chattanooga, gift of Mr. And Mrs. Norman Hirschl ▪ Page 95, Tennessee Historical Society ▪ Page 96, Frank H. McClung Museum, Knoxville ▪ Page 97, Tennessee Valley Authority ▪ Page 103, Department of Energy ▪ Page 113, Library of Congress Prints and Photographs Division ▪ Pages 120-121, The National Museum of the U.S. Army, Army Art Collection ▪ Page 125, Library of Congress Prints and Photographs Division

CUMBERLAND PLATEAU:
Page 128, Tennessee State Library and Archives ▪ Page 129, Mildred Lane Kemper Art Museum, Washington University in St. Louis. Gift of Nathaniel Phillips, 1890 ▪ Page 147, Tennessee State Library and Archives ▪ Page 149, Tennessee State Library and Archives

NASHVILLE:
Pages 152-53, Tennessee State Museum, Nashville ▪ Page 160, Hatch Show Prints ▪ Page 161 (top), Tennessee State Library and Archives ▪ Page 161 (bottom), Metro Board of Parks and Recreation, Nashville ▪ Page 166, Tennessee State Library and Archives ▪ Pages 168-69, Country Music Hall of Fame® and Museum ▪ Page 174 (bottom), Country Music Hall of Fame® and Museum ▪ Page 176, Fine Arts Center at Cheekwood, Nashville ▪ Page 178 (top), Vanderbilt University Special Collections and University Archives ▪ Page 179, Tennessee State Library and Archives ▪ Page 181, Fisk University Galleries, Nashville ▪ Page 186-191 (all), Michael Ochs Archives ▪ Page 194, Tennessee Historical Society ▪ Pages 196-97, The Hermitage, Nashville ▪ Page 199, Belle Meade Plantation

MIDDLE TENNESSEE:
Page 211, Library of Congress Prints and Photographs Division ▪ Page 220, Tennessee State Library and Archives ▪ Page 221, Tennessee State Museum, Nashville ▪ Page 234, Old Salem Inc.; Museum of Early Southern Decorative Arts ▪ Page 235, Mrs. Prentice Cooper ▪ Page 246 (top), Jerry Cooke/Sports Illustrated ▪ Page 246 (bottom), Hachland Hill Inn

WEST TENNESSEE:
Page 257, Library of Congress Prints and Photographs Division ▪ Page 260, Tennessee State Library and Archives ▪ Page 266, Tennessee State Library and Archives ▪ Page 269, John Bass ▪ Page 273 (bottom), Tennessee State Library and Archives

MEMPHIS:
Page 276, The New-York Historical Society ▪ Page 278, Library of Congress Geography and Map Division ▪ Page 279, Tennessee State Library and Archives ▪ Page 280, Memphis Shelby County Library ▪ Page 281, Frank Driggs Collection ▪ Page 283, Colin Escott/Michael Ochs Archives ▪ Page 286, Michael Ochs Archives ▪ Page 290, Library of Congress Prints and Photographs Division ▪ Page 293, Memphis Convention & Visitors Bureau

WALKS AND WILDFLOWERS IN TENNESSEE PARKS:
Page 304, Tennessee State Library and Archives

COMPASS AMERICAN GUIDES

Critics, booksellers, and travelers all agree: you're lost without a Compass.

"This splendid series provides exactly the sort of historical and cultural detail about North American destinations that curious-minded travelers need."
—*Washington Post*

"This is a series that constantly stuns us...no guide with photos this good should have writing this good. But it does." —*New York Daily News*

"Of the many guidebooks on the market, few are as visually stimulating, as thoroughly researched, or as lively written as the Compass American Guide series."
—*Chicago Tribune*

"Good to read ahead of time, then take along so you don't miss anything."
—*San Diego Magazine*

"Magnificent photography. First rate."—*Money*

"Written by longtime residents of each destination...these handsome and literate guides are strong on history and culture, and illustrated with gorgeous photos."
—*San Francisco Chronicle*

"The color photographs sparkle, the archival illustrations illuminate windows to the past, and the writing is usually of the utmost caliber." —*Michigan Tribune*

"Class acts, worth reading and shelving for keeps even if you're not a traveler. "
—*New Orleans Times-Picayune*

"Beautiful photographs and literate writing are the hallmarks of the Compass guides." —*Nashville Tennessean*

"History, geography, and wanderlust converge in these well-conceived books."
—*Raleigh News & Observer*

"Oh, my goodness! What a gorgeous series this is."—*Booklist*

COMPASS AMERICAN GUIDES

Alaska

American Southwest

Arizona

Boston

California Wine Country

Cape Cod

Chicago

Coastal California

Colorado

Connecticut & Rhode Island

Florida

Georgia

Gulf South

Hawaii

Idaho

Kentucky

Las Vegas

Maine

Manhattan

Massachusetts

Michigan

Minnesota

Montana

New Hampshire

New Mexico

New Orleans

North Carolina

Oregon

Oregon Wine Country

Pacific Northwest

Pennsylvania

Santa Fe

South Carolina

South Dakota

Tennessee

Texas

Utah

Vermont

Virginia

Washington

Washington Wine Country

Wisconsin

Wyoming

■ ABOUT THE AUTHOR

Robert Brandt is a Nashville writer whose works on Tennessee history, culture, and the outdoors include *Touring the Middle Tennessee Backroads* and *Middle Tennessee on Foot*. He is also author of the Sierra Club's *Tennessee Hiking Guide* and is a contributor to the *Tennessee Encyclopedia of History and Culture*.

Brandt's articles have appeared in the *Tennessee Historical Quarterly, Tennessee Conservationist*, the *Nashville Scene, Sierra*, and other periodicals. His history articles on Tennessee's bicentennial were featured in *The Tennessean*, and he frequently writes travel articles for the Nashville daily.

■ ABOUT THE PHOTOGRAPHER

Joseph Allen took up photography in order to document rare moments during extended backpacking trips, carrying a large-format camera into the backcountry. He now photographs subjects of architectural, historical, and cultural interest as well. His images have appeared in books, calendars, and journals including *Outdoor Photographer, Shutterbug*, and *Tennessee Conservationist;* he also teaches nature photography at Nashville State Technical Institute. Allen lives with his wife and two children on a ridgetop outside Nashville, and struggles to train his youngest to slow down for photo-ops.